P9-CEY-939

Children's Rights in the United States

For our children

———————— ✿ ————————

Kristen Hansen Perry and Laura Meaker Perry
Whose childhoods now are a tapestry of memories

Martin Brooks-Lesser
Whose childhood is unfolding in the splendor of daily discoveries

Allan Jefferson Wrightsman
Whose childhood communicated the essence of individuality

And for children everywhere
Who deserve the rights and respect of full personhood

———————— ✿ ————————

Children's Rights in the United States

In Search of a National Policy

Nancy E. Walker
Catherine M. Brooks
Lawrence S. Wrightsman

SAGE Publications
International Educational and Professional Publisher
Thousand Oaks London New Delhi

Copyright © 1999 by Sage Publications, Inc.

All rights reserved. No part of this book may be reproduced or utilized in any form or by any means, electronic or mechanical, including photocopying, recording, or by any information storage and retrieval system, without permission in writing from the publisher.

For information:

 SAGE Publications, Inc.
2455 Teller Road
Thousand Oaks, California 91320
E-mail: order@sagepub.com

SAGE Publications Ltd.
6 Bonhill Street
London EC2A 4PU
United Kingdom

SAGE Publications India Pvt. Ltd.
M-32 Market
Greater Kailash I
New Delhi 110 048 India

Printed in the United States of America

Library of Congress Cataloging-in-Publication Data

Walker, Nancy E.
    Children's rights in the United States: In search of a
national policy / by Nancy E. Walker, Catherine M. Brooks, Lawrence S.
Wrightsman.
        p.   cm.
    Includes bibliographical references and index.
    ISBN 0-8039-5103-5 (cloth: acid-free paper)
    ISBN 0-8039-5104-3 (pbk.: acid-free paper)
    1. Children—Legal status, laws, etc.—United States.
2. Children's rights—United States.   I. Brooks, Catherine M.
II. Wrightsman, Lawrence S.   III. Title.
    KF479.W35   1998
    323.3'52'0793—ddc21   98-19695

This book is printed on acid-free paper.

08 07 06   10 9 8 7 6 5

Acquiring Editor: C. Terry Hendrix
Production Editor: Sherrise M. Purdum
Editorial Assistant: Navair Kabakian
Typesetter/Designer: Janelle LeMaster
Cover Designer: Candice Harman

Contents

PART II: A PATCHWORK OF POLICIES

Acknowledgments

L ike raising a child, writing a book gives rise to a wide spectrum of emotions—joy and frustration, satisfaction and frustration, pride and frustration. The tasks of authorship, also like the tasks of parenting, can be both fulfilling and mundane. The latter certainly are made more bearable—and even enjoyable—when the authors, rather than working in isolation, are surrounded by a network of support, knowledge, and skill. We consider ourselves particularly fortunate in that regard and so give heartfelt thanks to the "extended family" that helped bring this project to fruition.

For their especially careful research, dogged determination, and general good cheer, we thank Kathryn A. Honecker, Jennifer S. Hunt, Isabelle Cherney, Mindy Weiner, Stephanie Weiland, Lori A. C. Komori, Michaela Culver, Rachel Jackson, Traci M. Gleason, Jessica S. Cain, Julie Galas, and Lisa Kellen.

For their perseverance in reading chapter drafts "under the midnight oil" and in providing particularly thoughtful critiques, we thank Karen Kassebaum, J.D.; George R. Lesser; Gary B. Melton, Ph.D., Kathryn A. Olson, J.D.; Stephen D. Starr, M.D.; and Harriet I. Walker.

For her careful typing of chapter drafts, we thank Katia Silva.

For their encouragement and moral support, we thank our colleagues in the Center for the Study of Children's Issues at Creighton University.

For provision of administrative support, we thank Michael Proterra, S.J., Dean of the Creighton College of Arts and Sciences; and Lawrence Raful, J.D., Dean of the Creighton School of Law.

Finally, for their unending patience, tolerance of our emotional vicissitudes, and unfailing kindness—not to mention their remarkable willingness to eat untold numbers of restaurant meals—we are especially grateful to our families and to our friends, without whom we would be so much less. Catherine Brooks thanks especially her little boy, Marty, who forgave his mother her absences and who gave her joy in his dancing and laughter upon her many late returns home.

PART I

Foundations

1

Children Are Persons . . .
Or Are They?

An Introduction to the Issues

Children have rights only if adults allow them.

—A child (1995)

Are children considered to be "persons" in the United States? The answer to that question depends on which court opinions one reads. Consider the following cases.

Tinker v. Des Moines Independent Community School District (1969)

On December 16, 1965, when 13-year-old Mary Beth Tinker arrived at her junior high school in Des Moines, Iowa, she was wearing a black armband. So was a friend, and so too—on the next day—was her 15-year-old brother, John. They and their parents were expressing their deep opposition to the war in Vietnam. Theirs was a silent protest; in no other way did they behave differently from their peers.

Word of their protest preceded their action. Two days before, the administrative staff had decided that any students wearing armbands would be told to remove them; if they did not, the students would be suspended from school until they did so.

The students refused; for this action, the Tinker children were disciplined by the school authorities. When the decision was appealed to the Supreme Court, it ruled (on a 7–to-2 vote) that such discipline was a violation of the children's rights of free expression (*Tinker v. Des Moines Independent Community School District,* 1969). In the majority decision, written by Justice Abe Fortas, the Court ruled that students are persons under the law and that their rights to free expression must be respected by the state: "Students in school as well as out of school are 'persons' under our Constitution" (p. 511).

This decision, along with others in the same era that dealt with specific rights (cf. *In re Gault,* 1967; *Planned Parenthood v. Danforth,* 1976), reflected the judicial system's view of children as a class having constitutional rights similar to those of the class of adults. But these court decisions "have failed to lead to such an equalization of children's constitutional rights" (Stier, 1978, p. 49). Instead, specific decisions subsequent to *Tinker* have given some classes of children protection for some constitutional rights but have denied children other fundamental rights.

Brown v. Board of Education (1954)

Even before the *Tinker* decision, the Supreme Court reflected an implicit assumption of the "personhood" of children in certain decisions, paramount of which is the 1954 decision in *Brown v. Board of Education.* By announcing that "separate educational facilities are inherently unequal" (p. 495), the Court affirmed the rights of all children to an educational setting in which each child is provided the same opportunity to learn regardless of his or her race.

Despite the time it took Chief Justice Earl Warren to orchestrate the unanimous vote and despite the upheaval it created in racially segregated school districts, *Brown* was an "easy" case in the sense that the decision was clear-cut. Granting children due process rights conflicting with those of parents was less straightforward. The case of *Parham v. J. R.* (1979) is illustrative.

Parham v. J. R. (1979)

In *Parham v. J. R.*, two institutionalized children challenged a Georgia law concerning commitment of persons under the age of 18 to mental hospitals. Both children had been in a mental hospital; one—referred to by the Court simply as "J. L." because of his minor status—had been there since he was 6 years old. In 1970, his mother had requested the hospital to admit him indefinitely. When the admitting physician interviewed J. L. and his parents, he learned that J. L.'s biological parents had divorced and that his mother had remarried. J. L. had been expelled from school because he was considered to be uncontrollable. The physician accepted the parents' evaluation that J. L. had been extremely aggressive, and he diagnosed the condition of "hyperkinetic reaction of childhood" in the child.

The other child, labeled J. R., was declared a neglected child and removed from his biological parents when he was 3 months old. At the age of 7 years, after having been placed in seven foster homes, he was admitted to Central State Hospital at Milledgeville. The admission team at the hospital determined that he had borderline retardation and an "unsocialized aggressive reaction of childhood." The team recommended unanimously that he would "benefit from the structured environment" of the hospital and would "enjoy living and playing with boys of the same age" (*Parham v. J. R.*, 1979, p. 590). J. R.'s progress was reassessed periodically, and the Department of Family and Children Services tried periodically—but always unsuccessfully—to place him in various foster homes.

In October 1975, J. R., through a guardian *ad litem*, filed a lawsuit requesting a court order that would place him in a less restrictive environment that was suitable to his needs. J. L.'s companion action was merged into that of J. R. They claimed that they had been denied liberty without due process of law as required by the Fourteenth Amendment, arguing that adults cannot be committed against their will to state mental hospitals without a full judicial hearing and legal representation and that children should have the same rights.

The lower federal court ruled in favor of J. R. and J. L., ordering Georgia to restructure its state mental health system to provide such children their procedural rights; it also granted the boys' plea for less restrictive treatment. The state appealed to the U.S. Supreme Court.

The Supreme Court's majority opinion was written by Chief Justice Warren Burger; in it, he made some "interesting" conclusions (Walding, 1990). He acknowledged that "it is not disputed that a child, in common with

adults, *has a substantial liberty interest* [italics added] in not being confined
unnecessarily for medical treatment" (*Parham v. J. R.,* 1979, p. 600). But he
concluded that "this interest is inextricably linked with the parents' interest in
and obligation for the welfare and health of the child" (p. 600) and that:

> The law's concept of the family rests on the presumption that parents possess
> what a child lacks in maturity, experience, and capacity for judgment required
> for making life's difficult decisions. More importantly, historically it has
> recognized that natural bonds of affection lead parents to act in the best
> interest of their children. (p. 602)

The Court explained that parental "errors" in such decisions could be checked
by the use of a determination by a "neutral fact finder" (p. 606) prior to the
child's admission to a hospital or institution. This function, Justice Burger
suggested, might be served by a staff physician. Such a person, in the mind
of the Court, did not have to be trained in the law.

The *Parham* decision has been interpreted as providing very little due
process protection for minors considered for commitment (Walding, 1990),
although the decision allowed individual states to provide more protections if
they so desired. The *Parham* majority also accepted as true the idea that
parents act in the child's interests in seeking psychiatric commitments. What
this means for a child in a for-profit psychiatric hospital setting in which
troubled or selfish parents seek respite was not considered by the Court (see
Chapter 7, this volume).

Another perspective acknowledges the intersection of the child's and
parents' interests:

> Although the conventional interpretation of *Parham* is that it pitted parents
> against children, the case initially was framed as focusing primarily on
> *substantive* due process (not who will decide, but what are they offered to
> choose). Neither parents nor children were given meaningful choices. Al-
> though parents and children have different specific interests, they have a
> convergent interest in family preservation. (G. B. Melton, personal commu-
> nication, October 12, 1997; see also Melton, Lyons, & Spaulding, in press)

Haley v. Ohio (1948)

In conjunction with the growing recognition of children as persons, the
Court gradually and on an issue-by-issue basis applied constitutional rights

to children and adolescents who came under the scrutiny of the criminal justice system. For example, in *Haley v. Ohio* (1948), the Supreme Court threw out as evidence a murder confession from a 15-year-old youth, extracted after 5 hours of intensive interrogation by the police. The Court concluded that "a 15-year-old lad, questioned through the dead of night by relays of police, is ready victim of inquisition" and that without aid of counsel a boy would not have a full appreciation of the circumstances surrounding him nor would he recognize that he had a freedom of choice (*Haley v. Ohio,* 1948, p. 600). The Court noted, "The Fourteenth Amendment prohibits the police from using the private, secret custody of either man or child as a device for wringing confessions from them" (p. 601).

In re Gault (1967)

Clearly, the most important Supreme Court decision in this category is that of *In re Gault* (1967). On June 5, 1964, Gerald Gault, age 15, was committed to the Arizona State Industrial Training School until he reached adult status—a term of 6 years. What was his crime? A few weeks earlier, he and a friend had telephoned a woman and made mildly lewd remarks to her. Although the opinion in *Gault* does not tell us just what the lewd remarks were, the Court stated that "[i]t will suffice for purposes of this opinion to say that remarks or questions put to her were of the irritatingly offensive, adolescent sex variety" (p. 4). If an adult had been convicted of committing the same crime, the penalty would have been a fine of $5 to $50 and no more than 2 months in jail.

Neither Gerald Gault nor his parents were represented by counsel at either of the two hearings that were held, and no one told them they had the right to counsel. The judge questioned Gerald at both hearings but did not tell him he had the right to refuse to answer questions. The complainant did not testify at either hearing. No record was kept of what transpired at either hearing. Nonetheless, Gerald was committed to the state industrial school for a period of 6 years.

The Arizona Superior Court found Gerald's commitment to be proper, and the Arizona Supreme Court affirmed that ruling. But the U.S. Supreme Court disagreed with the conclusion of the Arizona Supreme Court that had allowed children fewer procedural safeguards than those given to adults charged with criminal conduct. Thus, in the *Gault* decision, the U.S. Supreme

Court awarded to children the same rights it had made explicit for adults in earlier rulings (cf. *Gideon v. Wainwright,* 1963; *Miranda v. Arizona,* 1966).

Gault was a landmark decision for children in the United States. Recognizing the Fourteenth Amendment's application of the Bill of Rights to the states, the U.S. Supreme Court found that "neither the Fourteenth Amendment nor the Bill of Rights is for adults alone" (*In re Gault,* 1967, p. 12). In *Gault,* the Court recognized the importance of safeguarding children from unfair loss of liberty. In addition, it explicitly endorsed several rights for juveniles involved in criminal justice proceedings—rights to notice, to counsel, to confront accusers, and to cross-examine witnesses brought by the state. The Court noted that many existing juveile court procedures "either singly or in combination, all too often have resulted in depriving some juveniles of fundamental rights that have resulted in a denial of due process" (p. 18). The Court, therefore, required that the procedural due process protections of the Constitution be made a part of juvenile court actions.

The U.S. Supreme Court's recognition of these rights for juveniles served as an important affirmation of the child as a person entitled to constitutional rights. Children's advocates, therefore, hailed the *Gault* decision as an important step forward. But the Court's decisions following *Gault* have not always been so supportive of children's rights. For example, in *Bethel School District No. 403 v. Fraser* (1986) and *Hazelwood School District v. Kuhlmeier* (1988) (described below) the Court restricted children's right to free speech in school. And in *New Jersey v. T.L.O.* (1985) (also described below) the Court restrictged children's Fourth Amendment right to freedom from unreasonable search and seizure.

Bethel School District No. 403 v. Fraser (1986)

In April 1983, Matthew Fraser, a Tacoma, Washington, high school senior, made a six-sentence nominating speech at a school assembly in front of 600 students. He spoke on behalf of a friend who was running for student body vice president. Fraser said: "I know a man who is firm—he's firm in his pants, he's firm in his shirt, his character is firm—but most of all, his belief in you, the students of Bethel, is firm. . . . Jeff is a man who will go to the very end, even the climax, for each and every one of you" (quoted in Mauro, 1986, p. 2A).[1] The high school principal considered Fraser's comments to be sexually suggestive. He suspended Fraser for 3 days and dropped him as a possible graduation speaker. After his suspension, Fraser appealed; a U.S. Circuit Court of Appeals found in his favor, awarding him $13,000 in damages and lawyers' fees (Mauro, 1986). The school district then appealed. In a 7-to-2 vote, the Supreme Court upheld the suspension, observing that the speech contained "an elaborate graphic and explicit sexual metaphor" and provoked raucous behavior and simulated sexual acts by some students and embarrassment in others; it concluded that "vulgar and offensive" language is inappropriate in the public schools and is not protected by the First Amendment.

Hazelwood School District v. Kuhlmeier (1988)

A parallel case involved actions taken by school officials in a St. Louis suburb. Without telling the paper's staff, the Hazelwood East High School principal deleted two pages from the school newspaper, including one article on student pregnancies and another on the impact of divorce on students in the school. Both articles included comments from interviews with Hazelwood East High School students, but no names were used. The principal considered the articles to be "inappropriate, personal, sensitive, and unsuitable for student readers" (*Hazelwood School District v. Kuhlmeier,* 1988, p. 285), reflecting a nurturance orientation that children need to be protected by the authorities in society (see Chapter 4, this volume). The Supreme Court affirmed the constitutional right of the Hazelwood authorities to control the expression of students "so long as their actions are reasonably related to legitimate pedagogical concerns" (p. 261). In what Hentoff (1988) has called a "dramatic removal of First Amendment rights for public school students" (p. 340), Justice Byron White wrote that educators have the authority to censor or suppress "school-sponsored publications, theatrical publications, and other expressive activities that students, parents, and members of the public might reasonably perceive to bear the imprimatur of the school" (*Hazelwood School District v. Kuhlmeier,* 1988, p. 271). In addition, Justice White wrote that student speech can also be censored if it "associates the school with any position other than neutrality on matters of political controversy" (p. 271). In his dissent, Justice William Brennan accused the majority of justices of approving "brutal censorship" while giving educators the power to act as "thought police" (p. 285). He denounced the Hazelwood principal for his "unthinking contempt for individual rights" (p. 289).

New Jersey v. T.L.O. (1985)

In another decision reflecting a step back from awarding full "person" status to children, the U.S. Supreme Court, in *New Jersey v. T.L.O.* (1985), ruled that any public school student can be searched by school officials without a warrant on the basis of nothing more than "reasonable grounds for suspecting that the search will turn up evidence that the student has violated or is violating either the law or the rules of the school" (p. 326). The 14-year-old girl identified as "T.L.O." in court records was suspected of smoking in a rest room at Piscataway High School in New Jersey in March 1980. She was taken to the school office, where a vice principal opened her purse. He discovered a pack of cigarettes and also noticed a pack of rolling papers of the kind used in making marijuana cigarettes. He dug further and found marijuana and other drug paraphernalia. The girl was sentenced as a delinquent to 1 year probation that required her to attend a drug therapy program. The student claimed that the vice principal had acted unlawfully in searching her purse. The Supreme Court disagreed, substituting the school official's less protective "reasonable grounds" for the "probable cause" standard required for searches of adults. Once again, Justice Brennan wrote a minority opinion, noting that the majority opinion "portends a dangerous weakening of the purpose of the Fourth Amendment to protect the privacy and security of our citizens" (p. 357). He observed, "In adopting this unclear, unprecedented and unnecessary departure from generally applicable Fourth Amendment standards, the Court carves out a broad exception to the standards that this Court had developed over the years of considering Fourth Amendment problems" (p. 354).

Trends in Supreme Court Decisions Regarding Children's Rights

If we return to the question posed at the beginning of this chapter—"Are children considered to be 'persons' in the United States?"—one conclusion must be that the courts have answered in inconsistent ways. Certain pronouncements make the rights of children explicit, but other U.S. Supreme Court opinions reflect a paternalistic view. Moreover, as the constituency of the Court has shifted from predominantly liberal to predominantly conservative in the past 20 years, the majority members' opinions are increasingly unwilling to grant to minors those rights routinely acknowledged for adults.

Why is this? One difference between liberal and conservative judges is the sources they use in forming their opinions. The distinction is made between primary sources (cases, statutes, and regulations) and secondary sources cited in judicial opinions (Hafemeister & Melton, 1987). Secondary sources may be divided into two categories: legal secondary sources (articles in law reviews commenting on the law, and legal reference books and treatises) and nonlegal sources. The latter include all other secondary sources, including books and journals that report relevant social science research.

Hafemeister and Melton (1987) observed that the number of times a Supreme Court justice cites secondary sources is correlated with his or her judicial philosophy:

> Justices Brennan and Marshall [both now deceased], usually regarded as liberals on the Court, ranked first and second, respectively, in the frequency of such citations per page, with Justices commonly regarded as moderates (i.e., Blackmun, Stevens, and Powell) in the middle rankings. Brennan also ranked first in total citations of nonlegal sources, with Blackmun second. (p. 36)

At the opposite side of the political spectrum is Justice Antonin Scalia, who, in a case involving a death penalty appeal by a juvenile (*Stanford v. Kentucky*, 1989), rejected what he called "socio-scientific evidence . . . concerning the psychological and emotional development of 16- and 17-year-olds" (pp. 377-378). As Finkel (1995) noted, Justice Scalia consistently has considered social science studies to be irrelevant when deciding on constitutional law; for him, the only "empirical" materials of relevance in responding to such appeals are legislation and jury decisions. Chief Justice William Rehnquist also has been quite antagonistic toward social science research findings, although another conservative appointee, Justice Sandra Day O'Connor, has relied on *amicus* briefs from the American Psychological Association in some cases for which she has written the majority opinion (Finkel, 1995).

Thus, several factors may influence the members of the Court regarding children's rights. First, conservative justices are more likely to support nurturance rights for children, whereas liberal justices are more inclined to extend to children rights of self-determination. (See Chapter 4, this volume, for a discussion of the distinctions between these types of rights.) Second, justices differ on their willingness to consider social science findings to be "evidence." Third, it is likely that the justices differ in their knowledge of the stages of child development, including the ability to make informed decisions. It is not surprising, therefore, that the Court's decisions regarding the rights of children seem inconsistent.

If there is any consistency in the Supreme Court's decisions about children's constitutional rights during the past 30 years, it has been an erosion of the rights of "personhood" granted by the Court in decisions during Earl Warren's tenure as chief justice. It has been said that "the development of children's rights began with the Warren Court" (Sullivan, 1991, p. 1142), and advocates of self-determination rights were encouraged by such decisions as *Tinker* and *In re Gault*. Gradually, however, such advocates have come to recognize that the Supreme Court, "while acknowledging that the Constitution guarantees certain individual rights to children, has generally not applied stringent standards in determining whether the rights of children have been abridged or denied" (Sullivan, 1991, p. 1139).

Today, a paternalistic orientation toward children generally remains, as reflected in the *Bellotti v. Baird* (1979) decision. In that case, the Court cited three reasons why constitutional rights of children should not be equal to those of adults:

1. The peculiar vulnerability of children
2. Their inability to make critical decisions in an informed, mature manner
3. The importance of the parental role in child rearing (*Bellotti v. Baird,* 1979, p. 634)

U.S. Policy on Children's Rights: Does It Exist?

The Supreme Court's inconsistent rulings on children's rights beg the question: Does the United States have a coherent national policy on children's rights? In a word, the answer is no. Legal decisions, agency policies, and everyday practices involving children vary widely because no national policy is in place to guide decision making involving the "rights of children." The result is that decisions involving children are haphazard at best and inequitable or even damaging to children at worst.

The U.S. Constitution affords its citizens rights—rights of decision making, privacy and confidentiality, legal representation, self-determination, and so forth. There is no consensus, however, on the rights to which children are entitled—or even whether they are entitled to rights at all. Some argue that children have the right to be nurtured and protected; others contend that children should be afforded maximum opportunities for self-determination

(Rogers & Wrightsman, 1978). Still others argue that equal rights for children are neither in their best interest nor in that of society (Purdy, 1992).

Thesis and Purpose of This Book

Our view is that children are entitled to rights to nurturance, protection, and self-determination. Regarding the last, they must develop competency in decision making that will provide them the skills necessary to handle the right to self-determination in a mature fashion. In this regard, Brassard, Hyman, and Dimmitt (1991) noted:

> [I]t is in adults' best interests to prepare children to make decisions, take responsibility for their actions, develop an internal moral standard, and learn other tasks necessary for successful life as an adult. Children who don't develop these skills, which must be taught or modeled as they are not an automatic outcome of general development, do not magically come to possess them once they turn 18. It seems prudent to prepare children, in a developmentally responsive way, to learn to handle some constitutional rights and consequent responsibilities. (p. 376)

That concept is not new. Two decades ago, Rodham (now First Lady Hillary Rodham Clinton) argued that children should be granted rights appropriate to their maturational abilities (see, e.g., Rodham, 1973, 1979). Centuries before Rodham, John Locke (1690/1980) asserted:

> [W]e are born free, as we are born rational; not that we have actually the exercise of either: age, that brings one, brings with it the other too. . . . [M]ust not the child . . . be in subjection to his mother and nurse, to tutors and governors, till age and education brought him reason and ability to govern himself and others? The necessities of his life, the health of his body, and the information of his mind, would require him to be directed by the will of others, and not his own; and yet will any one think, that this restraint and subjection were inconsistent with, or spoiled him of that liberty or sovereignty he had a right to, or gave away his empire to those who had the government of his nonage? (p. 34)

Locke also noted that parents' responsibility for their children "created a duty not only to care for them but to see that they develop into reasonable beings" (cited in Purdy, 1992, p. 5). Brassard et al. (1991) framed the issue as follows:

> How do children develop the ability to handle constitutionally supported rights of decision-making, privacy and confidentiality, . . . legal representation, self-determination, and so on? How can adults find the balance of providing adequate guidance and support while allowing independent development? Both parents and educators have the difficult task of preparing young people for competency, while simultaneously ensuring that they are not endangering themselves or others. This entails a close monitoring of developmental ability, both from a general and individual perspective, and a tailoring of responsibilities and tasks to this assessment. (p. 376)

In this book, we argue that the lack of a national policy on children's rights in the United States is a major obstacle to ensuring that the best interests of children prevail. We contend that the United Nations Convention on the Rights of the Child (United Nations General Assembly, 1989) provides the appropriate foundation for U.S. policy because it "provides moral authority for all serious child advocates" (Melton, 1991, p. 349).

We further argue that the articles that constitute the Convention, coupled with empirical evidence regarding children's competency in making decisions, should form the basis for national policy on children's rights in the United States. We concur with Melton (1991), who commented:

> When practitioners and policymakers begin listening seriously to children, providing them with feedback, and perceiving problems from their perspective, we will be far along in building a child protection system that has a coherent sense of mission and that is driven by children's interests rather than a mindless, purposeless preoccupation with investigation. We will have a system that diligently strives to preserve families and to treat children with dignity. (pp. 349-350)

Our purpose in writing this book is to further those aims.

Part I provides an overview of children's rights in the United States. Chapter 2 describes historical and contextual perspectives for understanding the basic issues. Chapter 3 describes the United Nations Convention on the Rights of the Child and its relation to U.S. policy. Chapter 4 offers contrasting conceptualizations of children's rights and discusses how those perspectives inform policy decisions; Chapter 4 also delineates the development of children's competency in decision making.

Part II provides discussion of six policy areas involving the rights of children: rights within the family (Chapter 5), rights to social services (Chapter 6), rights in health care (Chapter 7), rights in education (Chapter 8), rights in juvenile law (Chapter 9), and rights in employment (Chapter 10). Each chapter in Part II describes the specific issue, presents a summary of related case law, reviews the results of relevant research studies concerning children's decision-making capabilities and limitations in that area, and discusses how the U.N. Convention offers guidance for U.S. policy decisions on that topic.

Note

1. From "Campaigning or Off-Color Orating?" by T. Mauro, March 3, 1986, *USA Today*, p. 2A. Copyright 1986, USA TODAY. Reprinted with permission.

2

From Property to Personhood

A Historical and Contextual
Perspective on the Rights of Children

> With no political power, no right to vote, and no assets,
> children remain the most vulnerable members of our society.
>
> —George H. Russ, Attorney and
> Adoptive Parent (1993)

In 1992, 11-year-old Gregory K. hired an attorney and "divorced" his mother, a woman who, according to court records, had been chronically neglectful and abusive not only to the plaintiff but also to his two younger brothers (Rohter, 1992; see Chapter 5, this volume, Box 5.5). The Florida trial court that heard the case decided in Gregory's favor, granting the dissolution of Rachel K.'s parental rights. Advocates cheered the victory for children's rights, but their celebration was short-lived. The following year, a Florida appeals court reviewed Gregory's case and declared that minors may not sue on their own to terminate their parents' rights. Although the court stopped short of removing the boy from his chosen adoptive situation, the opinion clearly reinforced a long-standing tradition of denying children rights to stand before the court and be heard on their own motion when they seek to alter their familial ties.

In 1993, Americans sat riveted to their televisions as the story of "Baby Jessica" unfolded (see Chapter 6, this volume, Box 6.4). In August of that year, a court removed 2-year-old Jessica from the custody of her caring adoptive parents in Michigan—the only parents she had ever known—and returned the distraught child to her biological father in Iowa.

How can we reconcile these opinions? As the decisions in these cases illustrate, U.S. national policies on children's rights are muddled. In fact, the United States lacks a coherent policy on children's rights. As Box 2.1 illustrates, the United States rules on each case separately instead of adopting a sensible, unified policy.

This lack of focus concerning children's rights seems alien in a country whose citizens deify rights. In the United States, people demand their constitutionally protected rights: the right to speak freely; the right to bear arms; the right to be protected from unreasonable searches, seizures, and arrests. People are indignant when someone threatens one of their "inalienable rights." Indeed, organizations designed to safeguard the rights of American adults (e.g., American Civil Liberties Union, National Rifle Association) have exerted impressive power.

But what of children's rights? Organizations chartered to protect children, such as the Children's Defense Fund International (CDFI) and the United Nations Children's Fund (UNICEF), certainly have advanced children's rights agendas. Nationally guided policies that inform the development of legislation and judicial oversight of children's issues, however, still are lacking in the United States. Why is this so?

One reason for the lack of a unified national policy on children's rights is that the development of such a position will require national consensus regarding the answers to some difficult questions: Do children have rights? Indeed, should they have rights? If not, why not? If so, who should determine the rights to which children should be entitled? At what age should children be allowed to exercise those rights? How should individual circumstances be added to the calculus? Most people agree that children have the right to be protected from danger and abuse. But do they also agree that children have rights to self-determination? Should children's voices be heard in a meaningful way? Should the best interests of the child take precedence over the desires of other interested parties?

Those thorny questions are rife with controversies that cannot be resolved easily. Indeed, resolution requires consideration of context—a theme that is repeated throughout this book. In our opinion, chronological age—perhaps the simplest of standards for making legal decisions regarding children's rights—tends to be a particularly poor criterion. Rather, the maturity of the

Box 2.1

A Sampling of Children's Rights Decisions in the United States

Date	Case/Document	Holding
1874	"Mary Ellen"	The American Society for the Prevention of Cruelty to Animals (ASPCA) prevailed in arguing that a girl, Mary Ellen, was covered under laws barring the barbaric treatment of animals.
1943	West Virginia State Board of Education v. Barnette	The Supreme Court ruled that public school students may refuse to salute the flag because of their religious beliefs.
1967	In re Gault	The Court extended to juvenile crime suspects the right to a lawyer, the same protection afforded adult defendants.
1968	Jehovah's Witnesses in State of Washington v. King Co. Hospital Unit No. 1	The Court allowed states to order blood transfusions for children over the religious · objections of their parents.
1969	Tinker v. Des Moines Independent Community School District	The Court ruled that children are persons. It also held that, as persons, schoolchildren are protected by the First Amendment to the Constitution and therefore may wear black armbands protesting war.
1970	Voting Rights Acts	Congress passed legislation allowing 18-year-olds to vote; the Constitution was amended accordingly 1 year later.
1979	Bellotti v. Baird	The Court ruled that minors seeking abortions could obtain approval from judges instead of parents.
1990	Baltimore City Department of Social Services v. Bouknight	For the first time, the Supreme Court appointed an attorney to protect a child's rights during pleadings in an abuse case.
1992, 1993	"Gregory K."	A Florida court ruled that minors may sue to terminate their parents' rights. One year later, an appeals court reversed that holding.

individual child must be considered within the context of the particular legal question to be addressed.

To provide a framework for discussion, we first consider the current status of children throughout the world. Next, we provide a brief history of children's rights.

Worldwide Status of Children Today

Children are the most vulnerable class of citizens. They are most influenced by, and least able to escape from, their particular circumstances. As a result, children suffer injustices that are less likely to be tolerated by adults. Consider, for example, these statistics on the welfare of children worldwide:

- In 1970, 26 million Latin American children under the age of 6 lived in absolute poverty; by 1980, that number had risen to 35.5 million. It is estimated that, by the year 2000, the number will reach 51 million (Jupp, 1990).
- In 1995, 14.7 million children in the United States (21%) were poor—almost twice the adult poverty rate of 11% (Children's Defense Fund, 1997).
- Approximately 35,000 children die each day from malnutrition and hunger (Vessels, 1997). One analyst noted, "Every time you take a breath, a child dies."[1]
- Five million African children died from hunger-related causes in 1984 alone (Jupp, 1990).
- In 1993, more than 50% of children in India, Bangladesh, and Yemen were moderately to severely underweight (UNICEF, 1993).
- In 1993, only 44% of children living in the least developed countries had access to safe water. Only 29% of that population had access to safe sanitation (UNICEF, 1993).
- In poorer nations, some 12 million children die every year because they do not have vaccines or sufficient food (Hammarberg, 1990).
- Approximately 60% of these 12 million child deaths are caused by preventable or treatable illnesses, including pneumonia, diarrhea, and measles (LeBlanc, 1995).
- In northeastern Brazil, women experience, on average, 9.5 pregnancies, 3.5 child deaths, and 1.5 stillbirths. A bereaved mother is told not to cry because "her tears will dampen the wings of her little angel so that she cannot fly up to her heavenly home" (Bross, 1991, p. 96).
- During 1993, 93% of girls in developed countries were enrolled in secondary school during 1993. By contrast, only 12% of girls living in the least developed countries and 35% of girls living in developing countries were allowed a secondary education (UNICEF, 1993).

- Today, between 30 million and 100 million children live on the streets of the world's cities (Jupp, 1990).
- In 1996, of Latin America's 197 million children, 15 million were believed to live on the streets, 6 million suffered from malnutrition, and 30 million worked without legal protection (Cevallos, 1996).
- In 1997, the International Labor Organization estimated that 120 million children between the ages of 5 and 14 were working full time, often in hazardous conditions (Stewart, 1997).
- In 1990, 88 million of the world's children were working under harmful conditions (Jupp, 1990)—a number that did not decline over a 7-year period (1990-1997), according to the International Labor Organization ("International Conference," 1997).

As these facts poignantly illustrate, childhood is not always a blissful time. Moreover, only in very recent times have children been considered a special class of persons deserving of protection.

Views Toward Children's Rights

Until modern times, childhood was an almost universally grim experience. For hundreds of years, children were treated primarily as chattel (Hart, 1991). They were bought, sold, cared for, and abandoned in much the same way as a pair of shoes. Pappas (1983) noted that children commonly were "neglected, abandoned, abused (sexually and otherwise), sold into slavery, mutilated and even killed with impunity" (p. xxviii). Reflect, for example, on the fate of one newborn brother of Henri IV of France: He was dropped and killed while being thrown from one window to another during a round of infant-tossing, a common 16th-century game played for the amusement of adults (deMause, 1975).

From antiquity to the 18th century, almost every child-rearing treatise advocated the corporal punishment—sometimes extreme—of children (de-Mause, 1975). Indeed, some individuals charged with the care and upbringing of children made meticulous records of their "exemplary" disciplinary measures. One German schoolmaster, for instance, reported administering "911,527 strokes with a stick, 124,000 lashes with a whip, 136,715 slaps with his hand and 1,115,800 boxes on the ear" (deMause, 1975, p. 85). In the United States, early state law supported adult control of children, even to the point of allowing capital punishment for unruly youngsters (Hart, 1991;

Horowitz, 1984). According to deMause (1975), "It took centuries of progress in parent-child relations before the West could begin to overcome its apparent need to abuse its children" (p. 85).

From the 16th through the 18th centuries, children's status gradually improved. During that time, minors were not accorded the rights of personhood, but adults slowly began to acknowledge children's economic worth in contributing to family work and in supporting parents in their old age (Hart, 1991). Over time, that recognition led to consideration of children as a special class requiring protection and nurturance. That nascent attitude gave birth to a 19th-century child-saving era focused on ensuring the health and welfare of children.

The philosophical perspectives of several individuals of that period—including John Locke, John Stuart Mill, and Thomas Hobbes—encouraged child protection. Their view was that limits should be placed on children's freedom until such time as the young were able to enter into covenants, to understand the consequences of their decisions, and to pursue reasoned self-improvement (Worsfold, 1974). Status as a person and its accompanying rights, they argued, should accrue only when a child developed such competencies.

The Children's Rights Advocacy Movement

The child-saving era developed further during the early years of the 20th century. During that time, adults began to espouse the view that not only did children require saving, but they also represented "the essential human resources whose mature form would determine the future of society" (Hart, 1982, p. 4). That "child-as-redeemer perspective" set the stage for compulsory education, child labor reform, and the development of the juvenile court system (Hart, 1991).

After several centuries of painfully slow progress, during the last half of the 20th century children's current status as persons finally emerged. In the case of *In re Gault* (1967), children charged with crimes in the United States were guaranteed the right to notice of charges, to counsel, to confrontation and cross-examination of witnesses, and to privilege against self-incrimination—the same rights that adult defendants had enjoyed for many years. Two years after the *Gault* decision—less than 30 years ago—children at long last were designated as persons under U.S. law in the landmark decision of *Tinker v. Des Moines Independent Community School District* (1969).

According children personhood status has led to an interesting feud between two proponents, however, both claiming to have children's best interests at heart (Rogers & Wrightsman, 1978). On the one hand, child salvationists argue that children's status as persons has provided justification for the preeminence of rights to their protection, including state assurance of their safety and nurturance, even when the children find such nurturance unpleasant or unhelpful. On the other hand, self-determination advocates have used children's personhood status as an argument for granting children considerable personal freedom over their own decisions and destinies, even when doing so might jeopardize their immediate safety. As pointed out in Chapter 4, resolution of this conflict in the United States may be difficult to achieve.

Documents Advocating Children's Rights

According to Hart (1991), "Twentieth-century history documents the shifts from adult to children's rights and from protection to self-determination rights for children" (p. 55). Several key documents provide support for Hart's claim.

1924 League of Nations Declaration of Geneva. The Declaration of Geneva, drafted in 1924 by the Save the Children International Union (SCIU), was the first official document to propose that children should be the first to receive relief in emergencies. After the Declaration of Geneva, "children first" became a fundamental tenet in the struggle for children's rights (Hammarberg, 1990).

1948 United Nations Universal Declaration of Human Rights. Two decades after the "children first" doctrine was proposed, the U.N. General Assembly voted to pass *A Universal Declaration of Human Rights* (December 10, 1948). The preamble to that document asserted that "recognition of the inherent dignity and of the equal and inalienable rights of all members of the human family is the foundation of freedom, justice and peace in the world" (Ku, 1979, p. 691). The Human Rights Declaration was significant for many reasons, not the least of which was that, in recognizing the rights of all members of the human family, children were not excluded from protection. The Human Rights Declaration, though, did not accord special status to children.

1959 United Nations Declaration of the Rights of the Child. A decade later, the United Nations adopted the *Declaration of the Rights of the Child* (November 20, 1959), which posited that "mankind owes to the child the best it has to give" (quoted in Ku, 1979, p. 744). The Declaration announced that children "shall be brought up in a spirit of understanding, tolerance, friendship among peoples, peace and universal brotherhood" (Principle 10, quoted in Ku, 1979, p. 746) and that children "shall in all circumstances be among the first to receive protection and relief" (Principle 8, quoted in Ku, 1979, p. 745). In other words, the Declaration advanced a protectionist agenda.

Specifically, the 10 principles contained in the 1959 document both expanded the rights previously proposed in the Declaration of Geneva and espoused new rights for children. Box 2.2 lists the principles of the U.N. Declaration of the Rights of the Child.

1989 United Nations Convention on the Rights of the Child. In honor of the 20th anniversary of the Declaration of the Rights of the Child, the United Nations designated 1979 as the International Year of the Child. Poland took a leading role in the celebration. The Polish delegation argued that because a declaration is no more than a statement of principles, the United Nations should draft a Convention with the express purpose of developing a legally binding international treaty governing children's rights (Hammarberg, 1990). In response to Poland's proposal, the United Nations Commission on Human Rights established a Working Group charged with completing the Convention by 1989, the 30th anniversary of the Declaration. To give impetus to the process, the Polish government presented a model Convention that served as the foundation for deliberations by the Working Group (Cohen, 1990).

On November 20, 1989, the United Nations adopted the Convention on the Rights of the Child. Hammarberg (1990) describes the Convention's landmark status:

> The primary focus of the Convention is "the best interests of the child." More than any earlier international agreement, the Convention recognizes children as human beings of equal value. It marks the end of the age-old idea that children, at least in legal terms, are no more than possessions of their guardians. At the same time, it recognizes children as children. The importance of a happy childhood is accepted for its own sake. (p. 99)

Each year since its adoption in 1989, increasing numbers of countries have ratified the Convention. As of April 1997, 191 countries had ratified the

---

Box 2.2

Principles of the U.N. Declaration
of the Rights of the Child (1959)

Principle 1   The child shall enjoy all the rights set forth in this Declaration. All
children, without any exception whatsoever, shall be entitled to
these rights, without distinction or discrimination on account of
race, colour, sex, language, religion, political or other opinion,
national or social origin, property, birth or other status, whether of
himself or of his family.

Principle 2   The child shall enjoy special protection, and shall be given
opportunities and facilities, by law and by other means, to enable
him to develop physically, mentally, morally, spiritually and
socially in a healthy and normal manner and in conditions of
freedom and dignity. In the enactment of laws for this purpose the
best interests of the child shall be the paramount consideration.

Principle 3   The child shall be entitled from his birth to a name and a
nationality.

Principle 4   The child shall enjoy the benefits of social security. He shall be
entitled to grow and develop in health; to this end special care
and protection shall be provided both to him and to his mother,
including adequate pre-natal and post-natal care. The child shall
have the right to adequate nutrition, housing, recreation and
medical services.

Principle 5   The child who is physically, mentally or socially handicapped shall
be given the special treatment, education and care required by his
particular condition.

Principle 6   The child, for the full and harmonious development of his
personality, needs love and understanding. He shall, wherever
possible, grow up in the care and under the responsibility of his
parents, and in any case in an atmosphere of affection and of
moral and material security; a child of tender years shall not, save
in exceptional circumstances, be separated from his mother.

Convention. Thus, of all the world's nations, only two have not ratified the
Convention: Somalia and the United States. Somalia, it should be noted,
currently does not have a governmental structure to ratify an international
treaty. What reasons can the United States provide for being the only remaining nation in the world that has not ratified the Convention? (See Chapter 3

Society and the public authorities shall have the duty to extend particular care to children without a family and to those without adequate means of support. Payment of State and other assistance towards the maintenance of children of large families is desirable.

Principle 7   The child is entitled to receive education, which shall be free and compulsory, at least in the elementary stages. He shall be given an education which will promote his general culture, and enable him on a basis of equal opportunity to develop his abilities, his individual judgement, and his sense of moral and social responsibility, and to become a useful member of society.

The best interests of the child shall be the guiding principle of those responsible for his education and guidance; that responsibility lies in the first place with his parents.

The child shall have full opportunity for play and recreation, which should be directed to the same purposes as education; society and the public authorities shall endeavour to promote the enjoyment of this right.

Principle 8   The child shall in all circumstances be among the first to receive protection and relief.

Principle 9   The child shall be protected against all forms of neglect, cruelty and exploitation. He shall not be the subject of traffic, in any form.

The child shall not be admitted to employment before an appropriate minimum age; he shall in no case be caused or permitted to engage in any occupation or employment which would prejudice his health or education, or interfere with his physical, mental or moral development.

Principle 10   The child shall be protected from practices which may foster racial, religious and any other form of discrimination. He shall be brought up in a spirit of understanding, tolerance, friendship among peoples, peace and universal brotherhood and in full consciousness that his energy and talents should be devoted to the service of his fellow men.

for detailed information about the Convention and its relation to U.S. policy; see also Cohen & Davidson, 1990.)

1990 Declaration of the World Summit for Children. Following the 1990 World Summit for Children, most countries agreed to draft "national pro-

grammes of action" (NPAs) for achieving basic social goals. According to
UNICEF (1993),

> Those goals include control of the major childhood diseases, a halving of
> child malnutrition, a one-third reduction in under-five death rates, a halving
> of maternal mortality rates, the provision of safe water to all communities,
> the universal availability of family planning information and services, and a
> basic education for all children. (p. 60)

Of the 139 countries that have signed the Declaration of the World Summit
for Children, 54 have finalized NPAs, 34 have developed draft forms for NPAs,
and 46 (including the United States) currently are preparing NPAs (UNICEF,
1993).

1992 United Nations Conference on Environment and Development. The
"Earth Summit" met in Rio de Janeiro, Brazil, in June 1992. The outcome of
the summit, endorsed by 118 of the world's heads of state, was the Rio Declaration and its action plan, known as *Agenda 21* (UNICEF, 1993). Agenda 21
reinforces the commitments made at the World Summit for Children, stating:

> Specific goals for child survival, development and protection were agreed
> upon at the World Summit for Children and remain valid also for Agenda 21.
> Supporting and sectorial goals cover women's health and education, nutrition,
> child health, water and sanitation, basic education and children in difficult
> circumstances.
> National Governments, according to their policies, should take mea-
> sures to:
>
> - ensure the survival and protection and development of children, in
>   accordance with the goals endorsed by the World Summit for Children;
> - ensure that the interests of children are taken fully into account in the
>   participatory process for sustainable development and environmental
>   improvement. (cited in UNICEF, 1993, p. 32)

One section of Agenda 21, Chapter 25, is specifically devoted to children
and youths. That chapter urges governments to:

- implement programmes to reach the goals set by the World Summit
  for Children;
- ratify and implement the Convention on the Rights of the Child;
- promote primary environmental care activities to improve the environment by meeting basic needs and empowering local communities;

- expand children's education, especially for females;
- incorporate children's concerns into all relevant policies and strategies for environment and development.

We agree with the goals of the documents described above as they relate to children's rights and urge the United States to take formal action to advance the agendas. Furthermore, we urge the United States to provide empirically sound and developmentally appropriate direction to national policy regarding children's rights.

Note

1. From "Fasting to Help Out the Hungry World Event Attracts More Teens This Year," by A. Vessels, 1997, *Richmond Times-Dispatch*, p. E10. Reprinted with permission from the *Richmond Times-Dispatch*.

3

Getting It Right

The United Nations Convention on the Rights of the Child

A century that began with children having virtually no rights
is ending with children having the most powerful legal instrument
that not only recognizes but protects their human rights.

Carol Bellamy, UNICEF Executive Director (1997)

On November 10, 1989, the United Nations adopted the Convention on the Rights of the Child (hereafter referred to as the U.N. Convention). This document is a seminal human rights treaty that defines minimum standards for civil, economic, social, cultural, humanitarian, and political rights for children throughout the world. As noted in Chapter 2, the U.N. Convention articulates a wider variety of rights than has been covered in any previous human rights treaty (Drinan, 1992). The U.N. Convention "affirms the right of all children to receive the protection and care necessary to ensure their well-being" (Limber, 1994, p. 10). Among the basic rights that the U.N. Convention guarantees to children are the rights to survival, participation in decision making, protection, and development (Limber, 1994).

The International Catholic Child Bureau (ICCB, 1995), located in Geneva, Switzerland, said of the treaty:

The United Nations Convention on the Rights of the Child is the most comprehensive international legislative framework for children to date. This treaty reaffirms the fact that children, because of their special vulnerabilities, need special care and protection. It defines the minimum standards of human rights for children and calls on governments to devote resources to implementing those rights. It emphasizes the central role of the family. It testifies to the vital role of international cooperation in improving the living conditions of children in every country. (p. 1)

According to the ICCB (1995), the U.N. Convention is the first international human rights document to say that

- a child's viewpoint should be heard and taken into consideration in all judicial and administrative proceedings affecting his or her future (Article 12)
- considerations of the child's ethnic, religious and linguistic heritage should be taken into account when providing alternative family care for the child (Article 20)
- child victims of abuse, neglect, exploitation and torture need and should receive physical and psychological rehabilitation and social reintegration (Article 39) (p. 3)

Four principles guided the U.N. Convention: (a) children's rights shall be ensured without discrimination, (b) all actions concerning children shall be decided by considering their best interests, (c) children shall have the right to express their own views to the extent they are capable of forming such views, and (d) provisions of domestic or international law more favorable than those of the U.N. Convention shall prevail where they exist (Marks, 1990).

Elements of the U.N. Convention on the Rights of the Child

The U.N. Convention consists of a preamble and 41 substantive articles. The preamble notes that the inherent dignity and equal and inalienable rights of all members of the human family "are the foundation of freedom, justice and peace in the world." It also proclaims that "childhood is entitled to special care and assistance" and that "the child, for the full and harmonious development of his or her personality, should grow up in a family environment, in an atmosphere of happiness, love and understanding." The preamble also recognizes "the importance of international co-operation for improving the living conditions of children in every country, in particular in the developing countries."

The substantive articles, Articles 1 to 41, extend civil, political, economic, social, cultural, and humanitarian rights to children (see Table 3.1). Each of the substantive articles delineates a specific principle or right. For example, Article 3 describes the doctrine of the best interests of the child. That article advocates for each child "such protection and care as is necessary for his or her well-being." At the same time, the U.N. Convention stresses that consideration of the evolving maturity and capacities of the child must guide the degree of freedom granted.

In addition, the U.N. Convention includes 13 procedural and implementation articles (Articles 42-54). For example, Article 43 requires the establishment of a Committee on the Rights of the Child, composed of "ten experts of high moral standing and recognized competence in the field covered by this Convention." Committee elections were held on February 27 and March 1, 1991, with members elected from Barbados, Brazil, Burkina Faso, Egypt, Peru, the Philippines, Portugal, the (then) U.S.S.R., Sweden, and Zimbabwe (Cohen & Miljeteig-Olssen, 1991).

The U.N. Convention requires participating governments to submit to the committee reports describing the extent to which they have complied with the provisions set forth in the articles. Article 44 places an obligation on participating governments to distribute their reports widely within their own countries. Article 45 provides that, after reviewing governmental reports, the committee may "make suggestions and general recommendations."

Ratification of the U.N. Convention on the Rights of the Child

Signing the U.N. Convention signals a nation's intent to pursue ratification; ratification of the Convention constitutes a higher level of commitment than signing. Ratification denotes a nation's "serious attempt to address the plight of children around the world" (Limber, 1994, p. 10). Countries ratifying the U.N. Convention, known as "States Parties," are obligated to work toward implementation of the rights enumerated in the treaty and to make periodic progress reports to the Committee on the Rights of the Child.

Table 3.1 Summary of Substantive Articles of the U.N. Convention on the Rights of the Child

Article	Summary
1 Definition of Child	Every person under 18 years, unless national law grants majority at an earlier age.
2 Freedom from Discrimination	Rights in the U.N. Convention apply to all children without exception; the state is to protect children from any form of discrimination or punishment based on family's status, activities, or beliefs.
3 Best Interests of Child	The best interests of the child are to prevail in all legal and administrative decisions; the state is to ensure the establishment of standards for the care and protection of children.
4 Implementation of Rights	The state is to translate the rights in this Convention into actuality.
5 Respect for Parental Responsibility	The state is to respect the rights of parents or guardians to provide direction to the child in the exercise of the rights in this Convention.
6 Survival and Development	The child has a right to life; the state is to ensure the survival and optimal development of the child.
7 Name and Nationality	The child has a right to a name and to acquire a nationality and to know and be cared for by parents.
8 Preservation of Identity	The child has a right to preserve or reestablish the child's identity (name, nationality, and family ties).
9 Parental Care and Nonseparation	The child has a right to live with parents unless this is deemed incompatible with the child's best interests and a right to maintain contact with both parents; the state is to provide information when separation results from state action.
10 Family Reunification	The child has a right to leave or enter any country for family reunification and to maintain contact with both parents.
11 Illicit Transfer and Nonreturn	The state is to combat the illicit transfer and holding of children abroad.
12 Free Expression of Opinion	The child has a right to express an opinion in matters affecting that child and to have that opinion heard.
13 Freedom of Information	The child has a right to seek, receive, and impart information through any media.
14 Freedom of Thought, Conscience, and Religion	The child has a right to determine and practice any belief; the state is to respect the rights of parents or guardians to provide direction in the exercise of this right.

(continued)

Table 3.1 Continued

Article	Summary
15 Freedom of Association	The child has a right to freedom of association and freedom of peaceful assembly.
16 Protection of Privacy	The child has a right to protection from arbitrary or unlawful interference with privacy, family, home, or correspondence, or attacks on honor and reputation.
17 Media and Information	The state is to ensure access to information and material from a diversity of national and international sources.
18 Parental Responsibilities	The state is to recognize the principle that both parents are responsible for the upbringing of their children and that parents or guardians have primary responsibility; the state is to assist parents or guardians in this responsibility and to ensure the provision of child care for eligible working parents.
19 Abuse and Neglect	The state is to protect children from all forms of abuse, neglect, and exploitation by parents or others and to undertake preventive and treatment programs in this regard.
20 Children Without Families	The child has a right to receive special protection and assistance from the state when deprived of a family environment and to be provided with alternative care, such as foster placement or Kafala of Islamic Law, adoption, or suitable institutional placement.
21 Adoption	The state is to regulate the process of adoption (including intercountry adoption), where it is permitted.
22 Refugee Children	The state is to ensure protection and assistance to children who are refugees or seeking refugee status and is to cooperate with competent organizations providing such protection and assistance.
23 Disabled Children	Disabled children have a right to special care and training designed to help them achieve self-reliance and a full and decent life in society.
24 Health Care	The child has a right to the highest attainable standard of health and access to medical services; the state is to attempt to diminish infant and child mortality, combat childhood disease and malnutrition, ensure health care for expectant mothers, provide access to health education, develop preventive health care, and abolish harmful traditional practices.

Article	Summary
25 Periodic Review	Children placed by the state for reasons of care, protection, or treatment have a right to have all aspects of that placement reviewed regularly.
26 Social Security	The child has a right, where appropriate, to benefit from social security or insurance.
27 Standard of Living	The child has a right to an adequate standard of living; the state is to assist parents who cannot meet this responsibility and to try to recover maintenance for the child from persons having financial responsibility, both within the state and abroad.
28 Education	The child has a right to education; the state is to provide free and compulsory primary education, ensure equal access to secondary and higher education, and ensure that school discipline does not threaten the child's human dignity.
29 Aims of Education	The states parties agree that education is to be directed at developing the child's personality and talents; to prepare the child for responsible life in a free society; to develop respect for the child's parents, basic human rights, the natural environment, and the child's own cultural and national values and those of others.
30 Children of Minorities	Children of minority communities and indigenous populations have a right to enjoy their own culture, practice their own religion, and use their own language.
31 Leisure and Recreation	The child has a right to leisure, play, and participation in cultural and artistic activities.
32 Child Labor	The child has a right to be protected from economic exploitation and from engaging in work that constitutes a threat to health, education, and development; the state is to set minimum ages for employment, regulate conditions of employment, and provide sanctions for effective enforcement.
33 Narcotics	The state is to protect children from illegal narcotic and psychotropic drugs and from involvement in their production or distribution.
34 Sexual Exploitation	The state is to protect children from sexual exploitation and abuse, including prostitution and involvement in pornography.
35 Sale and Trafficking	The state is to prevent the abduction, sale, and trafficking of children.

(continued)

Table 3.1 Continued

Article	Summary
36 Other Exploitation	The state is to protect children from all other forms of exploitation.
37 Torture, Capital Punishment, and Deprivation of Liberty	The state is to protect children from torture or other cruel, inhuman, or degrading treatment; capital punishment or life imprisonment for offenses committed by persons below the age of 18 years; and unlawful or arbitrary deprivation of liberty. Children deprived of liberty have a right to be treated with humanity and respect, to be separated from adults, to maintain contact with family members, and to have prompt access to legal assistance.
38 Armed Conflict	The state is to respect international humanitarian law, ensure that no child under 15 years of age takes a direct part in hostilities, refrain from recruiting any child under age 15 into the armed forces, and ensure that all children affected by armed conflict benefit from protection and care.
39 Rehabilitative Care	The state is to promote the physical and psychological recovery and social reintegration of child victims of abuse, neglect, exploitation, torture, or armed conflicts and to do so in an environment that fosters the health, self-respect, and dignity of the child.
40 Juvenile Justice	Accused children have a right to be treated with dignity. The state is to ensure that no child is accused by reason of acts or omissions not prohibited by law at the time committed; that every accused child is informed promptly of the charges, presumed innocent until proven guilty in a prompt and fair trial, receives legal assistance, and is not compelled to give testimony or confess guilt; and that alternatives to institutional care are available.
41 Supremacy of Higher Standards	The standards contained in this Convention do not supersede higher standards contained in national law or other international instruments.

The U.N. Convention was opened for signature on January 26, 1990. On that day alone, 61 countries signed the Convention, "a record first-day response" (UNICEF Child Rights, 1997a). Just 7 months later, on September 2, 1990, the Convention went into effect after the 20th state had ratified it. In only 7 years, the Convention was ratified by all but two nation states (the United States and Somalia; see Box 3.1).

Box 3.1

The Status of Ratification of the
U.N. Convention on the Rights of the Child

Countries That Have Ratified the U.N. Convention on the Rights of the Child:

Africa: Algeria, Angola, Benin, Botswana, Burkina Faso, Burundi, Cameroon, Cape Verde, Central African Republic, Chad, Comors, Congo, Côte d'Ivoire, Djibouti, Egypt, Equatorial Guinea, Ethiopia, Gabon, Gambia, Ghana, Guinea, Guinea-Bissau, Kenya, Lesotho, Liberia, Madagascar, Malawi, Mali, Mauritania, Mauritius, Morocco, Mozambique, Namibia, Niger, Nigeria, Rwanda, São Tomé & Principe, Senegal, Seychelles, Sierra Leone, South Africa, Sudan, Swaziland, Tanzania, Togo, Tunisia, Uganda, Zaire (now named the Democratic Republic of Congo), Zambia, Zimbabwe

Asia and Arabia: Afghanistan, Azerbaijan, Bahrain, Bangladesh, Bhutan, Brunei Darssalem, Cambodia, China, India, Indonesia, Iran, Iraq, Japan, Jordan, Korea (Democratic People's Republic), Korea (Republic of), Kuwait, Laos, Lebanon, Libya, Malaysia, Maldives, Mongolia, Myanmar, Nepal, Oman, Pakistan, Papua New Guinea, Philippines, Qatar, Samoa, Saudi Arabia, Singapore, Solomon Islands, Syria, Sri Lanka, Thailand, United Arab Emirates, Vanuatu, Vietnam, Yemen

Eastern Europe: Albania, Belarus, Bulgaria, Croatia, Czechoslovakia, Estonia, Hungary, Latvia, Lithuania, Poland, Romania, Slovenia, Ukraine, Russia, Yugoslavia

Latin America: Antigua and Barbuda, Argentina, Bahamas, Barbados, Belize, Bolivia, Brazil, Chile, Colombia, Costa Rica, Cuba, Dominica, Dominican Republic, Ecuador, El Salvador, Grenada, Guatemala, Guyana, Haiti, Honduras, Jamaica, Mexico, Nicaragua, Panama, Paraguay, Peru, St. Kitts and Nevis, St. Lucia, St. Vincent & the Grenadines, Suriname, Trinidad & Tobago, Uruguay, Venezuela

Western Europe and Others: Australia, Austria, Belgium, Canada, Cook Islands, Cyprus, Denmark, Finland, France, Germany, Greece, Holy See, Iceland, Ireland, Israel, Italy, Liechtenstein, Luxembourg, Malta, Monaco, Netherlands, New Zealand, Norway, Portugal, San Marino, Spain, Sweden, Switzerland, Turkey, United Kingdom

Countries That Have Signed (But Not Ratified) the U.N. Convention on the Rights of the Child:

Africa: Somalia

Western Europe and Others: United States of America

NOTE: We are grateful to Joe J. Mettimano of the United Nations Children's Fund (UNICEF) for his kind assistance in obtaining this information.

U.S. Failure to Ratify the U.N. Convention

Clearly, the world's interest in the rights of children has changed dramatically in recent years. Why, then, is the United States, a nation of comparatively great wealth and high stature, one of only two states not ratifying the U.N. Convention?

One reason is that, despite its rhetoric to the contrary, as former President Jimmy Carter has noted on several occasions, the United States generally has a lackluster record of ratifying major human rights treaties. As a result, it can talk about the importance of human rights without being held accountable by official international bodies.

Another explanation is provided by the structure of the government. In the United States, the states are allowed great discretion and power in legislating domestic issues (Cohen & Davidson, 1990). By ratifying the U.N. Convention, the federal government could be perceived as interfering with the individual states' power to create, amend, and adjudicate their own laws concerning children. Indeed, under President George Bush, U.S. progress toward signing the U.N. Convention "stalled amid concerns that it impinged upon states' rights" (Limber, 1994, p. 10).

A third explanation is that some rights accorded children under the U.N. Convention are not recognized as rights in the United States. For example, Article 28 asserts a fundamental right to education. The U.S. Supreme Court held in *San Antonio Independent School District v. Rodriguez* (1973), however, that children in the United States have no fundamental right to education. The Court stated: "Education, of course, is not among the rights afforded explicit protection under our Federal Constitution. Nor do we find any basis for saying it is implicitly so protected" (p. 35). That view was reflected in two cases decided during the 1990s: *Craig v. Selma City School Board* (1992) and *Hill by and through Hill v. Rankin County, Mississippi School District* (1993). Thus, the judicial branch of the government has found U.S. law to be less protective than the U.N. Convention.

Moreover, some U.S. laws actually conflict with the U.N. Convention's principles. For example, Article 28 states that "States Parties shall take all appropriate measures to ensure that school discipline is administered in a manner consistent with the child's human dignity." Although the U.N. Convention neither expressly nor implicitly bars corporal punishment in the schools, the Committee on the Rights of the Child is interpreting the Convention as forbidding corporal punishment (G. B. Melton, personal communication, October 12, 1997). Yet, in 23 of the United States, school officials are permitted by law to use corporal punishment, including—at least in Texas— the use of "deadly force" (Monaghan, 1997, p. A7).

Similarly, Article 37 forbids the use of capital punishment "for offenses committed by persons below eighteen years of age." Yet, since capital punishment was held constitutional in the United States in 1976, at least nine young men who committed murder as children have been executed in the United States (Saul, 1997). In fact, the last juvenile execution *worldwide* was Christopher Burger, executed in Georgia on December 9, 1993 (Saul, 1997). According to the Africa News Service (1997), since 1990 only five countries have executed people who were under 18 years of age at the time of the crime: Iran, Pakistan, Saudi Arabia, Yemen, and the United States. Indeed, the United States is keeping curious company on this issue.

In 1988, the U.S. Supreme Court interpreted the Constitution as permitting use of the death penalty for persons who commit murder at the age of 16 years or older (*Thompson v. Oklahoma,* 1988). In some cases, even younger children who commit murder may be executed, as Supreme Court Justice O'Connor noted in the *Thompson* case:

> Although a national consensus forbidding the execution of any person for a crime committed before the age of 16 very likely does exist . . . the Federal Government and 19 States have authorized capital punishment without setting any minimum age, and have also provided for some 15-year-olds to be prosecuted as adults. These laws appear to render 15-year-olds death eligible, and thus pose a real obstacle to finding a consensus. (p. 2689)

Finally, "widespread misconceptions about the Convention's intent and provisions, and a lack of public understanding about how this type of agreement is treated by our government, have induced a significant level of opposition to the [U.N. Convention]" (UNICEF Child Rights, 1997b, p. 1). Most of the U.N. Convention's opposition involves concerns related to national sovereignty and the parent-child relationship. Opposition groups contend, for example, that the Convention "usurps national and state sovereignty," "undermines parental authority," "would allow and encourage children to sue parents, join gangs, have abortions, etc. . . . ," and express fears that "the United Nations would dictate how we raise and teach children" (UNICEF Child Rights, 1997b, p. 1).

Thus, several reasons can be offered for why the United States Congress has yet to ratify the U.N. Convention on the Rights of the Child. On October

5, 1992, both the U.S. House of Representatives and the U.S. Senate failed to pass resolutions supporting ratification of the U.N. Convention (S. Res. 352; H. Res. 515).

Why the United States Should Ratify the U.N. Convention

The International Catholic Child Bureau (ICCB, 1995) articulated two important reasons why the U.S. should ratify the U.N. Convention:

> First, it would establish a useful framework and set clear guidelines by which legislators, officials at all levels of government, and private organizations and individuals can form policies, establish budget priorities, and shape programs to improve the situation of our children. Second, it would require our government to assess and report regularly on the condition of our children and our plans as a nation to make needed improvements. . . . In short, although many of the Convention's rights and protections for children are already reflected in the U.S. Constitution, state and federal law, and in other treaties the United States has ratified, the convention would establish moral and legislative guidelines to be used in the dialogue this nation needs to have on how to improve the welfare of our children. (pp. 2-3)

Similarly, the United States Committee for UNICEF (1997) concluded that "ratification of the Convention would promote a more supportive social and legislative environment for children and would assist in making children more of a national priority" (p. 5).

How Does the U.N. Convention Relate to U.S. Law?

The U.S. Constitution specifies that international treaties ratified by the Senate become law. Human rights treaties, however, typically have been considered to be "non-self-executing," which means that they require what is known as "implementing legislation" in order to have the force of law (ICCB, 1995). The U.S. Senate has the right to determine what type of implementing legislation to pass in each case. Thus, in the case of the U.N. Convention, the U.S. Senate has the authority to determine how the Convention will be interpreted by the U.S. courts. Specifically, the Senate may adopt "Reservations," "Understandings," or "Declarations" (RUDs) as part of the implementing legislation. *Reservations* withhold national assent to particular provisions of a treaty, whereas *Understandings* state the country's interpretation of particular provisions within a treaty. *Declarations* provide notice to other countries as to how a ratifying nation intends to implement specific treaty provisions. When a non-self-executing treaty is discussed, any proposed reservations, understandings, or declarations become the subject of open debate in the Senate.

Thus, although the U.N. Convention on the Rights of the Child contains certain provisions that conflict with U.S. law, the Senate could adopt RUDs that would resolve each of those discrepancies. Cohen and Davidson's (1990) edited volume *Children's Rights in America: U.N. Convention on the Rights of the Child Compared With United States Law,* published jointly by the American Bar Association Center on Children and the Law and the Defense for Children International-USA, provides a thorough analysis of the discrepancies and their potential resolutions.

RUDs were used in 1992 in ratifying another treaty, the Covenant on Civil and Political Rights, which has a prohibition on the execution of minors (United States Committee for UNICEF, 1997). In that case, the Bush administration chose to make a reservation, and the Senate gave its advice and consent to that reservation. The United States Committee for UNICEF (1997) noted: "The reservation affirms the right of U.S. states to make laws concerning the execution of minors, which essentially means that we did not ratify this part of the treaty. A similar action could be taken while ratifying the children's convention" (p. 4). Alternatively, of course, the Senate could propose legislation that would bring U.S. law in line with the provisions of the U.N. Convention. Either process is lengthy, however, as noted by the United States Committee for UNICEF (1997):

> One of the factors which makes ratification such a lengthy process in the U.S. is that the Senate attempts to ensure that all federal and/or state laws meet the standards of the treaty and, if necessary, enact new legislation before giving its consent. This is because the United States takes the position that the text of a human rights treaty itself does not *directly* become part of U.S. law. (p. 1)

Current Status of the U.N. Convention in the United States

On February 16, 1995, the United States signed the U.N. Convention, a step indicating its intent to consider ratification. Currently, President Clinton and his advisers are drafting a Statement of Reservations, Understandings, and Declarations. On completion, that statement will be presented to the Senate, along with the Convention, for its "advice and consent." If the Senate ratifies the Convention (amended by the RUDs), the president can certify that ratification to the United Nations.

More than 200 U.S. organizations and local governments support the U.N. Convention on the Rights of the Child. The list of supporters is long and varied and includes the American Red Cross, the American Public Health Association, the Child Welfare League of America, the American Bar Association, the Children's Defense Fund, the National Education Association, United Way International, the YMCA, the YWCA, Girl Scouts of the United States of America, and the National Governors Association, as well as some religious groups.

Some conservative groups, however, oppose the U.N. Convention, including the Christian Coalition, the John Birch Society, the National Center for Home Education, the Eagle Forum, and Concerned Women of America (United States Committee for UNICEF, 1997). According to the United States Committee for UNICEF (1997), "[t]hese organizations have made a significant effort to portray the Convention as a threat" (p. 2). Interestingly, in many cases, opponents have criticized provisions that were added by the conservative Reagan and Bush administrations during the drafting process, reflecting the rights children have under the U.S. Constitution (United States Committee for UNICEF, 1997, p. 2). With regard to the U.N. Convention's opposition, the United States Committee for UNICEF (1997) noted:

> These public efforts are reinforced by a number of Senators (mostly Republican) which [sic] oppose ratification of the Convention. Opposition in the Senate is led by Senator Jesse Helms (R-NC). Citing his opinion that the "United Nations Convention on the Rights of the Child is incompatible with God-given right and responsibility of parents to raise their children," and that "the Convention has the potential to severely restrict States and the Federal Government in their efforts to protect children and to enhance family life," Senator Helms, along with 26 cosponsors, introduced a Senate Resolution in June 1995 which urged the President to not transmit the Convention to the Foreign Relations Committee (which Helms chairs) for review. (p. 3)

The United States Committee for UNICEF (1997) has responded to the opposition's claims as follows:

Q: Does the Convention threaten a parent's authority or rights? Does it threaten the parent-child relationship?

A: No. In fact, the Convention repeatedly emphasizes the central importance of the role and authority of the family. . . .

Q: Does the Convention threaten our national sovereignty? Will the United Nations control our laws and children?

A: No. The Convention contains no controlling language or mandates. Moreover, under the supremacy clause of our Constitution, no treaty can "override" our Constitution. . . . Therefore, neither the United Nations nor the Committee on the Rights of the Child would have dominion, power, or enforcement authority over the United States or its citizens. . . .

Q: Does the Convention give children the right to sue their parents?

A: No. The Convention does not address this issue. . . .

Q: What does the Convention say on the issue of abortion?

A: Great care was taken by the drafters to keep the Convention on the Rights of the Child *neutral* on the question of abortion.

Thus, the opposition's major concerns regarding the U.N. Convention appear unwarranted.

The process of ratification itself, though, may be troublesome. Cohen and Davidson (1990) commented:

> The comprehensiveness of the Convention's text, coupled with the fact that many of the Convention's rights ordinarily fall within the . . . jurisdiction of state rather than federal law, raises the possibility that Senate review and debate over the Convention could get bogged down interminably. (p. iv)

Their comment has proved to be prophetic; nearly 3 years have passed since the United States signed the U.N. Convention (signifying intent to ratify) and—still—the document has not been forwarded to the Senate for official ratification.

G. B. Melton (personal communication, October 12, 1997) offered some words of encouragement regarding the U.S. position on the U.N. Convention:

> A strong argument can be made that the Convention is now customary international law and thus binding in the U.S., notwithstanding that the U.S. is not a party to the Convention. Compare, [for example], the Helsinki Accord, in which the U.S. recognized a number of human rights treaties as customary

law. Ironically, the Convention may have substantially greater legal enforce-
ability in the U.S. (where customary international law is trumped only by a
ratified treaty or the Constitution) than in most of the states parties to the
Convention.

Nonetheless, we contend that the failure of the United States to ratify the U.N.
Convention is symptomatic of a larger problem—namely, that the United
States has adopted no coherent policy on the rights of children. Two decades
ago, Rodham (now First Lady Hillary Rodham Clinton) argued that children
should be granted rights appropriate to their maturational abilities (see, e.g.,
Rodham, 1973, 1979). That view, which we endorse, is expressed by the U.N.
Convention as well. It is time—indeed, it has been time since January 26,
1990—for the United States to ratify the United Nations Convention on the
Rights of the Child.

4

Differing Views

Perspectives on Children's Rights and Competencies

> Children are often more capable of expressing
> preferences and participating in making major life
> decisions than is generally recognized . . . under the law.
>
> Gerald Koocher and David DeMaso,
> Researchers (1990)

The term *children's rights* evokes different meanings for different people. For some, the focus is on rights granted *to* children by society; for others, the emphasis is on rights possessed *by* children, which those children are free to use as they wish. Adults' conceptions and children's views of the acceptability of these rights may differ (Melton, 1980). Furthermore, different attitudes exist about what constitute the appropriate needs of children (Bross, 1991; Rogers & Wrightsman, 1978); such varying conceptions are especially influenced by the particular cultural background of the respondent (Cohen, 1990).

Perspectives on Children's Rights

A Cross-Cultural Perspective on Children's Rights

Chapter 3 described the United Nations Convention on the Rights of the Child (United Nations General Assembly, 1989). The international discussion that led to a formulation of children's rights reflects differing emphases from one society to another. Indeed, the drafting of each article involved careful selection of language designed to reflect multiple cultural perspectives.

For example, delegates reflecting the Islamic faith strongly opposed the inclusion of rights concerning freedom of religion, foster care, and adoption, on the grounds that such "rights" conflicted with their religious beliefs (Cohen, 1990). Therefore, the language of Article 20 of the U.N. Convention was carefully crafted to include a multicultural perspective. It states that when alternatives to care by the natural parents are in the best interests of the child, "such care should include . . . foster care placement, Kafala of Islamic Law, adoption, or if necessary placement in suitable institutions" (p. 39).

The specific manifestations of children's rights, evaluated against the various articles of the U.N. Convention, are inevitably related to the historical and political processes of a particular country. For example, Last and Ben-yamini (1991) evaluated the current status of a variety of rights of children in Israel, as reflected in Israeli laws.

But even within one society—especially one as diverse as the United States—conceptions of appropriate rights differ. The purposes of this chapter, therefore, are to examine ideologically differing conceptions and to describe a procedure for measuring these different perspectives. In addition, this chapter discusses empirical research findings regarding children's developing competencies.

The U.S. Supreme Court's Attitude Toward Children's Rights

Melton (1989) offered four empirically grounded reasons why adults should recognize the liberty and privacy interests of youth: (a) Increased control of one's fate is related to psychological well-being, (b) freedom of choice increases motivation and performance, (c) experiences of decision making enhance legal socialization, and (d) respect for privacy may solidify a sense of identity. As the contradictory examples described in Chapter 1 suggest, however, the U.S. Supreme Court has been less than forthright in the application of the principle that minors are persons under the law. In this regard, Melton noted:

[T]he Court has been reluctant to concede that adolescents can be competent decision makers, and it has frequently assumed that recognition of adolescents' liberty and privacy interests would result in great harm to the child, the family, and society. Most important, the Court has sometimes applied a lower level of scrutiny to abridgement of minors' constitutional rights than is applied to state intrusions upon adults' fundamental rights and, in so doing, has started with a *presumption* that age discrimination is constitutional. Rather than questioning whether the state has *compelling* interests (the usual standard) in infringement of minors' fundamental rights, the Court has frequently looked merely for *legitimate, significant,* or *rational* bases for limitations placed by the state on minors' exercise of constitutional rights. (p. 283)

Thus, the Supreme Court has offered inconsistent guidance with regard to children's rights.

Traditionally, the Supreme Court's assumption has been that parents will act in the best interests of their children. As well-publicized examples of abuse and abandonment of children by their parents show, however, this assumption does not always hold true. Implicit in this assumption is that parents "know better" than children about what the children's best interests are. At times, the courts have reified this doctrine. For example, in *Parham v. J. R.* (1979), Chief Justice Warren Burger wrote: "Most children, even in adolescence, simply are not able to make sound judgments concerning many decisions, including their need for medical care or treatment. Parents can and must make these judgments" (p. 604).

Recognizing the harms inflicted on children within their family settings in U.S. society or elsewhere, psychiatrists, social workers, psychologists, and some judges in the 1960s began to emphasize a new conception of children's rights, especially with regard to their custodial caregivers. Two books by Goldstein, Freud, and Solnit were quite influential in this movement: *Beyond the Best Interests of the Child* (1973) and *Before the Best Interests of the Child* (1979). It is important to note the opening preposition of those two titles: Goldstein et al. were arguing for a standard that amounted to the least detrimental alternative available to the child whose interests were being examined.

In accordance with this view, Reppucci and Crosby (1993) argued that, despite the popularity of the phrase, the *best interests of the child* is a concept generally devoid of objective substance. Several alternatives may be equally desirable—or equally undesirable—for the child who suffers maltreatment. As Reppucci and Crosby noted, professionals do not "currently have the ability to predict accurately in every case what behavioral alternative is best for any given child" (p. 5). Hence, a major function of research should be to determine what values or psychological assumptions are used by decision makers in guiding their "best interests" determinations.

Law professor Robert Mnookin (1978) has written eloquently on this point:

> Deciding what is best for a child often poses a question no less ultimate than the purposes of life itself. Should the decision maker be primarily concerned with the child's happiness or with his or her spiritual and religious training? Is the primary goal long-term economic productivity when the child grows up? Or are the most important values in life in warm relationships? In discipline and self-sacrifice? Are stability and security for a child more desirable than intellectual stimulation? . . . [I]f one looks to our society at large, one finds neither a clear consensus as to the best child rearing strategies, nor an appropriate hierarchy of ultimate values. In short, there is in our society no apparent consensus about the good life for children. (p. 164)

Conceptual Distinctions Among Rights to Protection, Self-Determination, and Entitlement

The Merriam-Webster dictionary (1993) defines a *right* as "something to which one has a just claim . . . the power or privilege to which one is justly entitled" (p. 1008)—in other words, any power or privilege vested in a person by laws or customs. This definition implies that rights have to be recognized by the society in which the rights claimant lives. At present, a vast disparity exists between elements in U.S. society as to what is and is not a right. Regardless, one can take the dictionary definition to mean that rights are rather specific—that we can identify topics or subject matter that serves as the contents for various potential "rights."

The issue is especially controversial when children's rights become the topic. Society, moving sporadically and goaded by the child advocacy movement in the mid-1970s and again in the early 1990s, would appear to be extending and clarifying the rights of children. For every person advocating for the expansion of children's rights, however, someone else seeks to keep children in their current status—or narrower.

Several reasons come to mind for justifying advocacy for children (Vardin & Brody, 1979):

1. Children are politically disenfranchised; they cannot vote and typically do not lobby.

2. Children are economically disadvantaged; they have no separate financial power or control.
3. The legal status of children remains, at best, ambiguous and subject to the conflicting, nonconsonant interpretations of the courts.
4. Children are especially vulnerable to abuse and exploitation by others.

Not only do attitudes in U.S. society conflict over the nature and breadth of children's rights, but the concept of *children's rights* is multifaceted and complex. One advocacy group may focus on one topic, such as nutrition, whereas another may concern itself only with children's rights under law. Other advocates may be working toward the expansion of services to be provided children by the institutions of society, whereas others may propose that the thrust should be toward children achieving the freedom to make those choices that influence their own lives. As Rodham (1973) put it, "Children's Rights" is a slogan in search of a definition; it lacks any "coherent doctrine regarding the status of children as political beings" (p. 1).

The advocacy literature reflects two orientations toward the extension of children's rights. The first, labeled the "nurturance orientation," stresses the provision by society of supposedly beneficial objects, environments, services, and experiences for the child. The second, labeled the "self-determination orientation," stresses those potential rights that would allow children to exercise influence over their environments, to make decisions about what they want, and to have autonomous control over various facets of their lives.

The Nurturance Orientation

The nurturance orientation is essentially paternalistic (or maternalistic), in that what is good or desirable is determined *for* the child by society or some subset of society, not *by* the child. The nurturance orientation reflects distress over the inadequate state of children's lives in the United States and elsewhere. For example, according to the United Nations Children's Fund (UNICEF, 1993), in the United States, one of every seven children is in a family that relies on a welfare check for survival. Infant mortality rates rank the United States—despite its affluence—as one of the worst (29th) among industrialized nations; in addition, more than 400,000 babies are born annually with alcohol- and drug-related problems (UNICEF, 1993).

The Child Welfare League and the Children's Defense Fund are two advocacy organizations seeking to fulfill nurturance rights for children. In a report issued in 1993, the Children's Defense Fund estimated that more than one fourth of the children residing in cities with a population of 100,000 or more lived in poverty—in a country in which less than 2% of federal spending went to Aid For Families With Dependent Children (now known as Temporary Assistance to Needy Families). Such organizations view certain interventions as essential manifestations of children's nurturance rights—for example, prenatal medical care; free, mandatory immunization; proper nutrition; universal early childhood education; paid maternal or parental leave; and family-support centers in neighborhoods.

A report published by the Carnegie Foundation in 1994 (cited in Elmer-Dewitt, 1994) presented the following findings:

- One out of every three victims of physical abuse is a child younger than 1 year old.
- More than three million American children are growing up in neighborhoods with high rates of poverty.
- About 60% of 2-year-olds have not had immunizations against the common childhood diseases.
- Nine out of every 1,000 U.S. babies die before their first birthday.

Similarly, books that appeared in the mid-1990s alerted the public to the inadequacy of childhood supports in contemporary life. For example, Leach (1994) proposed that children have the right to live in a world of familiar adults who will provide for their basic needs, protect them, and respond to them in caring and effective ways. Much of this is not new, of course—A Children's Bill of Rights is now more than 20 years old (see Maurer, 1974)—but the new thrust in such books is the assumption that, in today's world, parents cannot provide all of what their children need; for children's needs to be met, therefore, considerable outside help—especially governmental intervention—is required.

The founder and president of the Children's Defense Fund, Marian Wright Edelman, reflected the fundamental assumption of nurturance-rights advocates when she stated: "As adults we are responsible for meeting the needs of children. It is our moral obligation. We brought about their births and their lives, and they cannot fend for themselves."[1]

First Lady Hillary Rodham Clinton is another advocate for the adoption of children's nurturance rights. Because of her position, when her husband, then-candidate Bill Clinton, campaigned for and achieved the presidency, her views were subjected to intense scrutiny. Box 4.1 evaluates the reactions to her written and spoken words.

Box 4.1

Hillary Rodham Clinton's Position on Children's Rights

During the 1992 presidential campaign, Hillary Rodham Clinton's position on children's rights received extensive attention from the media. Some of the treatment was sensationalistic, but other reviews were informed and thoughtful.

Mrs. Clinton's position has been expressed in a variety of articles, book chapters, and speeches, extending back to 1973. She has stated that children, if they are competent, should be allowed to determine their own future (Rodham, 1973) and that they should be considered to be competent to make such decisions until they are proved to be incompetent. Although she believes that not all families are wise and knowledgeable, she does favor the principle of parental notification when an adolescent seeks an abortion.

Political conservatives, however, are critical of Mrs. Clinton's views because they believe that her approach puts the state in the position of parent (Charen, 1993). They are especially negative toward her support of nurturant rights, noting that greater funding for immunization, for example, may not alleviate the problem of communicable disease in children. One critic, Mona Charen (1993), concluded that many inner-city mothers already have access to free immunization programs but that the mothers lack the responsibility or motivation to see that their children are immunized.

Other conservative criticisms of Mrs. Clinton's views, such as those by former presidential candidate Patrick J. Buchanan, claimed that she had "compared marriage and the family as institutions to slavery and life on an Indian reservation."[a] But, in the views of legal scholars, such criticisms "grossly distort"[a] her position. In her article in the *Harvard Educational Review* (Rodham, 1973), when describing the legal status of children, Mrs. Clinton referred to several classes of people, including wives, slaves, and Native Americans who were historically treated as dependents, legally unable to speak for themselves. Her history is accurate.

More informed criticisms, such as those by the philosopher Christopher Lasch (1992), questioned her allegiance to the concept of *the family*. He wrote that "her writings leave the unmistakable impression that it is the family that holds children back, the state that sets them free" (p. 77).[b] Furthermore, she "gives us a make-believe world in which everybody pretends that distinctions between children and adults have no basis in fact, or at least defy generalization" (p. 78). If, Lasch asked, she assumes the competency of children, why does she favor parental notification on abortions?

---

a. From "Legal Scholars See Distortion in Attacks on Hillary Clinton," by T. Lewin, August 24, 1992, *New York Times*, p. A1. Copyright © 1992, 1993, 1997 by The New York Times Co. Reprinted by permission.
b. From "Hillary Clinton, Child Saver," by C. Lasch, 1992, *Harper's Magazine*. Copyright © 1992 by *Harper's Magazine*. All rights reserved. Reproduced from the October issue by special permission.

In summary, the nurturance orientation emphasizes the protection of children against abuses and the provision of services they otherwise might not have. This position clearly recognizes the inherent worth of children; in a sense, though, advocates of this view treat children as "objects" who lack human qualities of judgment and choice.

The Self-Determination Orientation

Whereas the nurturance orientation may be considered, albeit simplistically, to be "giving children what's good for them," the self-determination perspective argues for "giving children the right to decide what's good for themselves." Several book-length treatments of this viewpoint emerged in the 1970s and 1980s, including those by Cohen (1980), Farson (1974), and Holt (1974).

The separation of two types of rights closely parallels the distinction that Farson (1974) made between two classes of child advocates: (a) those interested in protecting children and (b) those interested in protecting children's rights. The distinction between self-determination rights and nurturance rights is related to that made by Rodham (1973) between the extension of adult rights to children and the passage of laws that recognize the needs of children as a special, dependent class of citizens. Adults' rights tend to fall into the self-determination classification (e.g., the right to enter into contracts, the right to vote, the right to choose legal counsel), whereas laws recognizing the needs of children tend to fall into the nurturance category (e.g., the right to an education and the right to an acceptable home environment, with the state determining the meaning of *education* and *acceptable*).

Self-determination rights have been advocated for virtually every type of right customarily given to adults. For example, Paul E. Peterson (1993), a professor of government at Harvard University, has proposed giving children the right to vote: "[A]ll citizens, even our youngest, should be given the right to vote, either by casting their own votes or by having their votes cast for them by their parents or guardians" (p. 25).[2] His rationale for this self-determination right is, ironically, a nurturant one: If children were given the right to vote, groups representing children would acquire status and power and thus insist that programs benefiting children be accentuated.

Perhaps the most radical of proposed self-determination rights is that of sexuality. Some sexologists advocate full sexual freedoms for children, arguing that even "young children should be allowed, and perhaps encouraged, to conduct a full sex life without interference from parents or the law."[3] Mary S. Calderone, while head of the Sex Information and Education Council of the United States (SIECUS), proposed that children have the right "to know about sexuality and to *be* sexual."[2] Although we disagree with such views, we report them to illustrate the extent of rights advocated by some individuals under the self-determination label.

Specific Rights for Children

The conceptual distinction between rights of self-determination and empowerment versus child protection rights is of paramount importance. So too is the content area because the favorability of attitudes toward the rights of children is likely to be dependent on the specific subject matter or content area. For example, it seems plausible that an individual might be supportive of giving children the right to make choices in the area of education and yet, at the same time, be strongly opposed to giving children the right to make their own choices regarding health care.

Bross (1991) extended Rogers and Wrightsman's two-factor conceptualization of children's rights. He argued that three types of rights may be afforded children: rights of protection, rights of choice, and rights of entitlement.

> Rights of protection include protection from violence, exploitation, and deprivation. These rights are not dependent on a person's capacity to reason. Rights of entitlement to education, health and employment can derive from private sources, the economy, or the government. Entitlement may or may not be conditioned upon the competency of the individual recipient. Rights of choice and practice in exercising rights of choice classically accrue to an individual only when competence is established, e.g., voting, signing binding legal documents, agreeing to medical care. (p. 90)

In another section of his article, however, Bross (1991) reflected the basic distinction between nurturance and self-determination when he wrote:

> A proper summary of the possible rights of children related to national development should include the need for protecting the passive child as well as enabling children to practice making responsible choices when they are able. (p. 95)

Measurement of Attitudes
Toward Children's Rights

Given this diversity and multiplicity of opinions and approaches to the topic, Rogers and Wrightsman (1978) proposed that it would be helpful to develop a *taxonomy* (a system for classifying) children's rights. Such a taxonomy would allow for the measurement of attitudes toward the rights of children and could be sensitive to differences in attitude among specialized advocates, as well as between advocates and non-advocates (Rogers & Wrightsman, 1978).

Annas and Healey (cited in Beyer, 1974) suggested that the most helpful way to conceptualize the various meanings of the term *right* was to place them on a continuum—at one end, the rights recognized by law; somewhere near the middle, those rights that probably would be recognized by a court of law as such if the occasion arose; and at the opposite end, philosophical or political statements of what the law of rights ought to be. Although a taxonomy need not reflect these distinctions, Rogers and Wrightsman (1978) chose to focus attention on the potential, rather than the legally recognized, rights of children. For their purposes, Rogers and Wrightsman chose to limit consideration to those potential rights of children being advocated by various individuals and groups. In identifying content, they also bore in mind Worsfold's (1974) prescription of the three features necessary in all systems justifying new rights for children: (a) The rights must be theoretically possible, (b) the rights must be universal in scope, and (c) the rights must be paramount in importance.

Relying especially on the Farson (1974) and Maurer (1974) typologies, Rogers and Wrightsman (1978) identified five basic content areas: health, education and information, economic, safety and care, and legal-judicial-political rights. Within each of these content areas is a dimension of self-determination and a dimension of nurturance, resulting in 10 categories within which to classify specific rights advocated for children. Examples of the rights that might appear within each category are presented in Table 4.1.

Attitudinal Instruments

Several researchers have constructed attitudinal instruments designed to tap the self-determination dimension. These instruments include A Survey of

Table 4.1 Examples of Children's Rights

	Conceptual Dimension	
Content Area	*Nurturance*	*Self-Determination*
Health	Free health care	Choice to refuse or accept treatment
Education and Information	Quality education	Choice not to attend school
		Choice of classes
Economic	Equal pay for equal work	Right to enter into binding contracts
	Protection from child labor	Choice of work assignments and hours
Safety and Care	Products safely designed	Choice of friends and play materials
	Living choice determined by 'best interests of the child'	Choice of where to live
Legal-Judicial-Political	Due process	Choice of legal counsel
	Decisions made in the child's 'best interests'	Standing to 'divorce' parents

SOURCE: Rogers and Wrightsman (1978)

Opinions Regarding the Discipline of Children (Itkin, 1952); Attitude Toward the Freedom of Children (Koch, Dentler, Dysart, & Streit, 1934); Attitudes Toward Parental Control of Children (Stogdill & Goddard, 1936); Attitude Toward Parental Control of Children's Activities (Stott, 1940); and certain subscales of the Parental Attitude Research Instrument-Revised (Cross & Kawash, 1968) and of the Inventory of Family Life and Attitudes (Platt, Chrost, & Jurgenson, 1960). Generally, all of these instruments focus on the "freedom" of children in the home environment but do not consider or measure what the "freedoms" of children should be in other settings or spheres of activity (e.g., economic, legal-judicial-political, health).

In an attempt to address this shortcoming, Rogers and Wrightsman (1978) developed a 300-item attitudinal measure known as the Children's Rights Attitude Scale (CRA). The scale consists of the 10 content-dimension subscales presented in Table 4.1, as well as 2 overall scales measuring the nurturance and self-determination orientations across content areas.

Group Differences on the
Children's Rights Attitude Scale

Rogers and Wrightsman (1978) administered the Children's Rights Attitude Scale (CRA) to 381 participants distributed across four groups: (a) juniors and seniors in a large metropolitan high school, (b) undergraduate education majors, (c) other undergraduates enrolled at two small liberal arts colleges and seeking degrees in fields other than education, and (d) adults enrolled in weekend and summer continuing education classes. The researchers asked individuals to respond to the CRA statements by assuming that the child to be rated was either 7 years of age, 11 years of age, or 15 years of age. Overall, no significant differences in mean scores emerged on any of the 10 subscales of the CRA, a finding that reflects an assignment of equivalent rights regardless of the age of the child.

The most striking difference among groups in regard to the nurturance subscales was that, on three of five subscales (Health, Safety-Care, and Education-Information) and on the overall Nurturance scale, high school students held attitudes that were significantly less favorable toward the extension of nurturant rights to children than those held by any other group. In contrast, education majors held significantly more favorable attitudes toward the extension of nurturant rights than did any other group. High school students in particular, and to a slightly lesser extent undergraduate education majors, held more favorable attitudes toward extending self-determination rights to children than did either adults or other undergraduates. In addition, females expressed more favorable attitudes toward the extension of nurturant rights to children than did males.

Rogers and Wrightsman (1978) found that some groups may be favorable toward the extension of both nurturant rights and self-determination rights within a given content area but that other groups may favor the extension of only one. For example, undergraduate education majors held very favorable attitudes toward the extension of both nurturant and self-determination rights in the content area of education-information, whereas other undergraduates were favorably disposed toward the extension of nurturant but not self-determination rights in this area.

Of the group differences, perhaps the most provocative result was that high school students, though less favorable toward society ensuring children the right to be nurtured, were generally more favorable than other groups toward the extension of self-determination rights. This finding stands in sharp contrast with Farson's (1974) prediction that children themselves will be most strongly opposed to the extension of self-determination rights for themselves. The empirical data suggest that older children will be more supportive of the extension of self-determination rights than will other groups, primarily because they are responding in terms of what they want (but do not have) for themselves. In contrast, other respondents are reacting to the extension of self-determination rights to a currently dependent and powerless class of individuals. Similarly, the reaction of high school students toward the extension of nurturant rights to themselves (as well as to other children) might be described in terms of residual resentment toward paternalistic societal policies directed at them.

In this regard, Holt (1974) suggested that "most young people, and at earlier and earlier ages, begin to experience childhood not as a garden but as a prison" (p. 133). Holt also noted that such children begin to experience childhood as not only confining but humiliating as well. Although resentment toward paternalistic policies may explain the less favorable attitude held by high school students toward extending nurturant rights, it should be noted that such resentment, if it exists, is apparently not a strongly held one: The average response of high school students to nurturant items was at the "agree somewhat" level.

Finally, it should be noted that even though Rogers and Wrightsman (1978) found group and gender differences in attitudes toward the extension of nurturant or self-determination rights to children, the clearest pattern was one in which respondents more strongly favored the extension of nurturant rights to children than the extension of self-determination rights. This pattern was consistently the case regardless of respondents' gender, group membership, or the content area involved. Across all participants, the average response to self-determination items was "neither agree or disagree," whereas the average response to nurturant items fell midway between the "agree somewhat" and the "agree strongly" levels. Apparently, people are more willing to try to make the dependent status of children more comfortable than they are willing to grant children freedom.

Helgeson, Goodman, Shaver, and Lipton (n.d.) provided further information on the effect of a child's age on attitudes about children's rights. Their study focused on self-determination rights in four general categories (legal rights, rights to information, expressive rights, and rights related to competence; see Table 4.2 for a list of the proposed rights used in their measure). The respondents were either university students or employees; they rated

Table 4.2 Examples From Helgeson, Goodman, Shaver, and Lipton's Scale of Rights

---

Scale of Legal Rights
  Rights to Privacy and Communication
    complete lawyer-client confidentiality
    complete psychiatrist-client confidentiality
    freedom to choose and practice any religion
    freedom against any search of oneself or one's property (e.g., by police,
      by parents) when a legal warrant has not been obtained
    testify in court against a close relative
      having one's own courtroom testimony be given as much weight as anyone else's

  Constitutional Rights
    a speedy trial
    trial by jury
    full due process of the law
    refusal to testify in court against oneself
    freedom to express one's opinions in a newspaper
    posting bail for self if arrested on a felony charge
    testifying on own behalf in court
    be informed by physician regarding the precise nature of one's medical condition
    be given accurate and complete information concerning the circumstances and
      cause of a relative's death
    attend the funeral of a relative or a loved one
    find out the location and identity of one's parents
    know if adopted

Scale of Expressive Rights
  Rights to Counter-Moral/Counter-Conventional Expression
    use swear words or obscenities in everyday conversation
    swear when angry
    masturbate in private as frequently as desired
    refuse to speak at any time if one chooses not to
    take the deity's name in vain at any time
    refuse to say prayers at dinner table if eating with parents and they expect prayers
      to be said before each meal
    speak back to an instructor at school
    remain silent when spoken to
    express unpopular opinions even if it may embarrass somebody else

  Rights to Emotional Expression
    scream at someone out of frustration
    cry loudly in public if upset or unhappy
    be grumpy toward others when in a bad mood
    cry to get attention
    yell at someone in authority if angry

Scale of Rights Requiring Competence
  Civil Rights
    drive a car if state driving test has been passed
    serve on the police force in some capacity
    vote in any governmental election
    own a handgun
    have a charge account or credit card in own name
    get married with the consent of only the spouse

  Rights Involving Personal Choice
    live with person(s) of own choosing
    freely choose with whom to associate in friendships
    leave and enter home at will
    select what clothing to wear every day
    read any book or magazine
    refuse to attend school

  Rights to Engage in "Vices"
    purchase sexually pornographic magazines
    engage in premarital sexual intercourse
    gamble at casinos
    drink alcohol for pleasure
    smoke cigarettes
    take amphetamines ("uppers") for other than prescribed medical purposes

  Health Rights
    refuse medications in a life-threatening situation
    determine how often to go to the dentist
    refuse to submit to a potentially lifesaving cancer operation
    refuse to take prescribed medication if not immediately lifesaving
    decide to be taken off artificial life-support system such as a kidney machine
    refuse to take prescribed tranquilizers if diagnosed as "hyperactive"

SOURCE: Helgeson, Goodman, Shaver, and Lipton (n.d.)

individuals aged 5, 9, 13, 17, or 30 years. Although Helgeson and colleagues found that the age of the person rated influenced the rights granted, the significant dividing point was between children aged 5, 9, or 13 years old and adults who were 30 years old.

Parents' Attitudes Toward Children's Rights

Another approach to the measurement of attitudes toward children's rights is to ask respondents to specify the ages at which they believe children should be allowed to participate in making decisions and the ages at which children and adolescents should be granted sole responsibility for making decisions. Tremper and Feshbach (1981) studied reactions to self-determination decisions in 14 content areas, including medical treatment, psychotherapy, custody after divorce, and birth control. Subjects who were mothers themselves were willing to allow children who were at least 15 years old to participate in making most of the decisions, but the majority of these subjects did not approve of granting children sole responsibility until age 18. As expected, the age specified was dependent on the specific decision: Self-care and management decisions, such as television watching and taking medicine, were permitted at younger ages than birth control or abortion decisions. Consistent with Rogers and Wrightsman's (1978) findings, younger respondents (adolescents) were willing to grant self-determination rights to people of younger ages than were the adults.

Information about parents' attitudes toward children's rights also was obtained by Grisso (1981), who administered 3 of the 10 CRA subscales to a set of parents. The three subscales used were Legal-Judicial-Political/Self-Determination, Legal-Judicial-Political/Nurturance, and Education/Self-Determination. For the first of these, Grisso deleted two items and replaced them with two new items:

1. Children should not be allowed to withhold information from police when the police suspect they have been involved in a crime.
2. When children are seen by a juvenile court because they are suspected of a crime, they should not have to give information about whether or not they were involved in a crime.

Grisso also varied the reference group of children. Half of the parents were instructed to complete the CRA subscales with boys of ages 10 to 13 in mind; the other half, with boys ages 15 to 17 as the reference group. Also, half of the respondents in each of these two groups were instructed to consider boys who had often been in trouble with the police, whereas the other half received directions to consider boys who had never been in trouble with the police. Thus, the reference groups for Grisso's study are much more circumscribed than the original CRA directions. Group comparisons still may be useful, however.

Approximately two thirds of the parents believed that juveniles should have the same rights as adults in court proceedings. Even more (73%) believed that a lawyer should be made available, but only 6% believed that a child should have the right to choose her or his own lawyer. Also, parents were opposed to children withholding information from the police (new item), a position consistent with their negative attitudes toward children's self-determination rights in legal-judicial settings. But generally, parents' responses on the Legal-Judicial-Political/Nurturance items were situation-specific. Grisso (1981) noted, for example, that

> parents' non-supportive view of the right to silence for juveniles would appear to be relatively specific to their dealings with legal or judicial authority, and might not be related to the general degree of autonomy or decision making which they allow juveniles in other social contexts. (p. 178)

Nurturance scores, in contrast, were quite positive; the parents' lack of support for some self-determination issues apparently was not attributable to a lack of concern on their part for protecting or nurturing their children (Grisso, 1981).

Differences in attitudes based on the age of the reference group or on their delinquency status were negligible. The tendencies were to have more favorable attitudes toward older rather than younger adolescents and to nondelinquent rather than delinquent ones. No statistically significant differences in any consistent direction emerged, however.

Children's Attitudes Toward Their Rights

What do children themselves think about their rights? Melton (1980) was the first to ask children directly about their perceptions. Rather than use a set of attitude statements, he composed 12 vignettes and individually administered them, in an interview format, to children in the first, third, fifth, and seventh grades; he named the instrument the Children's Rights Inventory (CRI). The topics of the 12 vignettes were as follows: (a) access to school records, (b) due process in school discipline, (c) freedom of the school newspaper, (d) choice of curriculum, (e) self-determination in custody hearings, (f) right to refuse medical treatment, (g) right to vote, (h) right to receive medical treatment when parents cannot pay, (i) age restrictions on employment, (j) seeking treatment without parents' consent, (k) privacy of a diary, and (l) older children ordering younger children away from a public park.

The following is an example of one vignette:

> Mark wrote a story for the school newspaper. In his story he said that he didn't like the school rules. The principal told him that he couldn't print his story. Should there be a rule or a law that a principal can decide if Mark's story will go into the newspaper? Why? (p. 187)

Melton scored respondents' responses in two ways: (a) the degree to which the respondent advocated the expression of a right by the child in the story and (b) the level of conceptualization. The scoring system resulted in participants being rated as functioning at one of three levels of reasoning: (a) authority-based (the lowest), (b) law-based, or (c) principle-based (the highest).

The vignettes reflect a combination of the two concepts of rights previously described, nurturant and self-determinative. Although the measuring device and the types of respondents differed from those of Rogers and Wrightsman (1978), the factor structure of Melton's (1980) instrument was the same: The first factor reflected attitudes toward self-determination rights, and the second involved attitudes toward nurturance of children.

Melton (1980) found that the children's ages and their socioeconomic status (SES) influenced their conception of rights. High-SES children tended to advocate more self-determination rights for children than did their low-SES counterparts. High-SES children also tended to move toward positive attitudes regarding children's rights about 2 years earlier on the average than did their low-SES peers. In addition, older children (approximately age 12) "perceived rights as being based more on criteria of fairness and competence to exercise self-determination (Level 2) than on what authority figures actually allow children to do (Level 1)" (p. 189). By fifth grade, both high- and low-SES children reached Level 2 reasoning, a result that indicates their views had shifted toward positive attitudes about children's self-determination rights.

Cherney and Perry (1996) investigated culture as another factor that may influence children's attitudes toward their rights. They hypothesized that because different cultures encourage different amounts of autonomy during childhood, cultural values might affect children's perceptions of their rights. Using Melton's (1980) Children's Rights Inventory, the two researchers contrasted the responses of three groups of 11- to 13-year-old schoolchildren: 46 relatively affluent Swiss French, Swiss German, German, and English children who attended school in Geneva, Switzerland; 29 low-income Anglo, African, Hispanic, and Native American children who attended school in

Nebraska; and 12 middle-income children who attended school in a rural area of Alberta, Canada.

Although the children in Cherney and Perry's (1996) sample came from disparate socioeconomic and cultural backgrounds, their responses to the CRI vignettes tended, on the whole, to be more similar than different. Overall, 91% of the children interviewed believed that children should have rights, although only 83% believed that children actually have rights. Interestingly, but not surprisingly, the low-SES U.S. children of ethnic minorities were least likely to believe that children actually are accorded rights.

The European children favored more nurturance rights *and* more self-determination rights than did either the Canadian or the U.S. children, even though the tradition in European philosophy has been to emphasize the need to protect children, as distinguished from the American philosophical tradition of emphasizing the autonomy (and hence self-determination) of the individual. Thus, like Melton (1980), Cherney and Perry (1996) concluded that socioeconomic factors are potent influences on children's conceptions of their rights.

The most salient finding, however, was that

> [t]welve-year-old children do not advocate indiscriminately for rights. Instead, they distinguish between those rights they believe they are entitled to exercise and those they feel they are not yet ready to handle. Twelve-year-old children in our sample seemed to recognize that most children have neither the judgment nor the experience of adults and could hardly be expected to judiciously exercise all adult prerogatives. At the same time, however, our study participants recognized that children are not merely objects or helpless organisms. The children in our sample believed that children should be empowered to make autonomous decisions if and when they are capable of doing so. (p. 248)

Similar conclusions were reached by Taylor, Adelman, and Kaser-Boyd (1984), who studied children's and adolescents' beliefs about the proper age for making autonomous decisions. Participants in the Taylor et al. study believed that the proper age for making decisions concerning daily activities (e.g., television viewing, clothes, friends) should be, on average, 12.3 years; that the age for major life events (e.g., leaving home, marriage) should be, on average, 14.8 years; and that the proper age for health decisions, on average, should be 15.1 years. With regard to those findings, Mann, Harmoni, and Power (1989) noted: "It is interesting that 15 years (approximately) is considered the appropriate age for autonomy in making major personal decisions as it corresponds to that age for which the research evidence [reviewed below] suggests a growth in competence" (p. 273).

Development of Competence in Decision Making

When are children competent to make their own decisions? That question is an important one because, as Melton (1989) noted, it is clear that "even for elementary schoolchildren, privacy and self-determination are psychologically meaningful" (p. 286). That question has no simple answer, however; the response depends on a given child's developmental maturity, training, and experiences, as well as the content area of the decision.

Several researchers have identified factors that comprise competence in decision making (cf. Grisso & Vierling, 1978; Janis & Mann, 1977; Koocher & DeMaso, 1990; Mann et al., 1989; Ross, 1981; Tancredi, 1982; Weithorn & Campbell, 1982). Some also have tested children's competence in making decisions in laboratory settings (cf. Mann et al., 1989; Weithorn & Campbell, 1982).

Definitions of Competence in Decision Making

Tancredi (1982) defined *competence* as the "capacity to make a rational or intelligent judgment" (p. 53). Janis and Mann (1977) described the "vigilant" decision maker as follows:

> a highly competent person who thoroughly canvasses a wide range of alternative courses of action, surveys a full range of objectives and values implicated by the choice, carefully weighs the positive and negative consequences that could flow from each alternative, intensively searches for new information, incorporates new information even when it is unpleasant, and plans for the implementation of the decision. (as cited in Mann et al., 1989, pp. 266-267)

Ross (1981) stated that the competent decision maker must master five skills: (a) to identify a set of alternative courses of action, (b) to identify appropriate criteria for considering alternatives, (c) to assess alternatives by criteria, (d) to summarize information about alternatives, and (e) to self-evaluate—that is, to verify the outcome of the decision-making process.

Weithorn and Campbell (1982) distinguished between *factual understanding* and the concept of *appreciation*. Factual understanding involves basic comprehension of information presented, whereas appreciation involves a more abstract understanding of the "nature, extent and probable consequences" of the decision (p. 1590). Weithorn and Campbell also hypothesized that formal operational thought (Inhelder & Piaget, 1958), which emerges in early adolescence, is prerequisite to appreciation, noting that formal operational ways of thinking "allow individuals to make choices after they have imagined where each of two or several possible courses of action leads" (p. 1590).

According to Koocher and DeMaso (1990), the elements of competence assessment include (a) understanding, (b) choosing, (c) reasoning, and (d) appreciating. Koocher and DeMaso noted that "these elements involve psychological aspects of comprehension, assertiveness and autonomy, rational reasoning, anticipation of future events, and judgments in the face of uncertainty or contingencies" (p. 69). With regard to those abilities, adults, on the one hand, are presumed to be competent under the law; they must be demonstrated by specific proof to be incompetent. Children, on the other hand, are presumed to be *incompetent* in most contexts unless deemed legally competent by a court under specific state statutes (e.g., a married minor, a minor enlisted in military service, a minor who is financially independent or who is living independently) or through testimony provided under oath. According to Koocher and DeMaso (1990), however, cognitive and reasoning abilities are not always addressed in court hearings held to determine competency.

Koocher and DeMaso (1990) suggested that "the ability to go beyond the present and conceptualize the future, including hypothetical or potential outcomes, is closely linked to stages of cognitive development" (p. 70). Evaluating children's time perspective is crucial in assessing their ability to weigh short-term and long-term consequences of decisions, they posited, noting that "[t]he ability to weigh probabilities and to make some kind of personal long-term cost-benefit analysis, a capacity generally absent in preadolescent children, is crucial to an informed decision" (p. 70). Generally, children between the ages of 7 and 11 years are able to integrate information and reasoning in a more logical and effective manner than is possible at earlier ages. The critical thinking abilities required for children to make decisions concerning their long-term best interests (e.g., hypothetical reasoning, cause-effect reasoning, understanding contingencies, and considering probabilities), however, generally do not appear until the early teen years, when formal operational thinking emerges (Inhelder & Piaget, 1958). Koocher and De-Maso concluded that a child's level of development—based on consideration of socialization, time perspective, and concept manipulation—must be considered when determining the child's competence.

Mann et al. (1989) provided the most detailed listing of the elements of competent decision making. They described nine essential elements: (a) choice, (b) comprehension, (c) creativity, (d) compromise, (e) consequentiality, (f) correctness, (g) credibility, (h) consistency, and (i) commitment.

Studies of Developmental Differences in Decision-Making Competence

Weithorn and Campbell (1982) tested the hypothesis that 14-year-old adolescents do not differ from adults in their capacity to provide competent informed consent or refusal for medical and psychological treatment. The researchers tested their assertion by comparing the performance of four age groups (9, 14, 18, and 21 years) on a measure intended to define legal standards of competency in medical decision making. The measure of competency included three components: (a) a series of four stories involving hypothetical treatment dilemmas, (b) an interview schedule, and (c) a scoring system to rate participants' responses. The researchers instructed the participants to consider themselves to be the characters in the stories and to select a treatment alternative in the hypothetical situations.

Weithorn and Campbell (1982) found significant differences among age groups to support their hypothesis that 14-year-olds and adults demonstrated equivalent levels of competence. Interestingly, although 9-year-olds demonstrated less competence, they clearly were not devoid of sound decision-making skills. The two authors concluded:

> In general, minors aged 14 [years] were found to demonstrate a level of competency equivalent to that of adults, according to four standards of competency (evidence of choice, reasonable outcome, rational reasons, and understanding), and for four hypothetical dilemmas (diabetes, epilepsy, depression, and enuresis). Younger minors aged 9 [years], however, appeared less competent than adults according to the standards of competency requiring understanding and a rational reasonable process. Yet, according to the standards of evidence of choice and reasonable outcome, even these younger

minors appeared competent. Children as young as 9 appear to be capable of comprehending the basics of what is required of them when they are asked to state a preference regarding a treatment dilemma. And, despite poorer understanding and failure to consider fully many of the critical elements of disclosed information, the 9-year-olds tended to express clear and sensible treatment preferences similar to those of adults. (pp. 1595-1596)

Mann et al. (1989) reviewed several studies of decision-making competency as they related to the nine elements of competent decision making they had identified. They concluded that although the United States rarely permits adolescents to make important legal decisions, Grisso and Vierling (1978) were correct in stating that "existing evidence provides no psychological grounds for maintaining the general legal assumption that minors aged 15 years and above cannot provide competent consent" (as cited in Mann et al., 1989, p. 275). Mann and colleagues concluded: "The evidence is sparse but suggests that many adolescents, particularly from mid-adolescence, demonstrate knowledge of the steps involved in systematic decision making and have the capacity for creative problem-solving" (p. 271).

The evidence on adolescents is not plentiful, but the information on the decision-making competence of younger children is essentially nonexistent. Certainly, younger children are competent to make some choices in their lives. Even a toddler can make choices between mutually acceptable options—whether to eat meat or cheese sandwiches for lunch, or whether to scribble on the drawing paper provided or to spend "time out" for scribbling on a wall. But when are children competent to make important life decisions—choosing which parent with whom to live following divorce, deciding whether to accept medical treatment, selecting the better educational alternative, and so forth? Research on the developmental competency of children to make decisions in those areas is profoundly needed.

Balancing the Rights of Children

In this chapter, we have sought to portray the various dilemmas inherent in conceptualizing children's rights. The complexity of the issues makes it clear that reaching a national consensus on the rights that children should possess will be no simple matter. We propose that ratification of the U.N. Convention is an important first step in the national process, although implementation of the Convention's principles in the United States and elsewhere will require a careful balancing of children's rights to protection, entitlement, and self-determination. We concur with Hart (1991), who suggested that a coherent policy regarding children's rights will provide

> ... an appropriate balance between protection and self-determination rights ... for children at every point in their development. To determine and support this balance will require the existence of (a) empirical evidence of need and readiness for various protection and self-determination opportunities throughout the developmental period, (b) a broadly supported positive ideology of the child, and (c) the active involvement of children in establishing their needs and rights. (p. 57)

Our thesis derives from Hart's comments: Children's rights must be considered in context. Before a decision is rendered in any case, a child's rights to protection, entitlement, and self-determination must be evaluated, including assessment of the particular child's level of maturity and developmental readiness for decision making; further, consideration of the environment in which the child lives must be taken into account. Our purpose in writing this book is to advance this thesis by exploring the kinds of decisions routinely faced by children, their families, and the state. Thus, in the chapters that follow, we apply the contextual consideration of children's rights in a variety of spheres: family (Chapter 5), social services (Chapter 6), medical and mental health (Chapter 7), education (Chapter 8), juvenile law (Chapter 9), and employment (Chapter 10). In each of those policy areas, we explore how children of various ages might participate in decisions that involve them. As Melton (personal communication, October 12, 1997) noted:

> The Convention requires not a specific level of *self-determination* at a given age (or level of competence), but instead encouragement of children's *participation*. The key question is not the *standard* for decision making, but instead the *structure* for participation, which is mandated even for young children.

Notes

1. From "They Cannot Fend for Themselves," by N. Traver, March 23, 1987, *Time,* p. 27. Reprinted with permission from Time Life Syndication.

2. Quote from "Give Kids the Vote" reprinted by permission of *Daedalus,* Journal of the American Academy of Arts and Sciences, from the issue titled, "Immobile Democracy," Fall 1992, Vol. 121, No. 4.

3. From "Cradle-to-Grave Intimacy," by J. Leo, September 7, 1981, *Time,* p. 69. Reprinted with permission from Time Life Syndicate.

PART II

A Patchwork of Policies

5

There's No Place Like Home

The Rights of Children Within the Family

> To hold that a child is the property of his parents is to deny the humanity of the child . . . [A child] "belongs" to no one but himself.
>
> Illinois Appeals Court Justice Dom Rizzi (1994)

Dorothy donned her ruby red shoes, clicked her heels three times, and chanted, "There's no place like home. . . . There's no place like home. . . ." This image from the movie version of L. Frank Baum's (1900) classic novel *The Wonderful Wizard of Oz* is indelibly etched in the memories of most American children. Dorothy's deeply felt wish to be returned to her family following a traumatic separation symbolically expresses the central place accorded the family in American culture.

In fact, the family is the organizing unit of cultures throughout the world. One critical function of the family is to foster the development of human competence and character of each family member. Therefore, any discussion of the rights accorded to or denied children must consider the family as the context in which those rights are to be weighed against the parents' rights.

In the latter half of the 20th century, the term *rights* has come to be used to describe the profound, fundamental needs of children, without which they are unable to develop into healthy adults. Inferentially, parents have recognized that their children have a right to progress to healthy adulthood, and we, the generations who go ahead of them, have a profound, fundamental need

69

that they do so. Hence, children are accorded the "right" to have their needs met to ensure their progress to adulthood, which in turn ensures the preservation of the human species; parents benefit more immediately in their children's return of care in their older years.

The global, international discussion of children's rights to have their tangible and intangible needs met, to enable their maturation, has gained great ground. In the United States, though, adults remain reluctant to recognize the "rights" model, including those rights that acknowledge a child's increasing capacity for self-determination.

Further complicating the discussion is the fact that single-parent families continue to increase in number, now constituting "the fastest growing segment of the American family unit" (Kennedy, 1997, p. 6). Sole parents face numerous challenges in doing the work intended for the two-parent structure. Congressional testimony regarding a field study illustrates the remarkable movement toward a considerable subculture of single-parent families in the United States:

> In just three decades, from 1960 to 1990, the percentage of U.S. children living apart from their biological father has [more than] doubled from 17% to 36%. . . . In 1965 only one out of thirteen births was out of wedlock[;] today it is one out of three; and for African American children it is even worse with 70% of births out of wedlock. For children born after 1980, it is projected that 70% of the white and 94% of the black children will have lived with only one parent before reaching the age eighteen [years]. (Fox, 1997)

The impact on children is unmistakable. Shepard (1997) reported that 70% of juveniles in state institutions grew up without fathers; moreover, girls who live in single-parent households are 53% more likely to give birth as adolescents and 164% more likely to give birth out of wedlock. Those percentages translate into extraordinary numbers: Edwards (1987) forecasted that the 27% of live births to unwed women in 1987 would lead to 1,000,000 children per year in single-parent families. He was not far afield. Eight years later, in 1995, 1.2 million children were born out of wedlock, approximately 32% of all births (Hsu, 1997).

The predominant type of right reviewed in this chapter, following the "best interests" catchphrase, is the nurturant one of deciding the child's situation in contexts involving families that are losing or have lost their viability. These contexts include divorce and the contested custody of, and access to, a child, foster care, and grandparents' visiting rights within families in disarray. Only in a few examples does the child's right to self-determination surface.

The lack of self-determinative rights of children is perhaps most prominent when a child's parents decide to divorce. The child has no influence on the decision to divorce or not, despite the fact that the adverse effects of divorce on children's functioning have been well documented (Camara & Resnick, 1989; Hetherington, Cox, & Cox, 1979; Wallerstein & Kelly, 1980). In each instance that children seek standing in their parents' divorce action, they have been rebuffed under the theory that they do not have a legally recognizable right to be heard. The child of a marriage that has been dissolved in a divorce action has no "standing" to attack the divorce decree or the grounds on which it was granted. Regardless of the detriments suffered by the child as a consequence of the divorce decree, the child has no right to seek redress by having the decree set aside because he or she had no standing to be heard at the time of the divorce action (see *Evans v. Asphalt Roads & Materials Company, Inc.,* 1952).

In a quest perhaps to sanction the married couple's right to divorce, one might assume that the long-term effects of the loss of the family on the child will diminish. The assumption that children are resilient and will eventually recover is challenged by a 15-year longitudinal study by Wallerstein and Blakeslee (1989). Their subjects were 131 children and adolescents from 60 divorced families in Marin County, California. Only about one tenth of the children in this study felt relieved when the quarreling parents separated, and these respondents tended to be the older children who had been the observers or recipients of physical abuse from one or both parents. Wallerstein and Blakeslee found, though, that young adults whose parents had divorced tended to be anxious, underachieving, self-deprecating, and, in some cases, angry.

Furthermore, Wallerstein and Blakeslee (1989) described a "sleeper effect" on females: Many of them seem to have adjusted to their parents' divorce well until adulthood, at which point they suffer "an intolerable level of anxiety about betrayal" (p. 62). They may drop out of college, become promiscuous in their sexual activity, or trap themselves in unsatisfactory relationships—all, according to the authors, to protect themselves from rejection, abandonment, and betrayal. Wallerstein and Blakeslee reported that this reaction occurred in fully two-thirds of the women they studied who were between the ages of 19 and 23.

Of children (male and female) whose mothers remarried, half said they did not feel welcome in the new family (Wallerstein & Blakeslee, 1989). Ten years after the divorce, more than one third reported having poor relationships with *both* parents (Wallerstein & Blakeslee, 1989).

Psychologist Urie Bronfenbrenner (1990) has noted that even young children who live in two-parent families with educated and well-to-do parents can be at risk—if both parents work outside the home and misjudge the proper priorities of conflicting demands of their personal needs, the family's well-being, the children's care, home maintenance duties, and work. According to Bronfenbrenner, these expectations can lead to an increasingly unstable, inconsistent, and chaotic daily family life, thus jeopardizing in some families the right and need of children to deeply attach to a caregiver.

Given the complexities of family life, meeting the needs of children—for stability and safety in housing, security in financial support, nutritious and plentiful food, developmentally appropriate education, permanence in their nurturing attachments, and an identity that allows them joy—seems overwhelming. Acknowledging a child's right to have those needs met should be of paramount national concern, however. We believe that the critical importance of meeting children's needs within the family should serve as a strong impetus for summoning the national will and resources necessary to provide adequately for the needs of children.

The U.N. Convention speaks clearly on this issue, as several articles of the Convention specifically address children's rights within the family. For example, Article 7 discusses children's right to know and be cared for by their parents. Articles 5, 14, 18, and 31 discuss parental responsibilities, as well as requirements of the state to respect the rights of parents (or guardians) to provide direction to their children. Articles 8, 9, 10, and 11 discuss the rights of children to family ties and reunification. The U.N. Convention clearly places central value on the family and honors the family as the context within which children should be nurtured and guided to adulthood and within which their rights should be expressed.

The Conflict Between Parents' Rights and Children's Rights

Focusing on the family enables us to look once more at the conflict between the rights of parents and those of children, a dispute introduced in Chapter 1. Generally, parents are expected to bear the responsibility for the care and protection of their children. Until passage of the Married Women's Property Acts—in the United States, from before 1850 through 1900 (Clark, 1987)—

the law and the community accorded legal rights to only one person in a family. Before that reform and other corrective legislation, only the husband could enter most professions, make contracts, give testimony, serve as a juror, or invoke other benefits of the law.

Generally, fathers, and more recently mothers, have had virtually absolute rights to make decisions involving their children; as Rodham (1973) observed, in 18th-century English common law the term *children's rights* was a non sequitur. Children were "prized possessions" of their fathers in William Blackstone's influential 18th-century commentaries on the law. Twentieth-century technological innovations remind us that property issues still are close to the surface. For example, the publicity over surrogate motherhood that surfaced in the late 1980s reflects a continuation of this assumption that parents somehow "own" their offspring. Box 5.1 describes the surrogate motherhood issue in more detail.

Then, in the early 1990s, the issue of ownership of fertilized eggs (*in vitro* embryos) marked the separation and divorce of one couple in Tennessee and set off a debate in law, bioethics, and medicine about possessing those frozen potential lives and paying for the support of the children when those lives moved from potentiality to reality (*Davis v. Davis,* 1990). The unprecedented custody action between the divorcing spouses concerned seven fertilized ova; the trial court declared that the "embryos" were children, not property, and awarded their care to the ex-wife, who wished to have them inserted into her uterus in an attempt to become pregnant. The use of the word *embryo* may be misleading, though:

> The technical term that some specialists like to use at this point is "pre-embryo," since the first dividing cells are not actually the cells that will become the fetal parts; they will split instead into what one physician calls "organizers," the cells that wait until they have implanted in the uterine wall and then direct other cells to begin developing as the earliest forms of the fetus.[1]

In the following year, the Tennessee Court of Appeals found that the seven fertilized and cryopreserved ova produced by Junior and Mary Sue Davis were the joint property of the Davises and that each had equal rights to control of the eggs. At the time of the conflict's resolution, the Davises had divorced and were married to other persons; neither of the Davises wanted the other as the parent of his or her children.

Box 5.1

Surrogate Mothers and Children's Rights:
The Case of "Baby M"

The controversy over surrogate motherhood surfaced in 1986 in the so-called Baby M case. Ms. Mary Beth Whitehead, a married woman who already had two children, agreed to be artificially inseminated and to surrender custody of the live born child for a fee of $10,000 and payment of all related medical expenses. She contracted with William Stern through a lawyer and the Infertility Center of New York. Stern's wife, Elizabeth, had a mild case of multiple sclerosis and believed that she would be at risk if she became pregnant, although she was not infertile. The Sterns paid the lawyer and the Infertility Center a significant fee for arranging the artificial insemination of Stern's sperm in Ms. Whitehead's uterus.

The Infertility Center examined and psychologically evaluated Ms. Whitehead. The psychologist who conducted the evaluation warned the Infertility Center that Ms. Whitehead demonstrated certain traits that might make surrender of the child difficult and that further inquiry should be made into this issue. But to inquire further might have jeopardized the Infertility Center's fee. The record indicates that neither Ms. Whitehead nor the Sterns were told of this finding, a fact that might have ended their surrogacy arrangement (Rae, 1994). The Sterns never asked to see the results of the assessments and seemed content with the assumption that the Infertility Center had completed the evaluation and apparently had concluded that there was no danger the surrogate mother would change her mind.

After the child was born, Ms. Whitehead came to regret her decision to relinquish the child. At her request, the Sterns allowed her to take the child for a week. But she

That issue of ownership continues to haunt other venues as well. Box 5.2 provides the cautionary tale of a child losing her rights to her mother in advance of a relinquishment of rights from her father. Her father's language betrays a remarkable lack of empathy with the child's situation.

Thus, families continue to experience the conflict between children's and parents' rights (see Box 5.3). But, in U.S. culture, parents' rights tend to predominate. The parents' rights perspective rests on four elements of the conventional credo of American society:

1. America is a familial, child-centered society in which parents are responsible for their own children and have primary control over them.

fled with "Baby M," going from New Jersey to Florida, where the child was recovered and returned to the Sterns. Ms. Whitehead then sued for custody of the child, noting that she had not accepted the $10,000 payment. In a decision announced in March 1987, Judge Harvey Sorkow ruled that Ms. Whitehead had not been coerced into signing the contract and that, therefore, it should be enforced. He referred to a woman "renting her womb" (thus reaffirming society's treatment of a child—or at least a fetus—as an article of property) and then concluded that the equal protection clause of the Constitution permitted a woman to sell her reproductive capacities (*Matter of Baby M,* 1988). He thus made a decision based on contract law, concluding that the mother had breached a valid contract when she refused to give up custody of "Baby M." The New Jersey Supreme Court, though, held Judge Sorkow's decision and rationale to be invalid.

Until that point, the issue of children's rights seemed superfluous to the case. The state supreme court's opinion, however, did not agree that it should be so.

In the light of the publicity over this case, as of 1997, eight states (Indiana, Kentucky, Louisiana, Michigan, Nebraska, New York, Utah, and Washington) and the District of Columbia had passed laws that restricted or outlawed surrogacy for pay. In addition, Arizona, New York, and Utah statutes also prohibit enforcement of unpaid surrogacy contracts (Kerian, 1997). In all, at least 18 states had laws banning commercial surrogacy in one form or another.

These laws generally reflect four concerns with surrogacy: (a) its commercialization, (b) the definition of *mother,* (c) the need to clarify parental rights, and (d) questions regarding whether such contracts are enforceable (Rae, 1994). But not all the laws are consistent with each other; the fee to the surrogate mother is prohibited in most—but not all—states. No national policy exists; as of 1997, no legislation had managed to work its way through Congress.

2. The community of adults, usually represented by the state, will not assume responsibility for the child unless the parents are unable to do so or will not do so or until the child breaks the law.

3. Because ours is a "child-loving society," nonparents and other adults representing the state want to, and will, do what is in the child's best interests.

4. Children need not or should not be participants with the family and the state in making decisions that affect their lives. (Rodham, 1973, p. 489).

The courts have advanced this credo by tending to assume a nurturance orientation when considering children's rights within the family. Drinan (1973) noted, for example, that "[i]n all matters where children are involved, courts have said with tedious regularity that the welfare of the child is the

---

Box 5.2

What Right to an Identity Does an "It" Have?

Shainea Mendez is 17 years old. Her daughter, Amy, is 2½ years old. Little in Shainea's life has been good for her, but one foster home—among the dozen or so placements she has endured in her life—stood out. In that home, the foster mother, Cathy O'Mealia, had won Shainea's trust and respect. So it was to Cathy O'Mealia that Shainea turned for her own daughter's placement. In May 1997, Shainea relinquished her rights to raise Amy, with the understanding that Cathy would become Amy's adoptive mother. After all, a psychiatrist had testified during Shainea's day in court that Amy would be devastated if she were to be separated from Cathy. "I wanted to give everything to my daughter that I possibly could,' Shainea [had] said. . . . 'It was the hardest thing I've ever done in my life. . . . I couldn't be selfish anymore' " (Brody, 1997, p. L01).

The state social service agency, the family court, Cathy, and Shainea thought that Amy's well-being was met in the adoption plan, that her best interests were finally settled in a permanent home with her identity as Cathy's daughter intact. No one counted on Amy's biological father claiming her.

Although Shainea says she told Rafael Longo, a friend of her older brother, of Amy's birth and his probable fatherhood 'from the start[,]' Rafael claims that he never knew he was a father until he saw a photograph of Amy in February 1997. The resemblance to his own baby pictures was striking, and a blood test confirmed his fatherhood. Of his daughter, Amy, he says, '*It's* something you made. *It's* something that looks like you. *It's* yours [all emphases added]' (Brody, 1997, p. L01).

---

supreme goal to be obtained" (p. 40). As a slogan or a moral principle, "the best interests of the child" appears on the surface to be child-centered. We recognize, though—within the framework of this book—that this guideline is nurturance-oriented and does not encompass the possibility of self-determination. That is to say, the child is not given any choice in the exercise of his or her rights—rights that, according to Rodham (1973), "are compulsory, not susceptible to waiver" (p. 493). For example, if the state concludes that some children have suffered severe harm while in the custody of their parents, the state may intrude into the family relationship and remove the children. Introducing the children's preferences into the judicial disposition of their familial status, however, seems to have gathered little respect from the federal bench and bar during the past 20 years or so, although the states have declared such expressions of preferences or wishes to be worthy of representation, as

Saying that his mother will raise her in Kissimmee, Florida, Rafael has sought custody of Amy from the state social service agency, which holds legal custody of the little girl until a decision is made in Cathy O'Mealia's adoption action. If the court allows Rafael's right to his biological daughter to take precedence over Amy's need for permanence and stability (and to be free from the "devastating" separation from her foster/adoptive mother), Amy will be moved by her father to Florida to be raised by her paternal grandmother.

Will Amy's interests be best served by that outcome? Rafael maintains that Amy "will get over any initial confusion" (Brody, 1997, p. L01). But she will see neither her birth mother nor her foster mother again. She will be expected to give up her primary attachments and do the hard work of attachment all over again to satisfy her biological father's right to possess the daughter he refers to as "It."

Rafael was arrested in July 1997 for possession of 52 bags of marijuana and was charged with the intent to distribute the drug. After initially denying knowledge of the drug's presence under his car seat, he pled guilty to possession 1 month later. Now, as the court weighs his right as a father, he is on probation for 1 year.

But what of Amy's rights? She has established an identity as Cathy's child and has formed a secure attachment to her. Amy's right to her identity and to decisions that are in her best interests—rights guaranteed by Articles 8 and 3 of the U.N. Convention—surely are at stake.

Her father, an admitted drug dealer, considers Amy an "It"—yet his rights to possess his child have prevailed. Under such circumstances, how can anyone say that any of Amy's interests have been protected, let alone her "best interests"?

SOURCE: Quotes from Brody, 1997, are reprinted with permission of *The Record* of Hackensack, N.J.

has the U.N. Convention (Article 12). Although Rodham's statement was written 6 years after *In re Gault* (1967) guaranteed to children and adolescents the legal, procedural, and substantive rights due to persons under the first 14 amendments to the U.S. Constitution, her comment reflects accurately the tension still present between an extant right and its effective invocation by the child involved.

Some advocates (e.g., Rodham, 1973) see the "best interests" standard as actually a rationalization by decision makers to justify their judgments about children's futures. The notion of best interests came into play when children were still considered to be the property of their fathers and was used to mandate courts and legislatures granting a divorce to consider a mother's relationship with her very young children and with her older female children. Perhaps the clear inference of child ownership, present at the inception of best

---

Box 5.3

Parents' Rights Versus Children's Rights

Ellen L. Hopkins (Hopkins, 1993) is the mother of a 12-year-old daughter, Kelly. One day, Kelly didn't come home from school. Because earlier her ex-husband had kidnapped and hidden Kelly, Ms. Hopkins's first thought was that this had happened again. Then she learned, however, that Kelly had told her friends on the school bus that day that she was running away.

That morning, before school, Kelly had been punished for "her continued refusal to clean up the mess she'd made." Ms. Hopkins's second husband, Kelly's stepfather, gave her "three whacks on the behind, open-handed, over her blue jeans." In 8 years, it was only the second time corporal punishment had been used on Kelly. Kelly reported her stepfather to the authorities with a charge of child abuse. She was brought home in a squad car. Ms. Hopkins writes:

> Don't get me wrong. I understand the need to protect innocent children. I know there are abusive parents and stepparents out there. But there must be evidence, not just the word of an angry child who thinks it is an easy way to get back at a parent. What are our rights?
>
> This episode has turned our lives upside down. My husband and I are professionals, active in the community, and it has impugned our reputations irreparably. . . .
>
> Is it just a coincidence that only the week before my daughter had completed a Child Abuse Prevention program in her school? It defined for her what constitutes "child abuse" in the eyes of the law. She knew exactly what to say to get everyone's attention. I would like to remove my children from this school system which, by its policies, encourages children to run to them in anger and to stick to their lies. (Hopkins, 1993, p. 26)[1]

---

1. From *Newsweek,* October 18, 1993, © 1993, Newsweek, Inc. All rights reserved. Reprinted by permission.

---

interests decision making (in 1837 in Great Britain and from 1813 in Pennsylvania and other states), has continued to color its application today.

Two Sources of Conflict

The courts become involved in the controversy between parental rights and children's rights in two identifiable types of situations; Mnookin (1975) refers to these as *private dispute settlement* and *child protection*. In the first type, the legal system intervenes to settle a family dispute, typically between divorcing parents. In the second type, the state seeks to protect the child from alleged inadequate or harmful action by the parent or parents. In protection cases, court action must be based on a factual finding of parental error. Thus, in protection cases, the legal tradition of respect for the privacy of the family gives way to judicial authority (Thomas, 1972).

This chapter discusses three issues related to private dispute settlement within families: (a) custody decisions, (b) children's right to sue their parents, and (c) grandparents' rights. Chapter 6 discusses child protection within the context of children's rights to social services.

Children's Rights in Custody Decisions

Before the reforms of the early 19th century, when a married couple divorced, the children of the family had no right to determine their future or their custody. After the reforms began, any apparent rights accorded the children were nurturant types, but even the nature of these has changed over the past century. For example, the "right" accorded children in the first reforms was the right to live with their mothers in infancy and, afterward, to have contact with her during their years until adulthood. Once they had reached adulthood, of course, sons could determine with whom they would associate—provided they could withstand the withdrawal of the purse, should their fathers be so inclined; a daughter could have such contact with her mother, depending on the inclination of the father, husband, or other male who asserted "protection" over the daughter.

Until the early 1800s, children were treated as chattel, or property, and were automatically assigned to the custody of the father as he was their "owner," with an attendant obligation to protect, financially support, and educate his minor children. But early in the 19th century, the parental-rights-and-fitness issue emerged, as did legal decisions that took into account the needs of the children involved; thus, the "best interests of the child" analysis emerged. The point in American legal history when "best interests" came into being was relatively soon after the United States was no longer a colonial ward of Great Britain and, except for the Louisiana Territory, had accepted British case law as its own jurisprudential history. Thus, it is useful to look at the emergence of "best interests" in Great Britain and then to examine its beginnings in the United States.

Trends in the Best Interests Standard

The British Common Law Tradition. Until 1836, it was accepted as fact that a father owned his children and that his wife, the mother of his children, submerged her identity before the law into that of her husband. As the children's "owner," the father had a legal right to the economic benefit of his children; he took their wages and, in exchange, was responsible for their support during their dependency, and for his daughters' dowry and his sons' education for later self-sufficiency. The children's mother was not considered to be a competent legal party to any court action, including her own divorce. As the children were the property of her husband, she had no right to receive custody, nor did she have any right to contact with the children who would then be her ex-husband's property, unless he allowed them access to each other.

The case known as *Rex v. Greenhill* (1836) precipitated the reform in Great Britain. In that case, a husband left his wife and family to set up life with his mistress. The wife left the marital home with her children and took them to live with her family because she needed their financial and emotional support. The marriage had three children, all daughters under the age of 6. Their father attempted to force a reconciliation with his wife by filing a *habeas corpus* action for the return of the children to him. The mother refused to return to the marital home and sought to keep the children in her own care. The court's conclusion was that no right existed under the law to deny the father custody of the children of the marriage. Interestingly, their mother took an action of self-help not unfamiliar in custody struggles today: She fled to continental Europe with her children (Klaff, 1982).

After the divorce action, the father's lawyer, Serjeant Talfourd, campaigned in Parliament for a change of the law under the notion of "natural justice." The resulting legislative reform, begun as Talfourd's eloquent speech to the Parliament (1837), became "Talfourd's Law" in 1839. That law provided the chancery court with the discretionary power to award custody of children under the age of 7 years to their mother and visitation rights to a mother of children of any age, provided the mother had not been found guilty of adultery. Hence, the so-called tender years doctrine came into being (Roth, 1977). In 1873, the tender years rule was modified such that mothers (again, absent adultery) could be considered for custody of children under the age of 16 years.

The tender years doctrine enjoyed widespread acceptance for a century. It presumed that the interests of all young children (regardless of their gender) and the interests of girls (regardless of their age) were best served by awarding custody to the mother, on the assumption that she was fit (Okpaku, 1976). With its presumption that the mother was best for rearing the child, the tender years doctrine usually put the burden of proof on the father, not only to show that he was an appropriate caregiver for his young children and for girls of any age but also to show that the mother was unfit (Wyer, Gaylord, & Grove, 1987). Unfitness was typically evidenced by the mother's adultery—to which, for a woman, there was no defense in the custody contest. Despite its many positive effects, though, the doctrine also served as an impediment to the expression of children's self-determination rights. The tender years doctrine served to protect children, not to include them in decision making.

The Best Interests Standard in the United States. The need for reform in the United States was expressed earlier. In the early 19th century, the view of families as patriarchal entities gave way to the newer ideal of democracies populated by individuals with inalienable rights—and obligations:

> The husband-father undertook an exclusive responsibility for productive labor. . . . The wife-mother was expected to confine herself to domestic activities. . . . The children of this marital pair were set off as distinctive creatures in their own right. (Demos, 1979, cited in Areen, 1992, p. 88)

Three U.S. cases, predating the Talfourd Act of 1839, illustrate this new way in which the custody of children was considered in the context of divorce. One, *Commonwealth of PA v. Addicks* (1813; hereafter referred to as *Addicks I*), involved a mother whose adultery ultimately interfered with her attempt to get custody. Absent the adultery, the court apparently was willing to award her custody of her children on the basis of the children's relationship with her; in fact, in *Addicks I* (1813) one finds the first language referring to the "tender years" of the children as a rationale for awarding custody to a mother.

The facts giving rise to *Addicks I* form an important backdrop for the court's first analysis that resulted in a custody award to a mother: The defendant woman's first husband, Joseph Lee, abandoned her and their two daughters, aged 10 and 7. At some time thereafter, she began a relationship with John Addicks, moved with her daughters to his home, and had a child by him. Four years later, her first husband returned and divorced her for adultery.

(Her cause of action against Lee for desertion had not yet ripened when he divorced her. Nor is it likely that, given her own adulterous acts, she would have been allowed to bring a divorce action even if sufficient time had passed to prove desertion because she could not have shown herself to be an innocent, injured spouse.) She then married Addicks; however, that marriage was held to be void because Pennsylvania law then prohibited a woman from marrying her paramour during her former husband's lifetime. In Lee's first *habeas corpus* action to retrieve custody of his daughters, the court remarkably broke with the chancery rulings of Great Britain and returned to a singular decision of the 18th century:

> [In 1763 . . .] in *Rex v. Delaval,* Lord Mansfield cast doubt on the inviolability of paternal rights for the first time when he denied a father's writ of habeas corpus for the return of an eighteen-year-old daughter. The young woman had been apprenticed to a musician who had subsequently delivered her to Lord Delaval for prostitution. Instead of restoring the girl to her father and mother, Lord Mansfield emancipated her. Since there was no precedent for refusing paternal custody of a minor, Lord Mansfield undertook to "clarify" the governing rule. Previous cases honoring paternal rights had been correct in result, he stated, but not in reasoning. Minors had been restored to their fathers (or legal guardian), not because the courts were bound to so deliver them, but because such a result had been appropriate on the facts of each case. The "true rule," therefore, was that "the Court are [sic] to judge upon the circumstances of the particular case, and to give their directions accordingly" [p. 914].
>
> [In another case . . .] Lord Mansfield followed his clarified rule and allowed a six-year-old child to remain with her mother where the father earlier had abandoned the family. Two rationales were advanced to support the holding. The broader rationale was that "if the parties are disagreed, the court will do what shall appear best for the child." This rule is nothing less than the modern "best interests of the child" principle. The narrower rationale was that a father who abandoned his parental duties forfeited his parental rights. This rationale has its modern counterpart in the "unfitness" doctrine under which a parent may be deprived of custody because of objectionable social conduct, often without regard to the children's welfare [*Blissets Case,* 1774]. (Klaff, 1982, pp. 337-338)

Thus, the Pennsylvania court, in *Addicks I,* relied on this remarkable pair of early British cases that had held no sway in Lord Mansfield's own country; the *Addicks I* court held that the father had no inherent right to possess his daughters, but rather that the daughters' welfare was to be considered the basis for the court's decision.

Two years later, in *Commonwealth of PA v. Addicks & Lee* (1815; *Addicks II*), the Pennsylvania court thought better of its earlier decision and awarded Lee custody of his daughters, again based on consideration of the girls' welfare. Although the earlier *Addicks I* court had expressed its disapproval of the mother's behavior with Addicks, that court went out of its way to note that her treatment of the children was without fault. The court also noted its concern about the effect of disruption in the relationship with their mother because of the children's "tender years" and their "need of a mother's nurturance" (*Addicks I*, 1813, p. 521). When the *Addicks II* court allowed the return of the children to their father's custody, it again cited the interests of the daughters, but this time it was the state's view that the girls, now 3 years older, had a more important interest at stake. The court believed that it was imperative the daughters learn that marriage was a sacred and inviolable contract that could be dissolved only by law and that they were to eschew their mother's bad example of creating a home with Addicks while she was still lawfully married to Lee. Note that emphasis is not on a woman's right to the companionship of her children in *Addicks I* or *II,* but rather on the tender (and then impressionable) years interest of female children in becoming good, law-abiding members of society. Thus, ironically, the daughters eventually were given over to the care of their father—who had abandoned them for 4 years of their early childhood—to teach them about the sacred duties of marriage.

Four years earlier, in *Prather v. Prather* (1809), an apparently blameless mother did receive custody of her youngest child, an infant. The father, though an adulterer, received custody of the older children under the property theory of male parenthood. Note that, again, the court's emphasis was not on a woman's right to companionship of her children in *Prather,* but rather on the tender years interest of the infant in remaining with her mother. The older children were not deemed to have a sufficient interest in staying in their mother's care; thus, their removal to their father was not prevented.

By 1830, a Maryland court was ready to give open support to the notion that a child had an important interest in remaining in his or her mother's care. In *Helms v. Franciscus* (1830), the court gave custody of a child of tender years to the mother after she had been granted a legal separation—on the basis that her husband had been living in open adultery with another woman. The innocent injured spouse received custody of the infant of the marriage, but again the father's right to the older children was upheld despite the fact that the man was an adulterer. The right of a father to ownership of his children was recognized, but the court acknowledged that the laws of nature require that a child not be snatched from a mother in infancy: A child should stay with the breast-feeding mother. Again, the emphasis is not on a woman's right to companionship of her child in *Helms,* but rather on the tender years interests of a breast-feeding child.

The Best Interests Standard Today. Arguably, the tender years rule was the first appearance of legal consideration of the needs of very young children; as such, it was a best interests standard. Once the tender years rule was fully accepted by U.S. divorce courts, fathers found the tables completely turned. For almost a century, the only way a father could gain custody over the children of the marriage, on legal separation or divorce, was to prove the mother's unfitness. During the peak of the tender years rule, the law was as gender-biased against men as it had been in favor of them beforehand.

The gender bias was declared unconstitutional by many states in the wake of the first gains of the women's movement. In *Ex parte Devine* (1981), for example the Alabama Supreme Court declared the gender-based tender years rule over when it found the doctrine to be unconstitutional. Similarly, a few years earlier, in *State ex rel. Watts v. Watts* (1973), New York's highest court, its Court of Appeals, found that any legal presumption against fathers was unconstitutional.

Other courts have found otherwise. Oklahoma's supreme court, in *Gordon v. Gordon* (1978), upheld that state's statutory preference for maternal custody "other things being equal" (Klaff, 1982, p. 372, footnote 10); in that case, the U.S. Supreme Court refused to hear an appeal from the state court's ruling (1978), in effect refusing to disapprove the state court's decision.

West Virginia's high court, however, has held the tender years rule to be constitutional on the basis of the following:

1. Men and women are not similarly situated when it comes to parenting, at least when a child is very young (e.g., breast-feeding).
2. The presumption in favor of mothers may be an appropriate offset to the historic disadvantages they suffered (*J.B. v. V.B.,* 1978).

As state courts dropped the tender years rule and its explicit preference for mothers, they retained the spirit of it in the name of "the best interests of the child standard." In essence, the tender years doctrine, which was aimed at meeting the needs of children, became gender neutral without losing the goal of appropriately addressing children's needs. Currently (with West Virginia as the exception), neither parent is presumed to have a superior right to the child (Wyer et al., 1987).

The Uniform Marriage and Divorce Act (UMDA, 1979), which has had a significant impact on the statutory reforms of many states, describes the following as among the factors a judge may consider in reaching a custody decision:

- The mental and physical health of all individuals involved
- The child's adjustment to home, school, and community
- Each parent's ability to provide food, clothing, medication, and other remedial care and material benefits to the child
- The interaction and interrelationship of the child with parents or other individuals who might affect the child's best interests (thus, in a general sense, the parent's lifestyle and the child's individual needs)
- The wishes of the parents and the child.

It is with respect to the last factor that children's rights to self-determination are beginning to emerge. At least 20 states permit children beyond a specified age to state which parent they prefer for custody. Some states specify an age, typically 12 or 14; others consider the maturity of the child's cognitive or emotional development. For instance, in the case *In re Marriage of Rosson* (1986), the court concluded that a child of a sufficient age and capacity to reason well enough to form an intelligent custody preference does have the right to have that preference seriously considered. But consensus is lacking on how much weight is to be given to the child's preferences. Sometimes the child's choice is considered only when other factors balance out the choice between parents (*Sharp v. Sharp*, 1973).

Family court judges, though, possess tremendous discretion in how they weigh different criteria and whether they even follow the preferences of the interested parties. Sales, Manber, and Rohman (1992), in a thorough review, concluded that often only slight consideration is given to the specific needs of each child who comes before the court, and, in fact, "surprisingly few state child-custody statutes explicitly include the needs of the child as a factor relevant to the application of the best-interests-of-the-child standard" (p. 24).

Evaluating Child Custody Decisions Under the Best Interests Standard. Under the gender-neutral standard of "best interests," judges gained great discretion in awarding custody. Even though psychologists are now being consulted by the courts and are asked to carry out evaluations about the child's best welfare (Skafte, 1985), a judge is not required to follow the psychologist's recommendations. In fact, judges' decisions may reflect their own stereotyped beliefs about what is in a child's best interests, beliefs that may or may not fit with empirical findings.

Furthermore, the laws of different states vary with regard to how much guidance they provide the judge and how specific the criteria are for decision making. As Wyer et al. (1987) observed, statutes usually do not

> guide the judge in deciding which of two fit divorcing parents is a superior caretaker where the primary differences between the parents are matters of parenting style (e.g., one parent is a stricter disciplinarian, one expresses affection more readily), or of notions about how to raise a child (e.g., one parent favors religious education, one favors secular education). (p. 4)

Some commentators (e.g., Coyne, 1992) even have suggested that the best interests standard is a misnomer. Their view holds that when one makes decisions regarding children's care and custody, one should use a "least worst" standard instead of a "best interests" standard, as Box 5.4 explains. Whichever view holds sway, we believe that children's voices should be heard in custody determinations.

Special Considerations

Deciding custody arrangements for children is rarely easy. But sometimes courts face especially challenging circumstances—for example, when the parent requesting custody (or even access) is gay or lesbian or when family members are of different races.

Custody When a Parent's Sexual Orientation Is Gay or Lesbian. Sharon Bottoms is openly lesbian; she has lived with another woman and—for some time—with her child, Tyler. But in March 1993, Sharon Bottoms' mother sued for custody of Tyler, claiming that her daughter's sexual orientation made her an unfit mother. A circuit court judge in Virginia agreed, citing a 1985 Virginia law saying that a parent's homosexuality is a valid reason for losing custody. He awarded custody of the 2-year-old boy to the grandmother, the first known instance of a judge awarding custody to a third person because of the parent's sexual orientation (Howlett, 1993). In 1993, though, in a clear victory for gays

---

Box 5.4

The "Best"–or "Least Worst"–Interests of the Child

The term *best interests* refers to the goal of the judicial determination in abuse, neglect, and dependency actions in juvenile court. The courts are charged with discovering and putting into place dispositions that will meet the child's best interests. This phrase, though neither advocated nor invented by the courts, came into popular use after publication of the series of books by Professor Joseph Goldstein, Dr. Anna Freud, and Dr. Albert Solnit: *Beyond the Best Interests of the Child* (1973), *Before the Best Interests of the Child* (1979), and *In the Best Interests of the Child* (1986). These books are an examination of information derived from the Yale University Child Study Center and the Hampstead Child-Therapy Clinic. In these books, the authors question the value and ability of any person's attempts to determine and put into effect the best interests of a child. The case goal that is offered by these authors to supplant the so-called best interests goal is 'the least detrimental harm.'

Another author, Professor Anne Coyne (1992), of the University of Nebraska at Omaha, has used a different phrase: 'finding the least worst solution.' Although the least worst solution may not be readily apparent to the lawyers and the judge in a particular case, focusing on the least worst solution, Professor Coyne says, will force the lawyers or judge to confront the perils in other choices available, thereby avoiding or mitigating them. A more productive goal than seeking the best interests, which may be unknowable, is to seek the least worst solution, which would help the professionals involved in the case avoid doing greater harm to a child who is already the subject of an abuse, neglect, or dependency action.

---

and lesbians, a Virginia appellate court overruled the judge and returned custody to Sharon Bottoms (*Sharon Lynne Bottoms v. Pamela Kay Bottoms,* 1994).

In fact, an increasing number of lesbian mothers and gay fathers are being permitted to have custody (e.g., *Doe v. Doe,* 1981). In some cases, however (see, e.g., *G.A. v. D.A.* [Missouri], 1987; *Jacobsen v. Jacobsen* [North Dakota], 1981; and *S.E.G. v. R.A.G.* [Missouri], 1987), a lesbian or gay parent has been denied custody—sometimes because the other parent is heterosexual, sometimes because the child may "suffer from the slings and arrows of a disapproving society" (*Jacobsen v. Jacobsen,* 1981, p. 81). The trial judge so ruled in the *Bottoms* (1994) case despite testimony by a psychologist, speaking as an expert witness, that children suffer no untoward effects from growing up in a home with two women who are engaged in a sexual partnership (pp. 486-487).

Research supports the claim by the psychologist; Cramer (1986), in a review of relevant research, concluded that "the evidence to date suggests that gay [or lesbian] parents raise children who are emotionally and sexually similar to those raised by non-gay [or non-lesbian] parents" (p. 506). The sexual orientation of a lesbian couple does not significantly influence the sexual orientation of any children in the home (Green, 1978; Hoeffer, 1981; Kirkpatrick, Smith, & Roy, 1981). A similar result was found in studying the children raised by a transsexual parent (Green, 1978).

What counted ultimately for Sharon Lynne Bottoms' child, though, when his grandmother appealed the adverse appellate court result to the Virginia Supreme Court, was the state's criminal code (*Pamela Kay Bottoms v. Sharon Lynne Bottoms*, 1995). Citing the intermediate appellate court's failure to give proper deference to the trial court's findings of fact regarding the child's best interests and the mother's fitness (*Bottoms*, 1995, p. 419), the Virginia Supreme Court reversed the decision of the intermediate appellate court and remanded the case to the trial court for implementation of its original order. Missing from the court's analysis is a discussion of the nexus between the unfitness of the mother—based on a per se finding by the trial court of unfitness because of her lesbian orientation (*Bottoms*, 1995, p. 421, dissenting opinion). The existence of such a connection between parental conduct or capacity to act and the child's well-being is the very issue that has occupied courts throughout the United States when they are called on to decide questions of parental fitness in custody cases (see, e.g., *Feldman v. Feldman*, 1974; *In re Marriage of Carney*, 1979; *Stewart v. Stewart*, 1988).

Custody After the Divorce of a Biracial or Multiracial Couple. What if a husband and wife of different races, who have had children together, decide to divorce? Some judges have assumed that such children's interests are best served by "placement with the potential custodian whom the child most closely resembles in terms of physical racial attributes" (Sales et al., 1992, p. 31). But some commentators have been critical of this determination.

In their extensive review, Sales et al. (1992) found no empirical studies on this specific topic, but they did conclude from the findings on adoptions by white families of nonwhite children that this procedure does not jeopardize the nonwhite child's racial awareness or identity. The transracial adoption issue raised by the National Black Social Workers Association that no white parent can properly raise a minority-race child to face the racism inherent in U.S. society (Simon & Altstein, 1977) seems to have given way somewhat to the needs of all children awaiting adoption and permanence (see, e.g., Adoption Assistance and Child Welfare Law of 1980).

Palmore v. Sidoti I (1984) represents the consonance between principle and the needs of a child. In this first of two cases to reach the U.S. Supreme Court (under the same name), the child of a dissolved marriage was placed in the custody of the white mother. The mother then began a relationship with an African American man—which angered the child's white father, who sued for custody of the child. The lower court awarded custody to the father on the basis of its perception of the child's interests being ill-served by living in a biracial home. The father argued his concern that his ex-wife was gratifying her own wishes to engage in the biracial relationship without heed to whether the child would suffer stigmatization from a disapproving community. The Supreme Court acknowledged that the lower state court had "correctly stated that the child's welfare was the controlling factor" (p. 434). The Supreme Court went on to declare, however, that the mother, who was in all ways an appropriate caregiver, could not be deprived of the child's custody and that the state court could not justify its action in reversing the custody award based on a racial classification. The Supreme Court recognized that although private biases cannot be changed by state action (and, further, that children should not be used to achieve change), state action cannot and should not give effect to those biases.

After being awarded custody by the Florida court—and while the Supreme Court action was pending—the father moved to Texas with the child. In *Palmore v. Sidoti II* (1985), the mother consequently attempted to have the U.S. Supreme Court enforce its decision in *Palmore I*. But the Supreme Court held that the Florida Court of Appeals was required to relinquish jurisdiction to the Texas courts under the Uniform Child Custody Jurisdiction Act (UCCJA). Thus, the father could not be subjected to Florida's jurisdiction after he had established his own domicile and that of the child in Texas according to the provisions of the UCCJA.

In *Farmer v. Farmer* (1981), a New York trial court examined how to weigh racial considerations in custody determinations. With all things equal, should race tip the scale in one direction or another? For example, should a child be placed with the parent whose race comports more closely with that of the child's appearance? In *Farmer,* the Court held that "[r]ace is not a dominant controlling or crucial factor[;] it is an element to be considered" (p. 590). Although the Court's resolution of the custody question appears to have rested heavily on the father's history of spousal abuse and violence, rather than on race, nonetheless, the trial court did a creditable job of laying out the majority and minority views on the issue of race in custody decisions.

Joint Custody. The most consistent innovation by the courts in the past two decades regarding divorce is the development of joint custody; statutes in an increasing number of states have come to favor it as an alternative to the traditional all-or-nothing approach to custody contests (Rohman, Sales, & Lou, 1990). Definitions of joint custody, however, differ widely from state to state. In few instances, the amount of time the child is in the physical custody of each parent is split relatively equally; in other cases, the child lives mainly with one parent, but both parents retain legal decision making with respect to the child's education, health, and welfare (Felner & Terre, 1987).

During the 1980s, joint custody was seen as a panacea to the problem of custody because it appeared to allow children to maintain their relationships with both parents, divorced fathers to maintain influence over the lives of their children, and divorced mothers to avoid the burden of being the sole custodial parent (Press, 1983). Weitzman (1985) offered two other reasons for the trend toward joint custody: (a) Fathers who continue to share custody of their children are more likely to make child-support payments, and (b) coparenting can reduce the conflict between divorced parents—in theory, at least.

Some research findings support this positive view of joint custody. Luepnitz (1982) compared joint-custody arrangements with single-custody homes and found that all the children in the joint-custody arrangements reported they preferred that system. Moreover, approximately half of the children in the single-custody homes wished for more contact with the other parent. In a follow-up of 43 of her 50 families, Luepnitz (1986) concluded that joint custody, at its best, is superior to single custody at its best but that by no means is one always better than the other. Shiller (1986a, 1986b) reported other positive effects: Boys have fewer behavioral difficulties in joint-custody arrangements (1986a), and children in joint custody retain more appropriate and realistic feelings about each parent (1986b).

Despite these positive findings, the concept of *joint custody* has also been criticized. Some argue that joint custody strains the ideal of "psychological parenting" after divorce—a hypothesis advanced by Goldstein et al. (1979), who defined a *psychological parent* as "one who, on a continuing, day-to-day basis, through interplay and mutuality, fulfills the child's psychological needs for a parent, as well as the child's physical needs" (p. 98). In fact, a child's need for environmental stability is considered by some to be the major obstacle to greater use by judges of the joint-custody arrangement (Clingempeel & Reppucci, 1982).

It is important to note that the early expectations about unqualified beneficial effects of joint custody have been tempered by research findings that are mixed (see Felner & Terre, 1987, pp. 126-134, for a general review). For example, Steinman (1981) interviewed 24 families, all of whom had agreed to joint-custody arrangements. Although many parents and children thrived under this system, about one fourth of the 32 children reported having a difficult time shifting back and forth between their two homes. One third of these children seemed "overburdened" and had noticeable adjustment problems. Furthermore, whereas some studies have concluded that fathers participating in joint-custody arrangements are less often late or delinquent in paying child support (Luepnitz, 1982, 1986; Waddell, 1985), at least one researcher reported no difference between joint-custody and maternal-custody arrangements (Lowery, 1986).

Likewise, it is not clear that joint custody reduces the level of antagonism between divorced parents (Sales et al., 1992). In this regard, Hauser (1985) concluded that "simply having the designation of joint custody does little, if anything, to ameliorate conflict; nor does it promote, support, or make possible appropriate communication, adequate to children's needs in a population of chronic litigators" (p. 581). Some studies, however, report no differences in conflict levels arising from different custody arrangements (Albiston, Maccoby, & Mnookin, 1990), and several report positive effects, such as greater cooperation between parents and a lower rate of further lawsuits (Ilfeld, Ilfeld, & Alexander, 1982; Luepnitz, 1986; Shiller, 1986a). Note, though, that judges may refuse to award joint custody if the parents are unable to demonstrate the capacity for cooperation with each other.

Given that joint custody only sometimes is helpful to children, can factors be identified that increase the likelihood of a beneficial result? If the parents have an amicable relationship, then joint custody tends to have no adverse effect on the emotional health of the children (Kline, Tschann, Johnston, & Wallerstein, 1989). A continuing conflict-riddled relationship between parents, however, can be detrimental to the children in a joint-custody arrangement.

Thus, Sales et al. (1992) concluded:

Factors that have been identified as important for joint custody to work beneficially for the children include the parents' willingness to share custody

and cooperate; their motivation to provide continued access to the other
parent; and their ability to separate their own feelings and issues about the
other parent from the child's needs and feelings, to empathize with the child,
to respect the other parent's bond with the child, to trust in the other parent's
parenting skills, and to maintain objectivity through the divorce process
(Keilin & Bloom, 1986; Steinman, Zemmelman, & Knoblauch, 1985; Shiller,
1986a; Volgy & Everett, 1985). The importance of the quality of the interpar-
ental relationship for the success of their joint-custody arrangement fits with
 Koch and Lowery's (1984) findings regarding noncustodial fathers; continued involvement of fathers with their children after divorce is predicted by
the relationship between the divorced parents rather than by the parent-child
relationship. (p. 33)

As the review implies in its last statement, the specific custody arrangements may be less influential on children's adjustment than the parents'
emotional stability and the amount of continuing conflict between them
(Grych & Fincham, 1992). In summary, Felner and Terre (1987) concluded:

> Perhaps the clearest statement that can be made is that no particular custody
> arrangement is "best." Arguments in favor of a presumption of one form over
> another are ill suited to the realities of family life and child development. The
> contention of Goldstein et al. (1973) that the child's relationship with the
> custodial or "psychological parent" may be damaged by the continued
> co-equal involvement of the noncustodial parent does not appear to be
> necessarily true in all cases. However, neither is the contention by joint
> custody advocates that joint custody is the best alternative for all children.
> (p. 140)

Children With Special Needs. For those children whose adoptions are made
less likely because of characteristics of the dominant culture, a designation of
"special needs child" has developed (Brooks, 1994). Children with physical,
mental, or emotional disabilities and children with racial or ethnic backgrounds or medical histories not desired by members of the dominant culture
are considered hard to be adopted or placed permanently. In response to these
situations, state social work agencies have developed subsidy systems to
encourage adoption and permanent placement for these children. Subsidies
for adoption may also be available to families considering the adoption of
siblings in order to encourage the continued connection between related
children (Brooks, 1994). Such procedures are consistent with the U.N. Convention's emphasis on ensuring children a right to be raised in a family
environment whenever possible.

The Right to Sue: Children's
Self-Determination Within the Family

Legal theory justifying the availability or absence of a particular remedy, especially in the area of family law, often lags behind the evolving culture of the United States. For example, in providing the right to children to sue their parents in the latter half of this century, the law finally has come to recognize the reality of children as more than parental property whose legal identity is subsumed into that of the father and, more recently, the mother. In this unique area—personal injury actions—the law recognizes most fully the child as a person separate from his or her parents. Furthermore, although a child cannot effectively pursue legal actions during his or her minority and while in the care of the wrongdoing parents, all states' statutes of limitations or case law take this disability into account, allowing children to sue for a period of time after reaching the age of majority regardless of when during childhood the compensable injury was inflicted.

The Parent-Child Immunity Rule

Can a child sue his or her parent for negligence that leads to injuries to the child? In the late 1800s and early 1900s, three state supreme court decisions established as part of U.S. common law what came to be called the *parent-child immunity rule* (Andell, 1973).

In the first case, Mississippi ruled that minors could not sue their parents for the bad acts committed by parents (*Hewellette v. George,* 1891). In the particular case, a daughter had sought recovery against her mother for wrongfully detaining her in an asylum, but the court thought the integrity of the family and the best interests of society barred a child from suing for personal injuries sustained at the hands of a parent (*Hewellette v. George,* 1891, p. 887).

Even more extreme in its reflection of parental immunity was a decision of the Tennessee Supreme Court (*McKelvey v. McKelvey,* 1903) denying a child recovery of damages from her father, who had criminally assaulted her. Two years later, in a similar decision, the Washington Supreme Court rejected a suit by a daughter against her father for raping her (*Roller v. Roller,* 1905). The rationale upholding the integrity of the family clearly had no place in these cases; true family integrity had been destroyed long before either court could have acted.

In justifying the immunity rule, state courts have cited several reasons for their decision: (a) the assurance of domestic tranquility, (b) the right of parents to discipline and control their children, (c) the danger of fraud and collusion between parent and child, and (d) the danger of draining family funds in favor of one child (Andell, 1973). Needless to say, decisions invoking the immunity rule and the rationales offered for them received strong criticism and dissenting opinions.

State courts began to restrict the use of parental immunity when the relationship at stake had gone beyond the bounds of parents' privacy interest in raising children. That privacy interest was recognized by the U.S. Supreme Court in *Meyer v. Nebraska* (1923) and *Pierce v. Society of Sisters* (1925). By 1930, the Supreme Court of New Hampshire allowed a child to sue his father for negligence when, employed by the father for the summer months, the child was injured when the staging on which the child was working collapsed (*Dunlap v. Dunlap,* 1930). The court held that, as the father had liability insurance, such insurance removed any danger of family discord (*Dunlap v. Dunlap,* 1930, p. 913); also, the insurance safeguarded against the drain of assets from the family for the benefit of a single member.

By the middle of the 20th century, support for parental immunity generally was beginning to erode. California's supreme court, which earlier had applied the parental immunity doctrine in its entirety, began to allow children to sue for damage awards when the parental act was willful or malicious. But even here, the recognition of children's rights was a reluctant one; in a pivotal case (*Emery v. Emery,* 1955), renowned Justice Traynor wrote:

> While it may seem repugnant to allow a minor to sue his parent, we think it more repugnant to leave a minor child without redress for the damage he has suffered by reason of his parent's willful or malicious misconduct. (p. 224)

Ten years later, the State of Washington further limited the immunity rule by excluding its application from incidents in which the wanton behavior on the part of the parent constituted an abandonment of the normal parent-child relationship. In *Hoffman v. Tracy* (1965), the state court wrote: "[A] parent who takes a child in an automobile with him and drives it while he is intoxicated is temporarily abdicating his parental responsibilities and is not entitled to the immunity" (p. 327).

The trend during the past three decades has been to abolish or severely restrict the immunity rule (Andell, 1973). The New York Supreme Court has gone so far as to declare that a child's right to sue his or her parents is an absolute right, one not dependent on the presence of insurance coverage (*Howell v. Howell,* 1969).

Thus, immunity from lawsuits commenced by one's children has generally been abolished by case law. For example, in California, the high court found that an unemancipated minor could maintain an action against his parent for negligence (*Gibson v. Gibson,* 1971). Overturning 40 years of precedence, the court found untenable the underlying reason for prohibiting such lawsuits: "bring[ing] discord into the family and disrupt[ing] the peace and harmony which should exist between members of the same household" (*Gibson v. Gibson,* 1971, pp. 916). Some 10 years later, an Arkansas court allowed an action brought by a minor child against his parent to go forward under a theory of willful and wanton conduct, arising out of the parent's intentional drunkenness before driving his car in which the child was a passenger (*Foldi v. Jeffries* [1983] provides a thorough discussion of the history of parental tort immunity). Finally, children who have suffered intentional harm at the hands of their parents have been allowed compensation in personal injury actions (see, e.g., *Wilson by Wilson v. Wilson,* 1984).

But the attempts of children to sue their parents for other relief, such as the termination of parental rights, have met with less success. The highly publicized case of "Gregory K."—who asserted his right to self-determination in his decision to "divorce" his mother—is a very specialized one (*Rachel K. v. Gregory K.,* 1992). Because of its unique nature, it is described in detail in Box 5.5.

Other children similarly situated as "Gregory K." was—in a state-licensed foster home and out of his parent's care for many years—have sought similar relief. Their fates have gone unnoticed as they have had to wade through the morass of state social service agency casework plans and federal rules (e.g., Adoption Assistance and Child Welfare Law of 1980). Through their law guardians, guardians *ad litem,* Court-Appointed Special Advocates, Foster Care Review Boards, and their persistent foster parents, however, those children, too, make their preferences known to the courts—as we believe they should. The consideration given those requests for relief has been increasing in weight during the past years (Sales et al., 1992), signaling increasing favor for according to children a right to self-determination.

Box 5.5

Can Children "Divorce" Their Parents? The Case of Gregory K.

Can a child sue his or her parents for termination of parental rights? That was the dilemma posed by the case of the 11-year-old Florida boy known in the courts as "Gregory K."—a child who had been moved from parent to parent, from house to house, from foster placement to foster placement, and even from state to state (Rohter, 1992). A lawsuit was brought on the boy's behalf to sever all legal ties to his biological mother so that he could be adopted by a foster family with whom he had been living (*Rachel K. v. Gregory K.*, 1992). His mother contested the suit, claiming that she had placed Gregory K. and her other two children in the state's care only for financial reasons and only temporarily.

Ralph and Rachel K. married in 1979; 1 year later, Gregory was born. In 1984, Ralph and Rachel separated, and Ralph was awarded custody of Gregory. But in 1989, the police filed a neglect complaint against Ralph; consequently, the state removed Gregory from Ralph's custody and placed him with Rachel, whom Gregory had not seen for 5 years. But the arrangement did not work out, so in September of that year Gregory was placed in foster care.

In June 1991, a trial judge, pursuant to a dependency action, ordered the Health and Rehabilitation Service (HRS) to transfer Gregory's case to its adoptions unit and to seek termination of Rachel's parental rights (Ralph previously had relinquished his parental rights). HRS terminated Rachel's parental rights in February 1992, but 1

Grandparents' Rights

A recently emerging topic of relevance is grandparents' visitation rights with their grandchildren (Thompson, Scalora, Castrianno, & Limber, 1992). Within the past two decades, each of the 50 state legislatures has given grandparents the right to petition courts for visitation privileges—even over parents' objections. This is quite a shift from the earlier common law tradition that gave parents autonomy over their children and delegated to parents the power to control interactions between grandparents and grandchildren. It reflects the social changes that have affected the family, including the higher divorce rate, the number of single parents, the increase in teenage pregnancy, and the abdication by parents of the right to raise their children in favor of their own parents, the children's grandparents.

month later, HRS reversed its position and recommended reunification of Gregory and his mother.

By then, though, Gregory had been living happily with his official foster parents, George and Lizabeth R., and did not want to return to his mother. So, in April 1992, he filed his own petition seeking to terminate his relationship with his biological mother and to be adopted by his foster parents. The boy and his attorney asserted that Gregory had a constitutional right to have his own views presented to the court, rather than being forced to accept what his parents, guardians, or other adults saw as his best interests.

In July of that year, in Orlando (Florida) juvenile court, Judge Thomas S. Kirk agreed to allow Gregory's lawsuit to go forward after ruling that the boy had the same constitutional right as an adult to protect his own interests—what seemed to be a landmark decision. The court then permitted Gregory to be adopted by his foster parents after concluding that his mother had effectively abandoned him. Advocates of children's rights to both self-determination and nurturance hailed this decision. But in 1993, the Florida Court of Appeals reversed the lower court's ruling although the appellate court stopped short of removing Gregory from his adoptive home.

So, whose rights prevailed in this case? Was Gregory successful in "divorcing" his parent? It is doubtful that the court's decision was intended to uphold his right to self-determination; more likely, the court's opinion was meant to support the view that Gregory had a right to be nurtured—affirming the primacy of the parent's right over the child's right, the child's need over the child's right.

Grandparents' Rights and the Best Interests Standard

To assert their new rights, grandparents must persuade the courts that they have standing to petition for visits or access; the courts then must determine whether it is in the best interests of the child to permit the contact. In fact, all the states require their courts to use this standard, but few state statutes identify the considerations inherent in the child's best interests, and explicit legislative definitions of these factors are even rarer (Thompson et al., 1992). The types of considerations usually referred to, however, include (a) the amount of prior personal contact, (b) the quality of the grandparent-grandchild relationship, (c) the lack of interference with the parent-child relationship, and (d) the child's preferences, if the child is "of sufficient age" in the judgment of the court (Thompson et al., 1992).

In a thoughtful review, Thompson et al. (1992) noted that despite the attractiveness of grandparent visits in the abstract, there are risks in mandating such a policy, as the grandchildren are the likely recipients of any visit-generated intrafamilial hostility (e.g., between children's parents and grand-parents). Thompson and colleagues concluded, therefore, that a policy insti-tutionalizing such procedures requires convincing evidence:

(a) that grandchildren necessarily benefit from visitation with grandparents (even over parental objections) and experience emotional losses when they are denied contact with them;

(b) that courts can effectively assess the child's best interests in determining whether visitation privileges should be awarded to grandparents or not; [and]

(c) that the potential benefits of visitation outweigh the indirect disadvantages that visitation statutes may impose on family functioning. (p. 299)

Their research, though, reveals the need to question the application of these criteria in most cases:

[j]ust as the parental autonomy tradition risks ignoring the significance of psychological parenting relationships that may exist outside the nuclear family, an exclusive focus on the child's "best interests" assumes that this standard can be validly and reliably applied by the courts. As this review has shown, there is reason to doubt that this is so, whether courts are adjudicating parental custody disputes, parent-third-party custody disputes, or grandparent visitation disputes. In each case, the complexity of assessing the child's best interests, together with a judicial tendency to rely on intuitive values concern-ing the family, often undermine valid determinations of a child's interest. When the uneven application of the best interests standard to visitation disputes is added to the uncertain benefits of visitation to children when they become enmeshed in intergenerational hostility, and the indirect conse-quences of visitation statutes for family functioning, it is reasonable to question how frequently children are, indeed, the beneficiaries of this statu-tory reform.

The parental autonomy tradition has, in fact, always had room for protect-ing the rights of individuals who have assumed a parent-like role in the child's life, as well as curbing abuses of parental prerogatives. But in grandparent visitation disputes, parent-like prerogatives are extended to family members who may not necessarily have assumed the role of psychological parent to the child, and it may be difficult for courts to determine when this psycho-logical parenting relationship really exists. Although these statutes derive, in part, from a cultural recognition of the importance of grandparenting and the value of intergenerational supports to children, these statutory prerogatives also derive from an effort to protect the interests of grandparents in the family. Grandparents have legitimate interests in their grandchildren, of course, which perhaps merit consideration in family law. The difficulty with grandparent visitation statutes is reconciling grandparents' and grandchildren's interests—which are not always coexistent—under a "best interest of the child" standard. As we have seen, judicial constructions of children's interests sometimes implicitly benefit grandparents and may, at times, function contrary to children's needs on some occasions while protecting them on others. (Thompson et al., 1992, p. 313)

Psychological Research on the Best Interests Standard and Grandparents

In their review of the empirical literature relevant to the issues set out above, Thompson et al. (1992) emphasized the diversity in interactions between grandparents and grandchildren. Neugarten and Weinstein (1964) defined five styles of grandparenting relevant in this regard:

1. The *formal* grandparent maintains an interest and involvement with grandchildren but clearly treats grandparenting as something different from parenting, leaving the latter strictly to the parents.
2. The *fun seeker* is informal and playful, viewing the relationship with grandchildren as a source of mutual pleasure.
3. The *surrogate parent* (which Neugarten and Weinstein observed only with grandmothers) takes on typical child-rearing responsibilities when the child's parent requests them.
4. The *reservoir of family wisdom* (primarily grandfathers) manifests an authoritarian style in which the grandparent keeps a distance from parents and grandchildren.
5. The *distant figure* is only infrequently and fleetingly available to grandchildren, typically on special occasions.

Surveys of the extent of contact between specific grandparents and their grandchildren underscore the diversity in their degree of involvement (Cherlin & Furstenberg, 1986; Kornhaber & Woodward, 1985). Furthermore, in one survey only 2% of grandchildren reported that they would turn to a grandparent for help with a personal problem, and only 15% even included a grandparent in their definitions of their family (Cherlin & Furstenberg, 1986, cited in Thompson et al., 1992).

Thus, to quote the conclusions of Thompson et al. (1992):

> . . . it appears that grandparenting is, at its root, a considerably more variable and ill-defined role than traditional conceptions would suggest. Moreover, current research does not clearly support the view that grandparents make unique contributions to their grandchildren's development, or even that the grandparenting role is itself consistently satisfying or meaningful to the adult. Instead, these studies suggest that the diversity of grandparenting roles and styles undermines any effort to portray grandparenting—and the benefits of grandparenting—in broad generalization. In other words, the grandparent-grandchild relationship is a *contingent* relationship: its benefits are not necessarily inherent in the relationship but depend on many other factors. (pp. 303-304)

Among these other influencing factors are the following:

- Age: Older grandparents are more likely to assume the formal style, whereas younger grandparents tend to be fun seekers (Neugarten & Weinstein, 1964).
- Socioeconomic, job, and marital status of the grandparents
- Ethnic or racial group: Some studies find that black grandmothers assume greater parent-like roles with their grandchildren, especially in lower-income families (Burton & Bengston, 1985).
- The geographical proximity of grandparents (Cherlin & Furstenberg, 1986; Tinsley & Parke, 1984) or their financial and physical ability to travel frequently
- The relationship between grandparents and their *own* offspring, the child's parents: Thompson et al. consider this to be the most important influence because, as the middle generation, parents mediate the relationship between grandparents and grandchildren into their respective roles (Robertson, 1975). If this relationship is positive and supportive, it encourages a multitude of benefits that reflect the rights of both generations (Thompson et al., 1992).

A divorce in the middle generation, of course, changes the grandparent-grandchild relationship. Maternal grandparents—assuming their daughter receives custody—may assume more responsibilities, from direct parenting to providing financial aid. Paternal grandparents may have reduced contact (but not always).

The Future of Grandparents' Rights

The rapid emergence of the demand for grandparents' rights in the past two decades implies that we may expect further issues for resolution in the near future. Already, one legal scholar (Ingulli, 1985) has asked whether the provision of visitation means that grandparents have the right to be notified—or even to intervene—in legal proceedings affecting the custody of their grandchildren.

In the rush to extend legislation, children's rights may be overlooked. Several proposals try to meet this need. First, California has mandated that grandparent-parent disputes must go to mediation before any judicial decision is made. Such mediation has the potential for diminishing the intergenerational hostility that harms the child (Thompson et al., 1992). Second, an appointment of a law guardian to represent the grandchild's interests would bring emphasis back to the child's needs because a guardian *at litem* traditionally only represents his or her own view of the child-client's best interests (Brooks & Stick, 1994). Both of these procedures also serve to put the brakes on a rampant awarding of court-enforced visits and access rights when they actually are *not* "in the best interests of the child."

Recommendations Regarding the Rights of Children Within the Family

The U.N. Convention provides helpful guidance on the issue of children's rights within the family. Articles 7 and 8 of the Convention acknowledge the child's right to an identity and to knowledge of his or her family and nationality. Those articles also guarantee children a right to know and be cared for by their parents. We believe that all children in the United States are entitled to an identity—specifically, the identity of the child within a particular family. In that context, children have the best opportunities to mature, to discover the world around them, and to learn the responsibilities of citizenship. Without identity, children have no solid foundation on which to build.

Further, we believe that children have a right to reliable satisfaction of their physical, emotional, cognitive, and spiritual needs. Where the family is lacking, the child is entitled to community support in order to attain these ends. Thus, as Article 9 specifies, when families cannot provide the foundation necessary to children's development or when living with the parents is deemed incompatible with a child's best interests, the state has an obligation to intervene. In such cases, though, children have a right to have their own needs heard and understood by judicial and other governmental bodies making decisions about their placement, custody, and well-being. A child's custodial care should be given to one parent or the other (or both) in accordance with the child's emotional, social, and cognitive needs—particularly the need to know one's siblings, one's parents, and both halves of one's extended family —as well as with the child's expressed preferences. Also, we believe that a child has a right to know his or her family's history and, whenever possible, to know and have the opportunity to form relationships with the members of the family of all living generations.

In addition, children have a right to be made whole for their losses and injuries, regardless of who is responsible for those harms (parents, state, or others). Although this is not to say that children should be expected or encouraged to bring legal actions against their parents or others, nonetheless, the United States, as a nation governed by law, should recognize the right of a child-citizen to the benefits accorded adults in the legal process.

Children's families are their first and most important caregivers and teachers. If children's voices cannot be heard in a meaningful way within the context of the family, how can anyone expect those voices to be heard in other contexts?

Note

1. From "The Real-Life Dilemmas of Frozen Embryos: A Tennessee Divorce Case Raises Questions the Law Hasn't Begun to Confront," by C. Gorney, June 26, 1989, *The Washington Post,* p. B01. © 1989, The Washington Post. Reprinted with permission.

6

When Parents Are Not Enough

The Rights of Children in the Social Service System

Self-sufficiency is such a strong value that it is almost sacrilege to question
it as a goal. I certainly support the goal that all adults should be independent and assume responsibility for themselves and their families.
However, individuals are not islands; our relation to society is inter-
dependent. We all exist in a social and economic context which can make
it more or less likely that efforts to assume family responsibilities will succeed.

Aletha C. Huston, Professor (1995)

A shy 8-year-old girl, "Lillian," is brought to a local hospital one evening
by her mother. A chance remark Lillian had made earlier that evening had
so enraged her mother's boyfriend that he hurt her badly in his venomous delivery of discipline. In the emergency room, Lillian, reading her mother's expression, knows not to reveal the identity of her attacker, but the look of fear
and deception that fills her face when authorities ask her the relevant question
betrays the truth; the adults interviewing her guess the right answer anyway.

All that Lillian wants is to go home with her mother, to help care for her
siblings, and to sleep in the bed she shares with her sister. But Lillian is told
that she will be staying in the hospital at least overnight and that when she
does leave, she will go to a stranger's home to live.

Lillian believes that the boyfriend is very important to her mother. But
each time she has been the victim of this man's anger, Lillian has wondered
about her own place in the family. She is confused about her mother's feelings
for her. Why does her mother allow the boyfriend to beat her? Does her mother

share the boyfriend's feelings of dislike and anger toward her? While she and her mother are absent, will the boyfriend be cruel to her younger brothers and sister?

Lillian knows—from her mother's eyes—that she cannot tell any of the strangers who surround her in the hospital about these fears. So, when interviewed, she tries to balance on the tightrope between her mother's expectations and her own need to return to her mother's care.

> What becomes very clear to Lillian early on is that she is alone in a maze of incomprehensible adult action. No one has made sense to her: not her mother, the doctors, the social workers, or the police officers. Her mother has betrayed her in a way that Lillian cannot articulate; the social workers and doctors who questioned her have tricked her by guessing the very information she has withheld and that she denies when asked directly; the police officers haven't arrested anyone even though she was convinced (and maybe secretly hoping) that an arrest would be made so she could be assured of sleeping safely in her own home. In refusing her the right to return home, the strangers around her are punishing her when she has done nothing wrong. Nothing makes sense to her, and no one—including Lillian herself—is proceeding in the way she has tried to direct. . . . Lillian's world had become an incomprehensible, unpredictable, frightening place for the horrible minutes of the beating she suffered earlier; she feels equally scared, confused, and helpless in the hospital emergency room. The one person upon whom she depends to get her home is without the power to do so. And so Lillian feels she is lost, actually, metaphorically, completely lost. (Brooks, 1994, pp. 3-4)

Sadly, Lillian's case is not unique; it is similar to hundreds of thousands each year in the United States alone (CDF, 1997). Indeed, the abuse of children by their parents is no secret in the United States; it is responsible for the annual removal of more than 500,000 children from their homes (Fine, 1992).

What rights do children have if they are abused by their parents? The courts may do as little as order the state to provide services to remedy family problems or as much as remove a child from her or his home and order the termination of parental rights. Here a dilemma results, as Fine (1992) noted:

> A decision to leave a child at home carries the significant risk of continued exposure to the condition which prompted court action. On the other hand, the seemingly safer alternative of removal does not necessarily result in a healthier environment. Not only is the act of removal disruptive to a child's emotional well-being, but it brings a child into a system fraught with shortcomings. (p. 128)

Humorist Art Buchwald, who bounced from foster home to foster home as a child, offered this revealing analysis of the problem and his personal response to it:

> The status of a foster child, particularly for the foster child, is a strange one. He's part of a no-man's land. . . . The child knows instinctively that there is nothing permanent about the setup, and he is, so to speak, on loan to the family he is residing with. If it doesn't work out, he can be swooped up and put in another home.
>
> It's pretty hard to ask a child or foster parent to make a large emotional commitment under these conditions, and so I think I was about seven years old, when confused, lonely and terribly insecure I said to myself, "The hell with it. I think I'll become a humorist." (cited in Goldstein et al., 1973, p. 157)

What rights do children have when the state must intervene in family affairs? This chapter addresses that question by considering three levels of state intervention: (a) provision of assistance to families that is intended to help them become self-sufficient, (b) intervention to stop neglect and/or abuse of children, and (c) removal of children to temporary or permanent alternative care. First, we consider children on whose behalf society expects the state to intervene—children whose parents cannot provide adequately for them. Next, we analyze the state's responsibility when parents inflict harm on their own children—that is, in cases of willful neglect or abuse or both. Finally, we consider children who are relinquished by their parents to the care of another, including that of the state—children who are removed to foster placement or permanent adoption.

Role of the State in Protecting Children's Rights Within the Family

Common sense suggests that governmental resources should unequivocally be placed at the disposal of children who are threatened with abuse from their own parents. We believe that state resources should also be made available to families to help them provide for children's basic needs. Huston (1995) suggested, however, that the United States is failing in this obligation:

> Relative to other industrialized societies, the societal contribution to rearing children in the United States is very small. We continue to assume that "other

people's children" are not our responsibility. Data gathered from seven other industrialized countries demonstrates that all but one of them have higher rates of direct transfers to families with children than the United States and that these transfers contribute significantly to their lower rates of child poverty. (pp. 310-311, citations deleted)

Why is this so?

Perhaps one reason is that, in American society, the right of family autonomy is a strong one, carrying with it a corollary principle of limited governmental intrusion into family life (Tyler, 1990). Furthermore, Tyler (1990) suggested that if public officials are made responsible for parents' harm to their children, then the government must specify "a more-or-less uniform national standard of parental conduct" (p. 14). Given disputes over what is acceptable discipline of children (e.g., should a parent strike a child in public—or at all?) and the cultural and ethnic diversity in American society, many shy away from governmental intrusion.

But others argue that children have a right to be protected and nurtured (Rogers & Wrightsman, 1978), so the state has an obligation to intervene when children's welfare is threatened. According to this view, the state must take action on behalf of children who are living in poverty or squalor, who are being abused or neglected, or whose parents cannot or choose not to raise them. In other words, the state must act in children's "best interests."

This view is consistent with the U.N. Convention. Article 27 guarantees children the right to a standard of living adequate for development in a variety of domains (in addition to survival and physical developmental alone), pro- vided with state assistance to parents if those parents cannot meet this responsibility. The Convention further charges the state with the responsibility for protecting children from all forms of abuse, neglect, and exploitation by parents or others (Articles 19, 34, 35, and 36). In addition, Articles 20 and 21 guarantee children the right to receive special protection and assistance from the state when they are deprived of a family environment and to be provided with alternative care if necessary (e.g., foster placement, Kafala of Islamic Law, adoption, institutional placement).

When Parents Cannot Adequately Provide for Their Children

Huston (1995) commented: "In the United States, children are more likely than any other age group to live in poverty, and U.S. children are poor much more often than children in most other industrialized nations" (p. 305). The *Kids Count Data Book*, compiled annually by the Annie E. Casey Foundation, supports Huston's assertion. The report distributed in 1996 noted that, with a child poverty rate of 26% before governmental assistance, the United States is third worst among developed countries; after governments have intervened to ameliorate poverty, the U.S. child poverty rate is far worse than the rest of the developed world (cited in "Young and Poor," 1996).

What data exist on rates of child poverty in the United States? The Costs of Child Poverty Research Project (CDF, 1994) reported the following startling facts:

- More than 14 million children in the United States are living in poverty.
- Nearly one out of every three American children (32%) experiences at least 1 year of official poverty before turning 16 years of age.
- Nearly one in two poor children (46%) lives in extreme poverty, in families with incomes below one-half of the official poverty line.

Moreover, the percentage of U.S. children living in poor families has been increasing for more than 20 years (Huston, 1997). According to the Annie E. Casey Foundation (cited in "Poverty Rate," 1996), the child poverty rate in the United States increased 50% between 1974 and 1994, and approximately 40% of poor Americans—more than 15 million people—had incomes less than half the official poverty threshold in 1994, compared with roughly 30% in the 1970s. Despite the rising poverty rate, however, "[b]etween 1981 and 1984 alone, federal outlays for programs affecting children decreased by 11%" (Garwood, Phillips, Hartman, & Zigler, 1989, cited in Huston, 1995, p. 307).

What explanations can be offered for these troubling statistics? The persistence of, and rise in, child poverty can be attributed to the following factors:

- Hourly wages have failed to keep pace with inflation (CDF, 1994).
- The value of the minimum wage has declined dramatically. According to Lazere and Ostrom (1994), "[i]n 1994, full-time work at the minimum wage [paid] only 75 percent of the federal poverty line for a family of three and only 59 percent of the poverty line for a family of four" (p. ix).
- Expansions of the federal earned income tax credit have only partially offset the decline in the value of the minimum wage and the shift toward lower-paying work (Lazere & Ostrom, 1994).

- The number of families headed by a single parent (usually the mother) has been rising (CDF, 1994).
- Even if they receive food stamps, many working families remain in poverty. The total income—including food stamps—of a family of four with a working parent falls nearly $1,000 below the poverty line, and larger families fall even farther below the poverty line (Lazere & Ostrom, 1994).
- The value of governmental assistance for poor families with children has been declining. For example, "[t]he inflation-adjusted value of Aid to Families with Dependent Children (AFDC) plus food stamps declined by 26 percent between 1972 and 1992" (CDF, 1994, p. 6)

In regard to the latter, Huston (1995) commented:

> Relative to other industrialized societies the societal contribution to rearing children in the United States is very small. We continue to assume that "other people's children" are not our responsibility. Data gathered from seven other industrialized countries demonstrates that all but one of them have higher rates of direct transfers to families with children than the United States and that these transfers contribute significantly to their lower rates of child poverty. (pp. 310-311; citations omitted)

According to *The State of America's Children: Yearbook 1997* (CDF, 1997), among industrialized countries, the United States ranks first in the number of millionaires and billionaires, first in defense expenditures, and first in Gross Domestic Product—but 17th in efforts to lift children out of poverty (p. xv). Results of inadequate assistance can be profound, as Box 6.1 illustrates.

These findings raise an important question: What should the role of the state be in providing assistance to families in need?

Role of the State in Providing Assistance

In the United States, self-sufficiency is highly prized, whether one endorses a liberal or a conservative political philosophy. According to Huston (1995), both liberal and conservative approaches tend to accept three assumptions:

> (1) Both assume that children's poverty is a result of parental inadequacy—that able-bodied parents ought to be able to support their children. Hence, the stated goal of most social programs for poor parents is self-sufficiency. (2) Both assume that responsibility for children's welfare resides almost entirely

---

Box 6.1

An Ounce of Prevention

"Bobby," a preschooler from New England, was bitten by a mosquito—a common enough childhood experience. When Bobby scratched the bite, though, it became infected. His parents, wanting to do the right thing for their son, took him to a physician, who prescribed an antibiotic. Bobby's father worked, but his family was poor and money was too tight for them to be able to buy the medication right away. Thus, as a direct result of the family's poverty, the infection grew dangerously out of control; Bobby was hospitalized for 3 days, receiving intravenous antibiotics (CDF, 1994, p. 45).

The total bill for Bobby's mosquito bite was approximately $2,500—more than 100 times the cost of the prescription medication his family could not afford to purchase on their limited income. In this case, as in thousands of others like it, an ounce of prevention (in the form of state assistance to lift families out of poverty) could have gone a long way toward reducing child suffering—and unnecessary taxpayer expense.

---

in the family, with little corresponding obligation of the community or the larger society. By comparison with most other societies, we emphasize individual responsibility almost exclusively, with the result that we have an imbalance between parental and societal responsibility for children. (3) Many decision-makers have an implicit belief that poor parents are unworthy or inferior—a view fed by racism and class prejudice that is often unspoken, but very real. (pp. 305-306)

Self-sufficiency, however, is not attainable if individuals cannot earn a living wage, if safe housing is unaffordable, or if disproportionate amounts of income—typically 22% to 25% of income in poor families—must be spent on child care (Huston, 1995). In such cases, the U.N. Convention asserts that it is the responsibility of the state to intervene—for example, by providing income supports or other forms of assistance. Huston (1995) offered a rationale for this requirement:

Direct aid to parents is one manifestation of the community contribution to the rearing of its children. Such aid reflects the reasonable assumption that people who are raising children are making a contribution to the larger society which should be supported by all. The society has an obligation to and an interest in its children. (p. 310)

During the past half-century, the U.S. government has attempted to meet its obligation to the welfare of its children through a variety of social service programs.

Previous Approaches. The first national program of support, known as Aid to Dependent Children (ADC; now more commonly known as Aid to Families with Dependent Children [AFDC]) was little more than 60 years old when it was dramatically reformulated as Temporary Aid to Needy Families, a part of the Personal Responsibility and Work Opportunity Reconciliation Act of 1996.

The history of national financial support to families in the United States is a rather short one, compared with that of other developed countries. However, national support did have a precedent in the form of state pensions for poor mothers (Blank & Blum, 1997).

ADC was a part of the original federal Social Security Act of 1935 and was designed to offer financial assistance to families in which the father was no longer providing support. ADC program guidelines were set by the federal government, but the states were in charge of the eligibility guidelines and benefits levels (Larner, Terman, & Behrman, 1997). Blank and Blum (1997) explained:

> In most cases, ADC added federal aid to state mothers' pension programs, which were assisting "deserving" poor lone mothers. Several features of the new ADC program kept states from abandoning their efforts following the passage of the Social Security Act [of 1935]. Federal ADC aid was contingent upon state contributions, and states were given considerable discretion to determine ADC eligibility and grant levels. For example, a state could continue to require that only children living in so-called "suitable homes" could receive assistance. Until they were struck down in 1960, these requirements were used to exclude "undesirable" families from aid, particularly children of never-married or African-American mothers. (p. 30)

One reason for the inception of ADC aid in the Great Depression was that fathers, then a family's traditional source of monetary support, were leaving their families in search of work when their local employment opportunities dried up. The absence of fathers, once an initiating cause, became an insidious requirement as ADC became the sole support of mothers in economically depressed inner cities and rural towns. Blank and Blum (1997) commented:

Concerns about whether the ADC subsidy inadvertently encouraged unwed motherhood arose early on in some states. From a federal perspective, these concerns were short-circuited by the perception that ADC was a program for families headed by widows. In 1939, however, Survivors Benefits were added to the mainstream Social Security program that separately aided widows—the most "deserving" of mothers—and left the ADC program to serve a caseload of apparently less deserving single mothers. (p. 30)

Blank and Blum (1997) further noted that, by the early 1940s, as births to unwed and divorced women began to match the number of children in households headed by widows, states began to exclude aid to children on the basis of their birth status. In the 1960s, as a 20-year migration from the South to the North culminated in millions of Americans—particularly African Americans—settling in urban areas, the courts forced the states to drop the normative eligibility criteria for ADC benefits. As a result, in part, of this dramatic demographic shift from southern rural to northern urban populations and, in part, the fairer eligibility standards, "[b]etween 1960 and 1970 [the ADC] caseload almost doubled" (Blank & Blum, 1997, p. 30).

The ADC denial to children of their unemployed father's presence in the home was a regrettable consequence of the original intent: "The American welfare system has its roots in the belief that children whose fathers died or abandoned them should be protected from destitution, as they are innocent of their parents' misfortunes and mistakes" (Larner et al., 1997, p. 5).

Attempts were made to correct that consequence in two federal moves, one in 1962 (42 U.S.C.A. § 606) and one in 1967 (42 U.S.C.A. § 651):

Partly reflecting concern that the [ADC] program's benefits and eligibility rules discouraged marriage, the program was renamed AFDC—Aid to *Families* with Dependent Children—in 1962. By 1967, federal law required state efforts to establish paternity for AFDC children and allowed aid to go to unemployed male parents with a work history. (Blank & Blum, 1997, p. 31, emphais in the original)

The latest federal reform, Temporary Aid to Needy Families (1996), follows in this line and adds the requirement of work in the near future, as well as a history of work, for both mothers and fathers. Many issues are raised by this latest reform legislation, not the least of which are the effect that mothers' absences will have on already impoverished children and the ability of mothers and fathers to maintain employment, given competing needs of the workplace and their children.

Welfare Reform in the 1990s. In August 1996, President Bill Clinton signed the Personal Responsibility and Work Opportunity Reconciliation Act, fulfilling his 1992 campaign pledge to "end welfare as we know it." At the signing ceremony, the president proclaimed, "We are taking an historic chance to make welfare what it was meant to be: a second chance, not a way of life" (Public Papers of the Presidents, 1996, #1484). The Personal Responsibility Act authorizes changes in several areas of social services:

Family Assistance
- Replaces the federal program known as Aid to Families with Dependent Children (AFDC) with a block grant to states to provide cash assistance to needy families under the program known as Temporary Assistance to Needy Families (TANF).
- Ends the guarantee of cash assistance to poor families, substituting state-determined eligibility criteria and benefit levels.
- Limits recipients to no more than 2 years of benefits without working.
- Places a 5-year lifetime limit on welfare benefits for adults.
- Requires that, to retain the maximum block grant funding, states have at least 50% of their single-parent welfare recipients working at least 30 hours per week by the year 2002.
- Continues Medicaid coverage for persons who leave welfare to go to work for 1 year after they leave welfare.

Supplemental Security Income (SSI)
- Tightens methods for determining whether children are eligible to receive SSI disability benefits by eliminating the Individual Assessment method of diagnosis for children.

Non-Citizens
- Prohibits future entrants from receiving benefits during their first 5 years in the United States.

Child Care and Support
- Consolidates seven current federal child care programs into a single block grant to states funded by two sources.
- Increases child care funding by more than $3 billion.
- Ends the duty to provide child care for the children of TANF recipients who participate in the Job Support program.
- Creates a new requirement for establishing paternity.
- Requires license revocation as a child support payment enforcement tool.
- Preserves the entitlement to foster care maintenance payments and adoption assistance for children in families that would have been eligible for AFDC.

Food Stamps

- Requires able-bodied food stamp recipients with no dependents to work at least 20 hours per week after receiving benefits for 3 months in any 3-year period.
- Prohibits most legal immigrants who are not citizens from getting food stamps.
- Reduces food stamp assistance for all families.

Passage of the Personal Responsibility Act has created a firestorm of reactions. Some (e.g., the Women's Alliance, 1994) have argued that welfare reform is a mistake, whereas others (e.g., Rector, 1996) have argued that it is a necessity. One argument of those who hold the latter view is that state social supports in the form of welfare payments make families too dependent on the government, creating what some individuals have referred to as "welfare moms" (see Box 6.2). As Huston (1995) pointed out, however, middle- and upper-income families seem to have few qualms about accepting state support in the form of deductions for mortgage interest and property taxes, subsidies for health insurance, and social security payments for senior citizens.

According to the U.N. Convention, children have the right to an adequate standard of living and the state has an obligation to assist parents who cannot meet this responsibility. Fulfilling this right does not need to be unduly expensive. Lazere and Ostrom (1994) suggested creating public-private partnerships to "make work pay." The researchers projected the following results of setting a state earned income credit at 15% of the federal credit and paying a minimum wage of $4.75 per hour:

- A family of four with one minimum wage worker would be lifted $150 above the poverty line in 1996, if the family also received food stamps.
- A family of four with one full-time minimum wage worker *not* receiving food stamps would receive an additional $1,518 in annual income—enough to eliminate more than one third of the $4,400 by which such a family would fall below the poverty line without any state action.
- A married couple (one of whom is a wage earner) with one child would reduce by half the amount by which such a family would otherwise fall below the poverty line.
- The income of a full-time working single parent with two children would be raised by $650—5% above the poverty line.

Lazere and Ostrom (1994) concluded that these actions—establishing a state earned income credit based on the federal credit and increasing the state minimum wage—"would establish a public-private partnership to make work

Box 6.2

The Myth of the "Welfare Mom"

The Myth	The Reality
"Welfare moms" have "kids for money."	Studies have not found a link between the AFDC grant and births outside marriage. Women on welfare have an average of two children, approximately the same number as women not on welfare.
"Welfare moms" get rich on welfare.	As of 1995, the average welfare benefit nationwide was $367 per month, or $4,400 per year—almost $9,000 less than the federal poverty line for a family of three.
"Welfare moms" don't work—and they don't want to work, either.	More than half of women who receive assistance are enrolled for less than 1 year; one quarter leave within 4 months; only one third stay more than 2 years.
"Welfare moms" cost the government too much money.	In 1995, federal social support programs for families cost only 1% of the federal budget; state programs averaged 3.4% of state budgets.

SOURCE: Mandell (1995).

pay enough to lift out of poverty a substantial number of Nebraska's working families with children" (p. xiii). Thus, we assert, meeting the guarantees of the U.N. Convention in this area may be a challenging task, but it is not an impossible one.

When Parents Harm Their Own Children

Early in 1993, most U.S. citizens were outraged when they learned that an Illinois couple had left their two young daughters home alone while the couple took a 9-day Christmas vacation in Mexico. The children, aged 4 and 9 years, were placed in foster care after the authorities learned of their situation. At a court appearance in February 1993, the couple—David and Sharon Schoo of Geneva, Illinois—denied the allegations of neglect and abuse described in the prosecutor's indictment. They contended that they had merely exercised their right to refresh themselves without the responsibility of their children. In their view, their children were without rights, even to have their most basic needs met.

The Schoos' two children survived this experience of temporary abandonment—physically, if not emotionally. But other children who are victims of parental neglect are even less fortunate; several hundred children in the United States lose their lives each year because of parental actions.

Lisa Steinberg was such a victim. Her adoptive father, Joel Steinberg, and his companion, Hedda Nussbaum, were educated and affluent. Education and financial resources, though, did not prevent Joel Steinberg from beating his 6-year-old child senseless and then leaving her unconscious for 12 hours in his Greenwich Village apartment. Hedda Nussbaum was present and a witness to Lisa's worsening condition through that awful night but took no actions to save Lisa, although Hedda also had been a victim of Steinberg's battering. After Lisa died from her injuries, Nussbaum became a witness for the state in its criminal case against Steinberg.

The Schoo and Steinberg cases help define the endpoints of a neglect-abuse continuum. At one end is the passive extreme of a temporary abandonment; at the other, is a lethal beating. Wrongful actions by parents fall along a continuum between these two endpoints—acts of neglect that force children to live in filth, exacerbating asthma and diseases of the immune system; acts of sexual use or exploitation that scar children's bodies and psyches; acts of violence that maim, torture, and even kill children. Sadly, these acts occur with disturbing frequency.

Scope of the Problems of Abuse and Neglect

Child abuse and neglect are at epidemic proportions in the United States. The Children's Defense Fund (1997) reported that, in 1995, some "996,000 children—more than 2,700 a day—were abused or neglected" (p. 51). One year later, the U.S. Department of Health and Human Services (DHHS) suggested that those totals were grossly underestimated:

The National Incidence Study (NIS) of Child Abuse and Neglect showed that child-serving professionals believed 2.8 million children were abused or neglected in 1993. That was almost triple the number of abused and neglected children reported by public agencies to HHS for that year. . . . Particularly

troubling was the NIS finding that the number of children seriously injured
nearly quadrupled between 1986 and 1993. (cited in CDF, 1997, pp. 51-52)

Thus, the problems of child abuse and neglect are serious ones for society.
The state must give adequate attention to resolving these problems if children
are to be guaranteed the right to be free from harm.

Neglect

Children typically are not neglected simply to facilitate their parents'
vacations. More commonly, children are left alone because of their parents'
drug addictions, criminal activities, or other irresponsible conduct. Sometimes older children of these parents are truant from school so that they may
provide caregiving for younger children in the family while the parents are
engaged in these activities.

But some children, lucky enough to have at least one parent as nurturer
and caregiver, fend for themselves while their parents work to provide life's
necessities. News accounts provide sobering examples of neglect emanating
from working parents' inability to secure appropriate care for their children.
One mother without the financial means or social resources to provide
appropriate care for her deaf and blind teenage girl with mild mental retardation came to the attention of the New Jersey state social service agency for
her neglectful conduct—leaving the girl in a locked car parked outside the
supermarket where she was employed (Associated Press, 1991). Another
mother lost custody of her 6-year-old daughter to the state for a period of time
because she could not find a baby-sitter. According to the Associated Press
(1991), the girl's case drew national attention and an outpouring of support
for single mothers who cannot find child care (p. A04). More tragic is the case
of a Wisconsin mother whose 2-year-old son became ill and therefore was
refused admission to day care. But the mother thought that she could not miss
work, so she bundled her child in warm clothes and kept him in her car outside
her place of employment. She checked him during her breaks and was
encouraged that everything seemed to be all right. But when the workday
ended, she arrived at her car to find her son dead (Child Health Forum, 1997).

Thus, neglect cases often illustrate the troubles of parents as well as of
children. Having a right to the community's resources—particularly to safe,
affordable care during work hours and to alternative care when children are
sick—would have made all the difference to these working mothers and their

children and to all the children left alone who do not have the ability to care for themselves. Having a right to its resources would also compel the community to recognize these parents and children as valued members.

Abuse

Abuse—the knowing, intentional, or negligent infliction of harm on a minor (Brooks & Stick, 1994)—is more difficult to comprehend. If parents are uneducated—regarding the stages and issues of child development, appropriate forms of discipline, and the symptoms of medical conditions, for example—it is easier to understand how negligent abuse might occur. When parents knowingly or intentionally inflict harm on their children, though, it shocks the conscience. How can parents commit such acts? Certainly, anyone who has parented can attest to *thoughts* of harming a child when the limits of patience have been reached, but an immense gap exists between having those thoughts and acting on them. Of course, children learn to imitate the behaviors they observe. Thus, when a child is raised in a violent home environment, that child is likely to grow into an adult who will imitate the disciplinary methods observed and received during childhood.

According to Article 27 of the U.N. Convention, children have a right to an adequate standard of living, and the state is expected to assist parents who cannot meet this responsibility. In addition, Article 19 requires the state to undertake abuse and neglect prevention and treatment programs. Thus, social service policies should aim first to prevent abuse and neglect through parent education and early intervention; if those efforts fail, however, the state must intervene to protect the children involved.

Federal Child Abuse Prevention and Treatment Act of 1974

The Federal Child Abuse Prevention and Treatment Act of 1974 has three provisions that are relevant to juvenile court abuse, neglect, and dependency practice; in order for states to receive federal funds for foster care and adoption programs, states must comply with the provisions of the act.

First, the law requires mandatory reporting of known or suspected cases of child abuse or neglect. Second, it provides for the placement of abused or neglected children in approptiate custody for the protection of the children's health and safety. Third, the act provides for cooperation between law enforce-

---

Box 6.3

Sample Definitions

Abuse is the knowing, intentional, or negligent infliction of or allowing the infliction of harm on a minor by (a) placing the child in a situation that does or will endanger her or his life or physical or mental health or (b) confining or punishing in a manner that is cruel in its nature, duration, or degree of force.

Battered child syndrome is a medical term of diagnosis used by a medical expert, usually a physician, to describe a pattern of symptoms in a child (who is usually less than 3 years old). This pattern of symptoms—on the basis of reliable, validated, scientific studies—shows that a child has suffered injuries that were not caused by accidental means. The symptoms include subdural hematomas, sometimes but not necessarily accompanied by skull fractures; healed and/or healing fractures or other bone injuries suffered over time; and soft tissue injuries. Typical of this syndrome is a history provided by a parent to explain the injuries that, in fact, is inconsistent with the injuries actually sustained by the child. Upon a diagnosis of battered child syndrome, it is logical to presume that someone caring for the child was responsible for the injuries.

Neglect is generally described as occurring when the parents have substantially and continually or repeatedly neglected their child and refused to give their child necessary parental care and protection. Neglect may thus be seen as a willful omission on the part of the child's caregivers to provide the child with an essential element of care, depriving the child of necessary food, clothing, shelter, or care. In some states (e.g., Nebraska), neglect also includes leaving a minor child unattended in a motor vehicle if such child is 6 years of age or younger.

---

ment officials and courts, as well as between law enforcement officials and the appropriate state agencies providing human resources (Brooks, 1994).

Specific definitions of neglect and abuse vary from state to state; however, several categories of neglect and abuse are generally recognized: abuse (including battered child syndrome and spiral-patterned fractures), sexual abuse, psychological abuse, risk of harm, and neglect (including medical neglect). Box 6.3 provides examples of those definitions.

Abuse and Neglect Reporting Laws

As a result of the Federal Child Abuse Prevention and Treatment Act of 1974, reporting suspected child abuse or neglect or both has been legally

Medical neglect is the willful omission to provide or cooperate with the delivery of essential medical care, absent religious proscription.

Psychological abuse, also known as emotional or mental abuse, involves intentionally, knowingly, or negligently causing injury to a child's psychological, emotional, or mental well-being. The acts or words that give rise to this harm are not easily characterized with precision; however, the resulting injury to the child is more readily described: low self-esteem, anxiety, depression, self-blame, and feelings of inferiority and isolation.

Risk of harm is a phrase used to justify state intervention in the life of a child who has not actually been harmed by her or his parents but whose siblings have shown those symptoms of harm. By citing risk of harm, the state may invoke court-ordered protections for the noninjured child, including removal from the parents' custody, with the expectation that intervention before harm occurs will prevent an actual harm from happening.

Sexual abuse is the illegal sexual use or exploitation of a minor by a parent, guardian, relative, acquaintance, or other person. Sexual abuse is perpetrated by force or persuasion or without the knowledge of the minor. Because of the child's minority and lack of power, it is presumed that the child has not and cannot consent to the sexual contact made with her or his person by the perpetrator.

Sexual exploitation is defined as allowing, encouraging, or forcing a person to solicit for, or engage in, prostitution, debauchery, public indecency, or obscene or pornographic photography, films, or depictions.

Spiral-patterned fractures, as they appear on x-ray films, are characteristic of traumatic, forcefully inflicted injury. Expert testimony from a radiologist may be necessary to identify such a fracture and to make the diagnosis of an inflicted injury.

SOURCE: Brooks and Stick (1994).

mandated for nearly 25 years. The reporting laws' history is well known, from its inception with an article published in the *Journal of the American Medical Association* (Kempe, Silverman, Steele, Droegemueller, & Silver, 1962) to the current trend toward denying immunity for reporters when the report is not substantiated (see, e.g., Connecticut, 1997). Reporting, as Justice Blackmun pointed out in the case of *DeShaney v. Winnebago County Department of Social Services* (1989, dissenting opinion), is federally mandated for the purpose of compelling the effective assistance of the state social safety net for the children on whose behalf reports are made.

Mandatory laws requiring professionals delivering health services to report abuse now are in effect in all 50 states. To qualify for federal assistance, states must grant immunity from prosecution to persons reporting instances of abuse and neglect (Danelen, 1991).

Even so, professionals may hesitate to make reports. Medical profession-als, for example, may be reluctant to report law violations by patient-members of their own social class (Chasnoff, Landress, & Barrett, 1990), as may psychologists and social workers. One survey concluded that between 30% and 40% of practicing psychologists fail to report cases of suspected abuse (Brosig & Kalichman, 1992).

The reason most often given for a failure to report is a concern over lack of definitive evidence. Other reasons, however, could be relevant as well. Friedrich and Boriskin (1976-1977) reported that some individuals believe that "only physicians' special skills and diagnostic abilities [are] sufficiently sensitive to accurately discriminate between accidental injury and parental abuse or neglect" (p. 210).

In most cases, social welfare agencies are entrusted with responding to, investigating, and making findings that either substantiate or repudiate alle-gations. They or local law enforcement agencies are empowered to remove children, either temporarily or permanently, from abusive environments. Although this approach seems straightforward, the situation actually is more complex. Sometimes, agency jurisdiction is unclear; at other times, agencies may find it difficult to communicate with one another:

> Responsibility and accountability for decisions are at stake, and these may be the subject of disagreements between responding agencies. For example, law enforcement officers and social service workers may disagree about the immediate steps to be taken in their responses to a given report of child abuse or neglect. Often, in such dialogue, a commonality of understanding is missing because of the jargon and the specificity of the language which govern professions such as law, social work, psychology, and medicine. (Brooks, Perry [now Walker], Starr, & Teply, 1994, p. 57)

Moreover, caseworkers often have inadequate training in child develop-ment, the application of diagnostic criteria, and cycles of abuse. For example, in New York State, caseworkers who investigate allegations of child abuse must have a college degree but are not required to have much training or experience in child development or psychology (Dugger, 1992).

Equally damning, social service agencies may rely on research that has not been subjected to peer evaluation and review, using such "evidence" to find "abuse" where no abuse in fact may exist. For example, in the category of undemonstrated validity, the works of psychologist and author Richard A. Gardner (cf. 1987a, 1987b)—accepted as valuable by many agency representatives—generally are not peer reviewed, are privately published, and do not take into account contradictory research published in peer review journals (Wood, 1994). Without sufficient training in necessary analytic skills, how can caseworkers be expected to evaluate such work? For example, how can they be expected to evaluate the validity of "an instrument for differentiating between bona fide and fabricated sex-abuse allegations of children" (Gardner, 1987b, p. 3) or claims that "parent alienation syndrome" (Gardner, 1987a) is a valid diagnosis?

In addition, clinicians are concerned about the possible negative effects that reporting could have on the therapeutic relationship. In essence, clinicians confront an ethical dilemma each time they face the prospect of reporting suspected abuse: Should they serve the best interests of the child (by reporting suspected abuse), or should they maintain the confidentiality of the adult client who is responsible for that child (by not protecting the child's rights)? With regard to this dilemma, Levine et al. (1991) commented:

> [C]ompliance with the mandatory reporting law may sometimes have nega-
> tive consequences for the therapeutic relationship and the process of treat-
> ment. However, our data also suggest that reporting may have the effect of
> strengthening the therapeutic alliance and have the potential for aiding in the
> long-term personal growth of the client and family. (p. 15)

Thus, the problems associated with mandatory reporting are complex, not given to ready resolutions. In this regard, Levine et al. (1991) concluded:

> [T]he requirement to report raises important ethical concerns. Our therapists
> generally accepted the law as a "necessary evil," and accepted the responsi-
> bility of protecting children, but they were still conflicted about much of what
> they had to do. Ethics can be argued in the abstract, but the principles have
> to be applied in concrete cases where conflicting demands and values can be
> identified. The dilemma of meeting ethical requirements of informed consent,
> and the fear that the information will inhibit disclosures important for therapy,
> or will affect the safety of the child, present us with a challenge to work out
> equitable principles that will protect the interests of child, parent and thera-
> pist. (pp. 12-13)

Although ethical considerations exist when professionals face the pros-
pect of reporting suspected abuse, we strongly believe that the rights of the child should prevail. Article 19 of the U.N. Convention clearly charges the

state with the responsibility of protecting children from all forms of abuse, neglect, and exploitation by parents or others; that requirement is appropriate.

State Response to Claims of Neglect or Abuse or Both

Although, according to the Federal Child Abuse Prevention and Treatment Act of 1974, state social service systems must respond to claims of abuse or neglect, often their responses are slow or inadequate or both. Even more disturbing (as we describe later in this chapter) is the U.S. Supreme Court ruling that the failure of social agencies to intervene and assist children does not give rise to private actions by those children against the agencies.

Several factors contribute to the problems of slow and inadequate agency response. One is that caseworkers frequently have too many cases to handle properly. Although the number of children reported to have been abused—especially those who have been seriously injured—has increased dramatically in recent years, the National Incidence Study reported that "the number of reports investigated by child protection agencies stayed about the same in each year, decreasing the percentage of children whose abuse or neglect was officially investigated from 44 percent in 1986 to 28 percent in 1993" (CDF, 1997, p. 52).

Another factor is that staff turnover tends to be high. For example, in 1991, four fifths of caseworkers in New York either quit or were laid off (Dugger, 1992). Also, when a problem is detected, services may be difficult to find (personal communication [to Walker], 1997). These conditions make it difficult to achieve the goals of keeping families together and preventing family breakdown.

Many authorities have considered the governmental response to family breakdown to be "clumsy, overintrusive, and the least calculated to accomplish the articulated social goal of keeping families together whenever possible" (Lowry, 1979, p. 56). One explanation for the problems in the process is that the state fails to recognize the child as a separate legal entity, with her or his own rights and interests. The viewpoint that values protection efforts above all else has created an orientation in which the child is merely a subdivision of the family and later a sheltered ward of the benevolent state (Lowry, 1979). The ancient view of the family's right to possession of the child persists, and once the child's place within the family is disrupted, there is little recognition of the child as an independent entity with rights of her or his own. As well, federal incentives that emphasized reunification of the child with the family further ignored the child's interest in true permanence in a timeframe that was meaningful to the child (42 U.S.C.A. § 671 [a][15]).

Recently, the U.S. Congress has passed legislation known as the Adoption and Safe Families Act of 1997, which seeks to overcome the shortcomings of the federal emphasis on reunion. In cases of abandonment, chronic physical abuse, sexual abuse, torture, or murder of a child's sibling by the parent(s), federal law now allows the state to forgo efforts at reunification without loss of funding subsidies.

What rights does the child have when a social agency fails to respond to indications that the child is at risk of (further) injury from a parent? The Supreme Court's answer is not as some would have expected. In the case of *DeShaney v. Winnebago County Department of Social Services* (1989), the Court concluded that the U.S. Constitution does not obligate state or local government officials to protect citizens, including children, against harm from private individuals. But this seemingly innocuous decision deals with a terrifying set of circumstances; in its 6-3 vote, the Court ruled that a failure of a public social welfare agency in Wisconsin to protect a young child from his father's brutal acts did not violate the child's constitutional rights.

The facts are straightforward: Joshua DeShaney was born in 1979; his parents were divorced in 1980, and his father was given custody. His father's second wife and others reported that the child was repeatedly beaten by his father. By the age of 4, he received a beating so severe that it destroyed half of his brain tissue; the resulting severe brain damage caused him to be mentally retarded and required his institutionalization. Today he remains in a persistent vegetative state.

His father was convicted of child abuse but served less than 2 years of prison time. His mother then brought suit against the Winnebago County, Wisconsin, Department of Social Services, claiming that its social workers had reason to know that the boy had been in danger while in his father's custody and that those social workers failed to intervene. Thus, the issue in *DeShaney* focused on whether the due process clause of the 14th Amendment gave a child the right to sue for damages against the state's social workers for their failure to protect him from harm inflicted by his parent.

Ultimately, the Supreme Court ruled that Joshua DeShaney's Fourteenth Amendment right—that is, the right not to be deprived of life or liberty without due process—had not been violated. The Court held that the Constitution does not require a state to protect a child from private harm but only against abuse of the state's own power. Chief Justice Rehnquist's majority opinion viewed the purpose of the due process clause as follows: "to protect the people from the State, not to insure that the State protected them from each other" (p. 196). Therefore, because Joshua was brutalized by his own father and not by an agent of the state, Joshua had no constitutional grounds to bring suit against the state.

The Court acknowledged that the social agency staff might have known that the boy was in danger. Periodically, the agency received reports that he was being abused, and at one point the agency even took custody but then returned the boy to his father's control.

Justice Rehnquist suggested that any state could enact a law that placed liability on such officials under similar circumstances, "but [the officials] should not have it thrust upon them by this Court's expansion of the Due Process clause" (p. 203). The majority opinion also brought in the parent-child relationship in defending the social agency's failure to provide effective assistance to Joshua:

> In defense of [the social service workers] it must also be said that had they moved too soon to take custody of the son away from the father, they would likely have been met with charges of improperly intruding into the parent-child relationship, charges based on the same Due Process Clause that forms the basis for the present charge of failure to provide adequate protection. (p. 203)

This is a surprising statement, given that most court opinions hold that when reason exists to believe that a child is being abused, the state must act to ensure the child's welfare (Orenstein, 1989)—a position consistent with U.N. Convention Article 19. The majority did point out that Joshua's lawyers relied on an argument that the state unconstitutionally denied Joshua the process due to him before it engaged in activity that severely infringed on his life and exercise of liberty (not effectively responding to reports of his need for assistance)—and did not argue for Joshua's right to due process before being denied an entitlement (effective state assistance in response to a report of abuse), which was statutorily mandated and conferred on others similarly situated.

In his dissenting opinion in the *DeShaney* case, Justice William Brennan wrote: "My disagreement with the Court arises from its failure to see that inaction can be every bit as abusive of power as action, that oppression can result when a State undertakes a vital duty and then ignores it" (p. 212). He thought the line between action and inaction was not as easily drawn as the majority opinion had suggested and that it did not consider the agency's duty to comply with the clear intent of the reporting statute, which was to safeguard children from caregivers who were dangerous to them.

The dissent by Justice Harry Blackmun is an impassioned one, criticizing the majority's rigid, formalistic determination to draw a line that separated state action from inaction. He urged a "sympathetic" reading of the Fourteenth Amendment due process clause, writing:

Poor Joshua! Victim of repeated attacks by an irresponsible, bullying, cowardly, and intemperate father, and abandoned by the respondents who placed him in a dangerous predicament and who knew or learned what was going on, and yet did nothing except, as the Court revealingly observes, "dutifully recorded these incidents in their files." (p. 213)

In general, one criticism of the majority decision is its failure to distinguish between children at risk of harm from their parents and those citizens in general who seek redress under the Constitution for negligently administered state services. Even if the state has no constitutional obligation to protect its citizens against the criminal acts of murderers, Joshua DeShaney "was not brutalized by an unknown, unforeseeable assailant; he was victimized by his father, a man in whose custody the state had watched his condition deteriorate for over a year" (Orenstein, 1989, p. 443). Children are not only more vulnerable than "citizens in general"; they also often lack alternative sources of help. As Orenstein (1989) has noted, even Chief Justice Rehnquist has acknowledged this point; in another case 5 years earlier, he had written:

Children, by definition, are not assumed to have the capacity to take care of themselves. They are assumed to be subject to the control of their parents, and if parental control falters, the state must play its part as *parens patriae.* (*Schall v. Martin,* 1984, p. 264)

The interpretation that agents of the state do have a responsibility was articulated in a 7th Circuit Court of Appeals decision, *White v. Rochford,* in

1979. One evening in 1976, police officers stopped a car for drag racing. In addition to the driver in the car were three children; the driver was their uncle. He was arrested and taken away. Despite his pleading with the police officers to help the children, they were left alone on the side of the Chicago Skyway. They did not know where they were and began walking along the eight-lane highway. Finally locating a telephone, they called their mother. As she had no car, she called the police department, which again refused to help. Finally, after a long wait in the cold and the dark, the children were rescued by a neighbor.

The circuit court concluded that the police officers, by their actions, had placed the children in great danger; the abandonment was a violation of the children's due process rights. Yet, as the *DeShaney* decision reflects, the courts still struggle over the implication of a failure to act. In the latter case, the Supreme Court majority chose to conclude negligence only when the state affirmatively acted to restrain an individual's freedom to act in her or his own behalf "through incarceration, institutionalization, or other similar restraint of personal liberty" (*DeShaney v. Winnebago County Department of Social Services,* 1989, p. 199). Thus, the Court creates a dubious difference, distinguishing a caseworker's failure to act to protect Joshua from a known assailant in *DeShaney* from the police officers' failure to act to protect the children in *White v. Rochford* from unknown potential assailants or unknown potential injuries arising out of the children's inability to comprehend and guard against dangers in their situation.

A decision by the Supreme Court 1 year after *DeShaney,* in the case of *Baltimore City Department of Social Services v. Bouknight* (1990), addressed again the clash of children's rights and constitutional restraints on state action. This time, the outcome favored the child's right to protection.

Jacqueline Bouknight's son, Maurice, was 4 months old when he was placed in foster care after having suffered extensive physical abuse, including multiple fractures of major bones. He was later returned to Bouknight's custody, in keeping with a juvenile court order for protective supervision, because she had agreed to cooperate with the Baltimore Department of Social Services and to refrain from physically abusing the child again. However, Maurice then disappeared; the authorities feared he was dead. When she refused to produce the child, Bouknight was placed in jail for civil contempt in April 1988.

The issue the Supreme Court faced in this case was whether the Fifth Amendment's clause protecting citizens from self-incrimination could bar the state from citing Jacqueline Bouknight for civil contempt and placing her in jail until she honored the court order to produce her child (Tyler, 1990). The Court's decision, by a 7-to-2 vote, was that the U.S. Constitution does not prevent the state from using its contempt powers to protect a child. Because she previously had agreed to an order of protective supervision, Bouknight's Fifth Amendment right was not violated when she was jailed to coerce compliance with the order to produce Maurice. In a sense, the decision was a narrow one (Greenhouse, 1990) because the Court ignored the broad spectrum of Fifth Amendment rights of all parents suspected of child abuse and concentrated on those of parents who had previous records of abuse and who were under protective custody orders to submit to periodic inspections.

How may we resolve the decisions in *DeShaney* and *Bouknight*? At first, they may seem contradictory. Instead, we may see them as "compatible holdings that define a narrow spectrum of constitutional protection for children" (Tyler, 1990, p. 14). Tyler writes:

> *DeShaney* holds that the Constitution cannot be used as a sword against the state even when the state fails to act to protect a child from parental harm. *Bouknight*, on the other hand, holds that the Constitution does not handcuff the state and prohibit it from acting to provide minimal protection to a child. (p. 14)

The Court in *DeShaney* was unwilling to hold that the state must act on peril of constitutionally imposed civil liability. *Bouknight*, by contrast, presented no such problem, for there the state wanted to act; it wanted to do what it could do in an obviously desperate situation, and the question was whether the Constitution denied it the authority to act.

The U.N. Convention provides guidance in this dilemma. Article 19 requires the state to

> take all appropriate measures to protect the child from all forms of physical or mental violence, injury or abuse, neglect or negligent treatment, maltreatment or exploitation, including sexual abuse, while in the care of parent(s), legal guardian(s) or any other person who has the care of the child. (Article 19 [1])

Further, Article 20 requires that special protection and assistance be provided by the state when a child is "temporarily or permanently" deprived of her or his family environment. Thus, according to the U.N. Convention, the children in *DeShaney, White,* and *Bouknight* all had a right to protection by the state—as they should.

When Children Are Relinquished by Their Parents

The consequences of losing one's parents in childhood are great. Inherent in that loss is the risk of becoming defeated in the ongoing struggle to attach successfully to a caregiver, because placing a child in a foster or adoptive home challenges that child's right to the "unbroken continuity of [an] affectionate and stimulating relationship with an adult" (Goldstein et al., 1973, p. 6). In addition, the child who loses parents risks losing an identity. Thus, the decision to remove a child, according to some authorities, must meet a higher standard than simply the "best interests of the child." Rather, a demonstration is needed of "substantial risk" of harm or "imminent" danger to the child (Institute of Judicial Administration–American Bar Association [IJA–ABA] Joint Commission, 1981). Although the ultimate decision is a legal one, we agree with Weithorn and Grisso (1987) that it must be guided by psychological knowledge and testimony.

Using "reasonable efforts" to achieve permanency for children has become the goal of the juvenile courts throughout the United States, due in large part to the financial persuasion of the federal government (see 42 U.S.C.A. 671[a][15]). The federal government, in order to continue funding state foster care programs, requires that in the juvenile court the state demonstrate, first, that efforts have been made prior to any removal of a child from her or his family home and, second, that efforts have been made toward reunification during the entirety of the child's placement outside the family home. These efforts must rise to a standard of reasonableness under the circumstances.

These reasonable efforts may be demonstrated by evidence of the circumstances of the particular child justifying immediate removal from the home, or they may be evidenced by attempts by the local social work office to meet the needs of the children within the home by providing various services and the failure of those provisions to make the home sufficiently safe for the child's continued presence there. Such efforts may include in-home family therapy, day care assistance, homemaker assistance, and drug and alcohol rehabilitation for an offending adult member of the home (Brooks, 1994).

Once a child has been removed from the family home, efforts toward reunification may be demonstrated by all of those services provided or attempted to be provided to the family, particularly to the adult parents, which would then have made the home safe for the return of the child. Efforts at reunification can include all of the above-mentioned services, as well as all efforts to facilitate visitation or other communication and contact between the removed child and her or his parents and siblings who remain in the home.

It is important to note that the parents' unwillingness to cooperate with these efforts, their noncompliance with services and the casework plan, and their willful or inadvertent refusal to have contact with the removed child can be used against them. One powerful use is to show that while reasonable efforts were made, those efforts were unsuccessful in preventing the removal or in reunifying the child with the parents. Conversely, the parents' willingness to cooperate, compliance with efforts and casework plan, and their attempts to have contact with their child provide defense counsel with powerful arguments on their behalf (Brooks, 1994). If, however, efforts are unsuccessful, the child may be removed to temporary or permanent care.

Congress amended this requirement of reasonable efforts findings in all cases in 1997. Under the Adoption and Safe Families Act, Congress exempted certain classes of cases from this requirement, citing a mandate that "the child's health and safety shall be of paramount concern" (H.R. 867, 1997, amending 42 U.S.C.A. 671 [a][15]). Today, reasonable efforts at reunification, which had been a source of painful delay and irremedial harm in the adoption of children, give way with a child if a court of competent jurisdiction has determined the following:

I. The parent has subjected the child to aggravated circumstances (as defined in state law, which definition may include but need not be limited to abandonment, torture, chronic abuse, and sexual abuse);

II. The parent has (a) committed murder (which would have been an offense under Section 1111 (A) of Title 18, United States Code, if the offense had occurred in the special maritime or territorial jurisdiction of the United States) of another child of the parent; (b) committed voluntary manslaughter (which would have been an offense under Section 1112 (A) of Title 18, United States Code, if the offense had occurred in the special maritime or territorial jurisdiction of the United States) of another child of the parent; (c) aided or abetted, attempted, conspired, or solicited to commit such a murder or such a voluntary manslaughter; or (d) committed a felony assault that results in serious bodily injury to the child or another child of the parent; or

III. The parental rights of the parent to a sibling have been terminated involuntarily. . . . (H. R. 867, 1997, 101 [a] [2] [d])

The Adoption and Safe Families Act of 1997 further provides for an accelerated schedule of permanency-oriented hearings (within 30 days of a judicial finding that reunification is not appropriate under 101 [a] [2] [d] [H.R. 867, 1997, 101 [a] [2] [e]).

Foster Care

Foster care affects thousands of children in the United States each year. The Children's Defense Fund recently reported that "[a]n estimated 468,000 children were in foster care during a one-day count in 1994—a 16 percent increase since 1990" (CDF, 1997, p. 52). Moreover, according to the report, "[m]ore than 1.4 million children lived with grandparents with no parents present in the household in 1995—up 66 percent since 1989" (p. 52).

Types of Foster Care Placements. In many of the dependency cases before juvenile courts, state-licensed foster care parents may be assigned to care for children on either an emergency or long-term basis. Brooks (1994) described the distinctions among several types of foster care: (a) emergency, (b) long term, (c) therapeutic, (d) adoptive, and (e) group or residential home.

An *emergency* foster care parent provides services, usually without notice, to children who have been removed from their family homes and who are in urgent need of care. It is not expected that children will stay in an emergency foster placement for more than a few days—until a long-term foster placement can be found or the children can be returned home to their parents. The length of time a child will stay in an emergency placement depends on the availability of longer-term foster care placements.

Long-term foster care may involve foster parents providing a home, clothing, food, education, and entertainment for as long as the child is placed outside the parents' home. Unfortunately, children often live in several foster homes before they are returned to their parents' care or freed for adoption.

Foster care also can involve the foster parents providing *therapeutic* placement for the child in their home. If the foster parents are providing a therapeutic home for the child, they are involved directly in the child's healing and recovery, typically from an emotional or psychological injury. Therapeutic foster parents are important to the child's therapy process, acting under the direct supervision of the child's psychotherapist.

Foster parents also may be *adoptive* parents. If the foster parents are interested in adopting the child in their care and if that child is subsequently freed for adoption through a termination of parental rights action or through a relinquishment by the natural parents, the foster parents may be considered first for adoption of that child. This action, of course, is contingent on whether they have formed a close and appropriate bond with the child.

When children have been freed for adoption through either surrender or termination of parental rights actions and there are no immediate adoption prospects for them, children may be placed in a preadoptive placement home, awaiting the identification of an adoptive home. Preadoptive placement parents provide the child with an interim safe place to live and sometimes are involved in readying the child for a move into adoption under the supervision of the child's psychotherapist.

Group homes and residential placements are also potential living environments for children in dependency actions. Group homes typically are provided to those children who are unable to settle themselves successfully into a regular family setting. Residential placements are typically psychiatric placements and are reserved for the most disturbed and psychologically needy children in dependency court actions.

Foster Care Review Boards. Foster care review boards, instituted under federal law (42 U.S.C.A. 675[5][B]) and operating in many states, provide periodic review of all children in out-of-home placements (Brooks, 1994). The local boards review social service agency files regarding the child and solicit input about the child's progress in placement and about the management of the child's case from a variety of sources: the child's social services case manager, foster parents, parents, guardian *ad litem,* and parents' counsel. The review board then may provide the juvenile court with recommendations regarding the child and any aspect of the child's continued placement or return home. Foster care review boards that require periodic review fulfill the spirit of Article 25 of the U.N. Convention, which guarantees children placed by the state for reasons of care, protection, or treatment have a right to have that placement reviewed regularly.

Adoption

The U.S. adoption pattern replaces one set of parents with another. This replacement model requires that the original parents' connection to the child be severed completely through a court-ordered termination or a voluntary surrender of parental rights, which leaves the child temporarily "parentless." A second set of parents is then provided to the child through a court-approved adoption. The child, in this way, at no time has two legally recognized fathers, mothers, or families. Implicit in this severance/replacement style of adoption is also the loss of siblings (unless they are adopted into the same second family) and all extended members of the original family.

This adoption practice is grounded in an ownership theory of children: No two fathers may possess or have a right to the same child. In an early form, adoption in ancient Rome was created to provide for the smooth transfer of property through inheritance and continuance of a family line when there was no male heir to receive the father's property and title (Brooks, 1994; Clark, 1987; Zainaldin, 1979). A father's rights once were to the labor and wages of the child (Brooks, 1994; *Ex parte Devine,* 1991; Rodham, 1973); now the law speaks of rights to companionship (*Stanley v. Illinois,* 1972) and family privacy (*Santosky v. Kramer,* 1982).

Today, adoption is seen as a benefit to the child, who is given a second family (*Santosky v. Kramer,* 1982). Severance of the original parental bonds, though, must be justified as in the child's "best interests" (*Santosky v. Kramer,* 1982). But the earlier property view of children continues to influence the way the child is assigned to a family: Rights of the parents are weighed against the lesser interest—the child's need for stability, consistency of care, and permanence (Goldstein et al., 1979).

In devising a system of child placement and adoption designed to distance the child from her or his biological family, jurisprudence in the United States created a scheme of child rearing that is foreign to many cultures, both within and outside the United States. Termination of all ties with an original family to create a new set of attachments with a separate family is unknown in such cultures, particularly among Native Americans (Brooks, 1994; Guerrero, 1979). Tribal traditions consider "adoption" to be the child choosing a substitute parent. Native Americans' spiritual bonds—between mother and child, father and child, child and family, as acknowledged in native peoples' cultural beliefs—make a severance incomprehensible among Native Americans (Brooks, 1994).

The traditional view in the United States, however, has been that children placed for adoption have no rights; the urgency of the problem seems to force a relinquishment of any potential rights. Recently, highly publicized cases have given prominence to this view and the resulting conflicts between the biological and adoptive parents' rights—while the rights of the child are shuffled aside. Box 6.4 describes such a conflict, the case of "Baby Jessica."

Elias (1993) suggested that adoption incorporates losses for all persons concerned: The birth parents lose their child, the child loses (often forever) a connection with the biological parents, and adoptive parents raise the child of another, often because they are unable to produce their own biological child (yet another loss). Losses were taken to an extreme in a second highly publicized case known as "Baby Richard" (*In re Petition of John Doe and Jane Doe, Husband and Wife, to Adopt Baby Boy Janikova,* 1994), described in Box 6.5.

Few adoptive persons will have access to so much information about their past as will Jessica/Sarah and Richard/Danny, although many adoptees do want knowledge about their biological mothers and fathers (Rosenberg, 1993). Still, some may fear a further abandonment if they seek contact with biological parents who reject their overtures. On the basis of her counseling with adoptive families, social worker Elinor Rosenberg (1993) concluded that adolescence for the adopted child can be an especially tumultuous time. As some adolescents decide that their birth parents must have been sexually irresponsible, they may even imitate this assumed tendency in an apparently unconscious effort to understand what happened (Rosenberg, 1993). Josselson (1980) noted that as adoptees attempt to integrate their pasts with their futures, they are hindered by the existence of two sets of parents and may experience an absence of generational sequence as a consequence of having been uprooted.

Empirical research is less conclusive on the proposition that adopted adolescents find the identity crisis especially difficult, as a review by Goebel and Lott (1986) revealed. For example, Reynolds, Levey, and Eisnitz (1977) found that adoptees' self-ratings of their childhood experiences were almost evenly divided between satisfactory and unsatisfactory, whereas in the general population, more self-reports were satisfactory (75%) than unsatisfactory (25%). In contrast, Ijams (1976) found no significant difference in the way these two populations viewed their family-rearing experience. Goebel and Lott (1986) found no differences in resolution of the identity/diffusion crisis. Comparisons of the capacity for intimacy—the major task of adolescence

---

Box 6.4

*The Conflict Between Biological Parents and
Adoptive Parents: The Case of "Baby Jessica"*

A wrenching battle over custody rights between two couples was portrayed on national television as millions watched "Baby Jessica" taken from her adoptive parents and returned to her biological parents (*Jessica DeBoer [a/k/a/ Baby Girl Clausen], by Her Next Friend, Peter Darrow v. Roberta and Jan DeBoer and Cara and Daniel Schmidt,* 1993).

In 1991, Cara Clausen, then 28 years old and unmarried, surrendered her infant daughter for adoption. In doing so, she named the wrong man—Scott Seefeldt—as the father and got his consent for the adoption. A married couple in another state, Jan and Roberta DeBoer, adopted the child 17 days after her birth and named her Jessica.

Ms. Clausen had broken up with Daniel Schmidt shortly after the child was conceived. Three weeks after she relinquished the infant, and regretful over doing so, she told Mr. Schmidt about the baby. Resolving to get the child back, Cara Clausen and Daniel Schmidt filed separate motions for the permanent return of their daughter.

In December 1991, they successfully argued in the Iowa courts that the adoption was not binding because the wrong "father" had been named (genetic tests proved Schmidt's paternity) and because Mr. Schmidt, as the natural father, had not relinquished his parental rights. The Iowa courts ordered the child returned to the Schmidts, but the DeBoers, living in Michigan, argued that their state had jurisdiction because Jessica was a Michigan resident.

In January 1992, the Iowa Supreme Court upheld the lower court ruling. Although the court questioned Daniel Schmidt's fitness as a parent, it held that his rights had priority over the baby's, and so she belonged with the Schmidts. But the next month,

---

according to theorist Erik Erikson (1963)—also have produced conflicting results. Ijams (1976) reported no difference between adoptees and nonadoptees, but Simmons (1979) found that adoptees had less capacity for identity.

But, as Goebel and Lott (1986) observed, perhaps such comparisons are too general; more relevant is whether adoptees who seek information about their birth heritage can be differentiated from those who do not. The motivations for such a search are themselves subject to several interpretations. Goebel and Lott (1986) wrote:

> The implication is that searching indicates failure to make satisfactory progress toward identity formation; that it stems from deficiency as opposed to growth motives. It could, however, be argued that search motivation would

Michigan Circuit Court Judge William Ager, Jr., awarded custody of 2-year-old Jessica to her adoptive parents, the DeBoers, on the advice of experts who said that the child would suffer permanent emotional damage if she were taken from the only parents she had ever known.

One month later, in March 1993, the Michigan Court of Appeals overturned Judge Ager's ruling and, concurring with the Iowa courts, ordered the child returned to the Schmidts. In April, Cara Clausen and Daniel Schmidt were married; later, they had another child.

That summer, the Michigan Supreme Court confirmed, on a 6-to-1 vote, that Michigan had no jurisdiction in the case. The court ruled that Jan and Roberta DeBoer were required to return 2-year-old Jessica to her biological parents in Iowa the next month.

On August 3, 1993—at the age of 2 $\frac{1}{2}$ years—Jessica DeBoer was relinquished to her "new" parents, who renamed her Anna Jacqueline Schmidt. The Schmidts refused the DeBoers any further contact with the child.

Six months later, the Schmidts reported that things were fine. They noted that the child was toilet trained within a month of returning to Iowa and had given up her bottle and pacifier—right on the developmental schedule (Ingrassia & Springen, 1994).

These signs are encouraging, but the jury is not yet in on the "Baby Jessica" case (and others like it). Disorders associated with disrupted attachments may not appear for several years following the initial loss. Often, they emerge when adolescents or young adults attempt to form mature, intimate relationships but find they cannot do so because they cannot trust that the person loved always will "be there" for them.

Thus, this incident left many observers with a sickening realization of the power of a traditionalist society that dictates that biological parents have a "right" to their offspring—even when they have not seen them for years.

seem to be more typical of individuals who are in a moratorium [period] seeking a basis for decisions, or of those who have already become achieved, than of those who are neither committed nor struggling to arrive at adult decisions. (p. 12)

Research reflects individual differences in reactions, lending support to both interpretations. For example, Baran, Sorosky, and Pannoz (1975) reported that although not all searches have happy endings, most searchers report that they feel glad they did it, that birth parents were generally pleased to reunite, and that their adoptive parents' feelings were not hurt. But other studies have concluded that those adoptees who search report lower levels of satisfaction with their relationship to their adoptive parents, as well as having

---

Box 6.5

Losses All Around: The Case of "Baby Richard"

In 1994, an Illinois judge ordered that "Baby Richard," then 3 ½ years old, be taken from his adoptive parents, with whom he had lived since he was 4 days old, and be given to his biological father (who had never even seen him) (*In re Petition of John Doe and Jane Doe, Husband and Wife, to Adopt Baby Boy Janikova*, 1994). The circumstances were broadly similar to the "Baby Jessica" case.

Daniela and Otakar Kirchner were not married when Daniela became pregnant. After they broke up, he returned to Czechoslovakia in January 1991, 2 months before the birth. She then gave up her child for adoption, telling Otakar that the child had died. Only when the child was 2 months old did the biological father learn of the adoption. After the couple reconciled—and later married—he asserted his rights.

The Supreme Court of the State of Illinois endorsed the judge's decision to award custody to the Kirchners—despite protests, including one by the governor of Illinois. The U.S. Supreme Court denied review of the case upon receiving the appeal petition.

This case surfaced again in the summer of 1997, when "Otto" Kirchner left his marital home to live with a girlfriend. Daniela Kirchner, having no legal relationship with her birth son, was left as his sole custodian. She filed a petition in court to reverse her relinquishment of her parental rights. The judge hearing the case ordered a home study before ruling on the petition. Realizing that she may have opened for review the entire question of her son's custody, Daniela asked to withdraw her petition. Her request to the court that her petition be dismissed without prejudice raised the issue of "forum shopping" for the judge, who then ruled against the request—a remarkable result apparently without legal precedent. But on Daniela's appeal to the state supreme court, the trial judge was ordered to allow the withdrawal. Now Daniel—formerly known as Richard Warburton ("Baby Richard")—lives with his birth mother and father, who has returned to the marital home.

---

received less adequate amounts of information about their birth parents from their adoptive parents (Loper, 1977; Yerger, 1981).

The mixed set of effects also is illustrated in the conclusions of researchers Aumend and Barrett (1984), who reported lower levels of satisfaction with parents among searchers but also that searchers knew more about the medical, educational, and occupational backgrounds of their biological parents than did nonsearchers. This interaction also was found in a study by Goebel and Lott (1986).

Furthermore, Goebel and Lott (1986) concluded that adjustment to adoption in their sample of adolescents and adults aged 18 to 35 years was affected more by family and personal attributes than by whether the adopted person had engaged in a search. Adoptees reported less opportunity to obtain information about their biological past than nonadoptees assumed to be the case. The authors noted:

> Non adoptees seemed unaware of what might be called the "closed record psyche"; the fact that many adoptive parents do not have much information about the biological heritage of their adopted child, and that they also sometimes feel threatened and fear competition for the love of their child if the biological past should become a reality. (p. 29)

Adoption Assistance and Child Welfare Act of 1980. Subsection (a) of the Adoption Assistance and Child Welfare Act of 1980 dispenses federal payments for state foster care and adoption programs, provided a state complies with certain requirements set out in the Act: The state will monitor, make periodic reviews of the programs, and report to the U.S. Secretary of Health and Human Services; provide safeguards restricting disclosure of information about individuals involved in the programs; create a reporting system for "suspected instances" of child abuse and neglect; develop standards for establishing and maintaining foster homes; and provide for periodic review of those standards and fair hearings for individuals with claims against the state regarding these programs. Two other very important provisions of the Act are (a) the requirement that "reasonable efforts" be made "to prevent or eliminate the need for removal of the child from his [or her] home" and "to make it possible for the child to return to his [or her] home" (Section 671 [a][15]); and (b) the required creation of a foster care review system to review required case plans for every child in foster care (Sections 671 [a][16] and 675 [5][B]; Brooks, 1994, p. I-2).

These requirements are consistent with the U.N. Convention. Article 9 guarantees children a right to live with their parents unless this is deemed incompatible with the child's best interests. Article 20 guarantees children a right to receive special protection and assistance from the state when deprived of a family environment and to be provided suitable alternative care (e.g., foster placement or Kafala of Islamic Law, adoption or institutional placement). Article 21 directs the state to regulate the process of adoption; Article 25 guarantees children placed by the state in alternative living arrangements a right to have all aspects of that placement reviewed regularly.

Recommendations Regarding the
Rights of Children in the Social Service System

When families cannot provide adequately for their own children, the state has a moral obligation to intervene, whether that intervention takes the form of temporary assistance, removal of children for their own protection, or termination of parental rights. In any of these situations, though, state intervention should not be "done to" children. Rather, in each case, the rights of children— to both protection and self-determination—should be respected.

Intervention in the Form of State Assistance

When families cannot make ends meet, the government should provide temporary assistance—a "helping hand"—to help families become self-sufficient. But governmental policies should not exacerbate the problem. Something is very wrong with the system when governmental policies, for example, drive families further into poverty, prevent them from obtaining adequate health care and quality child care, or make employment less economically viable than living on governmental assistance. Such policies obstruct children's right to an adequate standard of living (U.N. Convention, Article 27). Therefore, professionals must assess very carefully how "welfare reform" in the United States affects the welfare of its children.

Intervention in Cases of Abuse or Neglect

Children are not property; as persons, they deserve to be nurtured, loved, cared for, respected, and treated with dignity. If families, despite education and assistance, cannot fulfill these requirements—and certainly if they inflict harm on their children—then the state must intervene. We endorse reasonable efforts to reunify families and to provide education and supports for parents who can benefit from such assistance. Always, however, the safety and well-being of children must be of paramount concern. Article 19 of the U.N. Convention is unequivocal on this point:

> (1) States Parties shall take all appropriate legislative, administrative, social and educational measures to protect the child from all forms of physical or mental violence, injury or abuse, neglect or negligent treatment, maltreatment or

exploitation, including sexual abuse, while in the care of parent(s), legal guardian(s) or any other person who has the care of the child.

(2) Such protective measures should, as appropriate, include effective procedures for the establishment of social programmes to provide necessary support for the child and for those who have the care of the child, as well as for other forms of prevention and for identification, reporting, referral, investigation, treatment, and follow-up of instances of child maltreatment described heretofore, and, as appropriate, for judicial involvement.

We wholeheartedly agree.

Intervention in Cases of Foster Care and Adoption

Several factors argue for a different way of caring for the nation's children when they are in need of state intervention to effect temporary or permanent relinquishment of parental rights. As this chapter has documented, the U.S. foster care system is rife with problems: multiple placements in foster care; repeated unsuccessful attempts at returning children to their family homes under the federal requirement to reunify a child with the family, unless reasonable efforts to return the child safely have been undertaken and have failed; the high correlation between children in the care of state social service providers and children in the care of state departments of corrections. Thus, the rights of foster children—as guaranteed by the U.N. Convention—currently are not adequately protected in the United States.

When permanent termination of parental rights is necessary, adoption, despite its drawbacks, still appears to be a child's best hope for optimal development. Adoption provides the opportunity for permanency and uninterrupted attachments that foster care typically lacks. But permanency alone is not sufficient; other rights of children must be safeguarded in the process of adoption because, despite policies that seem to suggest otherwise, children are *not* chattel. Article 20 of the U.N. Convention guarantees children the right to receive *special* protection and assistance from the state when they have been deprived of their family environment. Thus, plans for adoption should include the following: (a) a route to successful attachment and permanent placement for very young children who have little chance of returning to their family homes before they reach their first birthday; (b) permanent placements for children in homes where they have already attached to nurturing caregivers; and (c) open adoption when the children's interest in maintaining sibling or extended family ties so warrants.

7

Being Patient With Patients

The Rights of Children
in the Health Care System

Asking children for their opinions about and input
into treatment decisions is an idea whose time has come.

Judith Ann Erlen, Nurse (1987)

Eight-year-old "Alice" faced the prospect of undergoing organ transplantation, a procedure she already had endured once. She refused the second operation, electing instead to go home and spend her remaining days with her family. In time, without the potentially life-saving operation, Alice died (Franklin, 1994).

Should such a young patient have been permitted to make a life-or-death decision? Does an 8-year-old child have the right to consent to or refuse medical treatment? Can such a young child give truly informed consent—which requires understanding the risks and benefits of various alternatives?

The medical staff who attended Alice firmly believed that she understood the implications of her decision. One said:

The discussion of her death was at first done on an abstract level, it was then expressed by symbolism and finally openly discussed without distress. Many colleagues are shocked that such a young patient was "allowed" to make such a decision. But this child was adamant that for her the burdens outweighed the benefits, and her parents respected her wishes. (Franklin, 1994, p. 33)

This decision, so respectful of the child's wishes, is, however, an anomaly. Generally, the voices of children are not heard when adults make medical and therapeutic decisions affecting them. Evans (1995), for example, reviewed 15 cases involving life-sustaining treatment for minors and found that the child's stated wishes were considered in only two (13%) of the cases. Why are children so routinely excluded from expressing their opinions with regard to medical decisions that directly affect them?

Why Children's Voices Typically Are Not Heard

In the common law tradition, competent adults have complete autonomy over their own bodies, including the right to consent to or refuse medical treatment. More than 100 years ago, Justice Benjamin Cardozo wrote:

> No right is held more sacred, or is more carefully guarded by the common law, than the right of every individual to the possession and control of his own person, free from all restraint or interference of others, unless by clear and unquestionable authority of law. (*Union Pac. Ry. Co. v. Botsford,* 1891, p. 251)

To consent effectively to medical treatment, individuals must be informed of both the potential benefits and the risks of the medical condition and proposed procedures. The law takes this right of adulthood very seriously. Indeed, "[a] physician or other health care provider who performs a procedure against the patient's will or for which the patient has not consented has committed an 'unauthorized touching,' and may be liable for battery" (Skeels, 1990, p. 1204).

In addition, the common law right to self-determination regarding one's own body and the constitutional right to privacy appear to guarantee a competent adult the right to refuse even life-saving medical treatment. In other words, the U.S. Supreme Court has said that competent adults have the right to die rather than submit to unwanted medical intervention. The caveat here is that the individual making such a decision must be both adult and competent. Children are not presumed competent under U.S. law.

Another reason why children may not be given an opportunity to be heard stems from the view that children are naturally dependent on their parents for support and guidance and that parents are believed to have the best interests of their children at heart (Brian-Mark, 1983). A more utilitarian reason was offered by Mnookin (1995), who suggested that because parents are financially responsible for the medical care of their children, they should be entitled to choose the method of treatment.

A common theme underlies all of these reasons. In the United States, minors generally are considered to be incompetent to give informed voluntary consent; included in that disability, of course, is consent to medical procedures.

The Competing Rights of Parents, Children, and the State

Minors traditionally have been considered to be legally incompetent because of their immaturity and lack of experience. Therefore, the state has asserted a right to exercise its *parens patriae* authority when dealing with minors. Using this power and in the guise of the "knowledgeable parent," the state may limit a minor's ability—and even the parents'—to make legal decisions, such as decisions regarding medical procedures. The state is said to don its *parens patriae* mantle to safeguard the health and welfare of children. In a landmark decision in support of the state's ability to intervene in family matters, the U.S. Supreme Court held:

> Parents may be free to become martyrs themselves. But it does not follow that they are free, in identical circumstances, to make martyrs of their children before [their children] have reached the age of full and legal discretion when they can make that choice for themselves. (*Prince v. Massachusetts,* 1944, p. 170)

But the state must balance its *parens patriae* interest against the nearly absolute right of parents to make decisions for their children. In the United States, parents have the right to the custody and care of their children, as well as the right to raise their children according to the dictates of their own conscience. The First and Fourteenth Amendments to the U.S. Constitution guarantee parents the right to raise their children without undue interference from the state, and the courts consistently have recognized that the relationship between a parent and a child is constitutionally protected. In *Stanley v. Illinois* (1972), for example, the Supreme Court emphasized that a parent's right in child rearing "undeniably warrants deference, and, absent a powerful countervailing interest, protection" (p. 651). This fundamental right includes parents' right to make medical decisions for their children (*Custody of a Minor,* 1978).

In addition, the state must balance its *parens patriae* interest against the rights of mature minors to bodily self-determination. Although most minors are presumed incompetent under the law, the Supreme Court has recognized that some minors possess the maturity to make certain constitutionally protected decisions. In *Planned Parenthood of Central Missouri v. Danforth* (1976), the Court held that minors, like adults, were entitled to constitutional rights—including the right to seek an abortion. The Court ruled that, to restrict a minor's constitutional right, the state must demonstrate a "compelling interest"—unnecessary in the case of an adult (Skeels, 1990).

The Illinois Supreme Court concluded in *In re E.G.* (1989) that the determination of maturity requires clear and convincing evidence:

> If the evidence is clear and convincing that the minor is mature enough to appreciate the consequences of her actions, and that the minor is mature enough to exercise the judgment of an adult, then the mature minor doctrine affords her the common law right to consent to or refuse medical treatment. (p. 111)

According to Wadlington (1973), cases in which physicians have been relieved of liability in providing non-emergency medical care based only on minors' consent have the following elements in common:

> (a) treatment was undertaken for the benefit of the minor, not a third person,

> (b) the minor was near majority age (at least 15 [years]) and was considered to have sufficient mental capacity to understand the nature and importance of the medical procedure, [and]

> (c) the medical procedure was not serious in nature. (p. 119)

Not surprisingly, these three rights—of children to bodily self-determination, of parents to make decisions for their children, and of the state to impose decisions in its *parens patriae* capacity—do not always dovetail. As a result, the Supreme Court has been faced with some intriguing dilemmas centering on medical and mental health decisions involving children.

Children's Rights in Medical Care

To abridge the rights of parents or mature minors or both in cases involving medical decisions, the state must show that to not intervene would constitute neglect. In other words, state intervention is appropriate only if parental conduct threatens a child's safety or health. In most cases in which a child is being deprived of medical services, a hospital administrator or a social services worker petitions the court to have the child declared neglected. Often, the court is requested to appoint a guardian *ad litem* for the child for the purpose of ensuring that proper treatment is administered. In weighing the evidence, the court must consider the state's child neglect statutes, particularly its medical neglect law.

When Parents Invoke the Rights to Privacy and Parental Autonomy

In some cases, parents have made medical decisions regarding their children on the basis of the constitutional right to privacy and the right of parental autonomy as interpreted by the U.S. Supreme Court. As early as 1925, in *Pierce v. Society of Sisters,* the Court stated that the right of parental autonomy is constitutionally protected. In *Parham v. J. R.* (1979), the Court stated that the "high duty" of a parent discussed in *Pierce* includes recognizing illnesses and seeking medical advice for children.

The state, though, may invoke its *parens patriae* power to protect children despite the assertion of parental autonomy if the parents' medical choice results in "neglect." In *In re Philip B. v. Warren B.* (1979), the Supreme Court recognized the right of parental autonomy and required that the state defer to the wishes of the parents under normal circumstances; the Court went on to note that the state has "a serious burden of justification before abridging parental autonomy by substituting its judgment for that of the parents" (p. 51). In *Philip B.,* the Court focused on the child's best interests, ultimately deciding that the operation opposed by the parents should not be performed because the risks outweighed the potential benefits to the child.

Similarly, the Massachusetts Supreme Court used a balancing approach when arriving at its decision to appoint a guardian who was to be in charge of reauthorizing chemotherapy treatments for Chad Green, who was suffering from acute lymphocytic leukemia (*Custody of a Minor,* 1978). After complete remission of Chad's symptoms was obtained by chemotherapy, his parents discontinued the treatment because of their child's discomfort with the regimen. Instead, they substituted a dietary program.

The court weighed the interests of all parties involved—the child, his parents, and the state. The court affirmed that parents have the primary right to raise their children according to their own wishes but held that a child may be taken from the custody of the parents on a showing that the parents are not willing to provide proper physical care. According to the court, such a showing had been found because the disease would have been fatal if left untreated and chemotherapy was the only treatment offering not only prolonged life but permanent remission of symptoms. In contrast, the program suggested by the parents had no proven value in accepted medical practice. The court concluded that when a child's life is in danger because of parental refusal to provide treatment, the state's interest in protecting the welfare of the child supersedes that of the parents.

Similarly, in *Matter of Hofbauer* (1979), the court affirmed parents' right to select medical treatment for their children but stated that the most important factor in deciding if a child is being deprived of proper medical attention is whether the parents have chosen an "acceptable course of medical treatment in light of all the circumstances" (p. 941).

When Parents Invoke the Right to Freedom of Religious Expression

The issue of state intervention in family medical decisions is particularly complicated when religious beliefs come into play. Some religions do not permit such practices as interpersonal blood transfusions (e.g., Jehovah's Witnesses) or the use of pharmaceuticals or surgical procedures (e.g., Christian Science). Parents who are members of such faiths may invoke the free exercise of religion clause of the First Amendment when placing constraints on medical treatment for their children.

The Supreme Court has held, however, that although parents certainly have the right to exercise their religion freely, that right is not absolute. The state can interfere with an individual's free exercise of religion if the state's interest significantly outweighs the interest of the individual—that is, if the state has a compelling interest. In *Prince v. Massachusetts* (1944), for example, the Court held:

> Neither the rights of religion nor the rights of parenthood are beyond limitation. Acting to guard the general interest in youth's well being, the state as *parens patriae* may restrict parental control. . . . Its authority is not nullified merely because the parent grounds his claim to control the child's course of conduct on religion or conscience. . . . The right to practice religion freely does not include liberty to expose the community or the child to communicable disease or the latter to ill health or death. (p. 166)

At what point does the state's interest in protecting children from neglect outweigh parents' interest in the free exercise of religion? Certainly, when a child's situation is life-threatening, the state has been permitted to substitute its judgment for that of the parents.

For example, in *State v. Perricone* (1962), a child's heart condition required surgery, which, in turn, would necessitate a blood transfusion. The boy's parents, who were Jehovah's Witnesses, consented to the surgery but refused to allow the blood transfusions, which were prohibited by their religion. At trial, two doctors testified that if the surgery and transfusions were not performed, the child would die. The trial court applied the state's neglect statute and held that it was necessary for the state to intervene to protect the child's welfare; thus, the court overrode the parents' wishes. According to the New Jersey Supreme Court, the actions taken at the trial level were part of the "sovereign right and duty to care for children, and protect them from abuse, neglect and fraud" (p. 475).

In *People in Interest of D.L.E.* (Colo. 1982), a parent refused, on religious grounds, to give her child medication to control his epileptic seizures. Evidence indicated that if the boy stopped taking the medication, his seizures would result in a life-threatening situation. The court held:

> A child who is treated solely by spiritual means is not for that reason alone dependent and neglected, but if there is an additional reason, such as where the child is deprived of medical care necessary to prevent a life-endangering condition, the child may be adjudicated dependent and neglected. (p. 274)

More recently, in *Walker v. Superior Court* (1988), a California court ruled that parents using faith healing must also provide medical care or else they can be held criminally liable. In *Walker,* the Supreme Court of California found a parent guilty of involuntary manslaughter and felony child endanger-ment for the death of her child when she chose spiritual healing over medical attention. In commenting on this case, Gathing (1989) noted:

> The court determined that the California religious exemption did not preclude manslaughter liability, that treatment by prayer alone could constitute crimi-nal negligence despite the good faith belief of the parents, and that prosecuting faith healing parents for manslaughter did not violate the state or federal constitutions. (p. 589)

The decisions in *Perricone, D.L.E.,* and *Walker* reflect the spirit of Article 6 of the U.N. Convention on the Rights of the Child (1989), which articulates children's right to survival and development. But the Supreme Court's rulings in other cases may run counter to another Convention article—Article 24—which ensures that children have the right to the highest attainable standard of health.

The case of *In re Green* (1972) is illustrative. Ricky Green, a 16-year-old, suffered from paralytic scoliosis. He was confined to a wheelchair, unable to stand because of the collapse of his spine. Doctors recommended an operation that would add bone to his spine, but they stated that the surgery required the use of blood transfusions. Ricky's mother refused to allow the transfusions because they violated her religious beliefs. A Pennsylvania court, in arriving at its decision not to override the wishes of the mother, considered the fact that the child's life was not in danger nor was it necessary that the operation be performed immediately. The court stated:

> As between parent and state, the state does not have an interest of sufficient magnitude outweighing a parent's religious beliefs when the child's life is not immediately periled by his physical condition. (p. 392)

Clearly, the quality of Ricky's life and his suffering were insufficient grounds on which the state court was willing to require medical care.

A result consistent with Article 24 of the U.N. Convention has been obtained in other cases, however. In *Muhlenberg Hospital v. Patterson* (1974), for example, a New Jersey appellate court ruled that a transfusion could be given to an infant over the religious objections of the parents. Although there was only minimal danger to the child's life if the procedure was not performed, evidence showed that without the transfusion the child would suffer severe and irreparable brain damage, resulting in mental retardation. The court held that it was in the "best interest of society" that a child be protected from severe and irreparable brain damage (p. 503). Another court reached a similar conclusion 15 years later in *In the Matter of Tara Cabrera* (1989). In that case, medical evidence showed that although the child was not in imminent danger of death, failure to provide blood transfusions to alleviate her sickle cell anemia would result in a 70% chance of stroke—the consequences of which could include paralysis, mental retardation, and loss of speech.

In *In the Matter of Kevin Sampson* (1970), a New York court weighed the potential good of the operation opposed by the parent against the risks involved. Kevin, age 15, suffered from neurofibromatosis, a condition that resulted in a massive deformity on one side of his face. The disease neither threatened his life nor seriously affected his health. As in *Perricone*, Kevin's mother consented to the surgery but refused to allow blood transfusions. In reaching its decision to permit the transfusions, the court quoted an appellate division decision, *In the Matter of Seiferth* (1955):

> It is not necessary that a child's life be in danger before the court can act to safeguard his health or general welfare. . . . It is immaterial that his physical life is not in danger . . . what is in danger is his chance for a normal useful life. (p. 653)

As these cases illustrate, if evidence is clear and convincing that a child's life is endangered when parents refuse medical treatment on religious grounds, the state is compelled to assume its *parens patriae* role. In this regard, Andersen (1993) commented: " . . . if religiously motivated conduct could not be regulated by the state, then one whose religion calls for human sacrifice would be free to kill whomever he or she wished in the name of freedom of religion" (p. 770). If the situation is not life-threatening, however, the courts must consider both the "best interests of the child" and the totality of the circumstances, including the risks placed on the child and the quality of the child's life in the event that treatment is provided or withheld.

We would argue that, in considering the totality of the circumstances, courts must be mindful of another factor—the child's wishes. In *In re Green* (1972), the Pennsylvania court considered whether the parent's religious beliefs were paramount to the decision of the child. Ultimately, the court remanded the case so that the wishes of the child could be determined—an action that is consistent with Article 12 of the U.N. Convention, which gives children the right to express their own views. We believe that the court took appropriate action in that case. But that action requires the answer to an important question: When are children competent to make medical decisions?

Children's Competence to Participate in Medical Decision Making

In Theory at Least

Billick (1986) noted: "One of the factors necessary for informed competency is judgment and wisdom. These factors usually increase with increasing age" (p. 306). According to Piagetian theory (Inhelder & Piaget, 1958), children below the age of 7 years typically are not capable of logical thinking and therefore should not be considered competent to give informed consent, which requires understanding and weighing potential risks and benefits (see Chapter 4). In this regard, Billick (1986) commented:

> Before the acquisition of logical thinking, it is proper to give the decision-making power to the appropriate guardian. Even from early recorded Western history, the early Christian church has held children under the age of 7 years nonaccountable for mortal and venial sins. In the Roman Catholic tradition, children at age 7 years begin to receive the sacrament, which provides absolution from sin. It is not necessary before age 7 years because the child is not capable of sinning. The child lack[s] religious and moral *mens rea.* (p. 307)

Therefore, parents or other adults must make important decisions for children under the age of 7.

Logical thinking emerges and grows between the ages of 7 and 11 years, a period Piaget referred to as *concrete operations* (Inhelder & Piaget, 1958). But the mental abilities of children during this phase, though improving, are not yet fully mature. Erlen (1987) suggested the following:

> Although children in the concrete operations period might not be able to identify risks and benefits and to consider future implications of a treatment decision, these children should not be ignored. Instead, they at least should be able to exercise their right to assent and dissent to treatment depending on their level of understanding and competence. (p. 158)

Some commentators (e.g., Weithorn & Campbell, 1982) have suggested that true informed consent is possible only after an individual reaches the Piagetian level called *formal operations* (Inhelder & Piaget, 1958). At that stage, a person is capable of independently generating a list of possible outcomes for a given situation, considering the risks and benefits inherent in each outcome, weighing the alternatives in an objective manner, and selecting an appropriate outcome based on that rational process. Even most adults, though, do not master that abstract level of reasoning (Inhelder & Piaget, 1958). When presented with alternatives (as might occur, for example, in an informed consent document), however, individuals who reason at the level of concrete operations should be capable of weighing the alternatives and making an informed choice. Because these abilities are established by age 12 for most individuals, Billick (1986) suggested:

> The average 12-year-old child has achieved the minimal mental capacity and moral reasoning that is expected of all adults. In terms of Piagetian development, the 12-year-old child has achieved concrete operations and can do average adult reasoning. The acquisition of abstract reasoning or Piagetian formal operations occurs only in approximately one third of the population. Clearly, this could not be a minimal standard for adult responsibility. Although less established, Kohlberg's studies with boys and Gilligan's studies with girls [on moral reasoning] support the age of 12 as the time when most children have achieved a morality that recognizes that society makes rules and regulations for the greater good of all. This same level of moral development is the predominant level in the adult population. . . . The average adult has concrete operational cognition and conventional morality of society. Because these are adequate for adults, I believe that they should also be acceptable as a standard for juveniles. When juveniles achieve these levels, in my opinion, there should be a presumption of developmental competency. (pp. 304-305)

On the basis of this reasoning, Billick (1986) recommended a developmental model for involving children in making important life decisions (see Table 7.1). Billick's model presumes that children have the competency ascribed in Table 7.1 "unless certain circumstances (mental retardation, severe psychosis, medical conditions, etc.) could be demonstrated to impair the expected level of competency" (p. 308).

Erlen (1987) offered a means for addressing Billick's concern that the greatest difficulty with his model involved decisions made by children between the ages of 7 and 11 years, the ages during which children's logical

Table 7.1 Billick's Model of Children's Competency to Make Decisions

Age of Juvenile (years)	Person Competent to Make Decisions and Bear Responsibility
0-6	Parent
7-8	Parents with child participating
9-11	Parent and child jointly
12-14	Child with parental ratification
14-on	Child

reasoning abilities are only beginning to blossom. Erlen's *participation in treatment decisions model* (1987) is based on Leiken's (1983) discussion of "the ethical and legal aspects of the processes of assent, dissent, and consent in minors and their relationship to the child's development" (Erlen, 1987, p. 157). The model assumes that, with increasing age and competence, children should take increased responsibility for treatment decisions.

In the participation in treatment decisions model, the first level of participation is *assent:*

> Assent . . . implies agreement or concurrence with a decision made by others based on a valid understanding of the proposed course of action. Assent requires that the child be informed about a proposed treatment or plan of care and be included when the decision making occurs; however, the child is not in the position to overrule the parent's decision. Through assent, the parents and health professionals seek the child's cooperation and keep the child's interests central. In decisions involving choices about which way to do a procedure or when to do it, the child is given the opportunity to be more in control and to make choices, although the overall treatment decision is out of the child's hands. (Erlen, 1987, p. 158)

Consider, for example, the case of Kristen, age 8, who has chronic asthma. She has been rushed to the hospital on several nights for emergency treatment and now is hospitalized for secondary infections associated with her acute condition. Several medications are required to alleviate her medical problems, but the medications have very uncomfortable side effects. Still, it is imperative that Kristen assent to treatment. Although her parents are the ones giving consent, Kristen's needs and values are recognized and included in the decision making. She is given choices about the placement of intravenous tubes (in the left or right arm), the timing of treatment procedures for which there is no overriding medical consequence (before or after eating lunch), and so forth. Thus, Kristen's parents and health providers respect the child's personhood by working to obtain her assent to the necessary procedures and treatments.

According to Erlen (1987), children who are at the level of concrete operations should have the right to assent to medical treatment. Such young children's involvement in assent is consistent with Articles 12 and 13 of the U.N. Convention, which give children the right to express their own views, and the right to seek, receive, and impart information, respectively.

The next level of the model of participative decision making is *dissent.* Erlen (1987) notes: "With dissent there is a difference of opinion, a lack of agreement, and a withholding of assent" (p. 158). As children progress through concrete operations, they become capable of reasonable dissent because "they develop a better understanding of relationships and can understand cause and effect. They develop a clearer understanding of their values. Thus it becomes possible to determine whether there are rational reasons for the child's dissent" (p. 158). Thus, Leiken (1983) concluded, "If there is evidence that the minor has sufficient knowledge and understanding of the illness and its treatment, the dissent should be taken seriously" (p. 174).

Erlen (1987) provides the following example: For 4 years, Larry, age 10, has undergone chemotherapy for leukemia. One day, Larry dissents to chemotherapy because an important Cub Scout dinner will be held in 2 days. He wants to be able to be with his friends at the dinner because it will be his last meeting with them. He asks to wait to have the chemotherapy until after he has attended the dinner. Larry's reasoning and request are determined to be rational, so his decision to dissent is respected and enacted.

The third and most advanced level of the model involves informed *consent,* which takes place when all elements—comprehension of information, as well as volition and competence to consent—are present. Children who provide informed consent receive and comprehend age-appropriate information that is sufficient to make a sound decision and voluntarily consent to the treatment or procedures proposed; there is no coercion or pressure.

Erlen (1987) offers the example of John, age 15, who arrives at the emergency room with an apparently broken arm. John's parents are out of town and cannot be reached. When the necessary medical procedures are explained to John, he is able to restate them in his own words. He also can identify the adverse consequences if his arm is not set. John's comprehension suggests that he is capable of giving informed consent.

The theoretical models proposed by Billick (1986) and Erlen (1987) offer valuable food for thought. Despite their rational appeal, however, they do not provide information about children's actual competence to participate in medical decisions.

Studies of Children's Participation in Medical Decisions

Grisso and Vierling (1978) conducted a systematic examination of the existing research in developmental psychology and concluded that children of at least age 15 years are usually no less competent than adults. The research review also suggested that although minors below the age of 11 years generally do not meet the legal criteria for competent consent, 11- to 14-year-olds may be able to consent independently for limited purposes.

Weithorn and Campbell (1982) tested 96 children and young adults for developmental differences in competency to make informed treatment decisions. They found that 14-year-olds did not differ overall from 18- and 21-year-olds. Even 9-year-olds, though "less competent than adults with respect to their ability to reason about and understand the treatment information," did not differ from older respondents in their "expression of reasonable preferences regarding treatment" (Weithorn & Campbell, 1982, p. 1589).

Similar results were obtained by Kaser-Boyd, Adelman, Taylor, and Nelson (1986), who investigated children's understanding of the risks and benefits of psychotherapy. In their study, all children ages 10 to 19 years demonstrated the ability to understand and identify risks, benefits, and meaningless factors in hypothetical treatment dilemmas.

Evans (1995) provided a summary of the facts in *In re Guardianship of Myers* (1993), which poignantly demonstrated that the court could deem a 14-year-old child competent to make a decision about withholding medical care that would result in her death (see Box 7.1). Evans commented: ". . . this opinion demonstrates that judges, by giving weight to a minor's expressed preferences, recognize that many children do understand and can meaningfully participate in treatment decisions" (p. 37).

Although some (e.g., Czajkowski & Koocher, 1987) have suggested that patient involvement at an early age may add unnecessary stress to the treatment dilemma, others (e.g., Melton, 1981) have contended that such involvement could be beneficial because of a resultant increase in sense of control and mastery. In a review of the literature, Carter and St. Lawrence (1985)

Box 7.1

The Facts in In re Guardianship of Myers *(1993)*

In October 1992, Carla Myers, age 14 years, suffered multiple injuries, including a severe head injury, in a two-car collision. She lost consciousness during the accident and slipped into a coma. The next month, Carla was transferred to a terminal care hospital. After a discussion with her doctor, Carla's father requested that her artificially administered nutrition and hydration be removed. In December, Mr. Myers's request was granted. Five days later, the nutrition and hydration were reinstated after Carla's mother objected to the removal. Each parent then applied to the county probate court for appointment as guardian of Carla. At the hearing, the court appointed as Carla's guardian an attorney who formerly had been a nurse with extensive emergency medical treatment experience.

In January 1993, the court heard testimony from Carla's parents, as well as from two neurologists and one internist. All three physicians agreed that Carla was in a persistent vegetative state. Tests indicated no cortical function and only limited brain stem function. Carla was completely unresponsive to all levels of stimuli. The three physicians agreed that she had no chance for any meaningful recovery.

In addition, Carla's siblings, Tim and Penny, testified that, "on several occasions prior to the accident, Carla had stated that 'she wouldn't want to go through life like that.'" These statements were purportedly made by Carla subsequent to separate incidents—specifically, "after watching a movie concerning removal of life support systems, and again upon visiting a relative in the hospital who was on life support systems due to severe brain injury" (*In re Guardianship of Myers*, 1993, p. 665).

Carla's guardian recommended that the feeding tube be removed. The county prosecutor stated that neither the state nor the county would find criminal liability if the hydration and nutrition were removed. Carla's parents agreed with the recommendations, and life support was removed; Carla subsequently died.

This case is meaningful for a variety of reasons, not the least of which is that the court recognized that children can meaningfully participate in treatment decisions. In *In re Guardianship of Myers*, the court gave weight to a minor's expressed preferences regarding her own death.

reported, for example, that minors who were involved in treatment decisions differed in several ways from those who were not involved: (a) improved psychological and physical recovery from surgery, (b) more rapid recovery, (c) increased compliance with professionals' recommendations, and (d) improved perceptions of treatment efficacy. Winick (1991) and Tremper and Kelly (1987) also found that ensuring patient choice enhanced patient compliance and facilitated goal achievement—two elements associated with treatment success.

Lewis and Lewis (1990) reported two studies of children's participation in treatment decisions. In 1977, they studied the ability of children to participate in the process of informed consent for a swine influenza vaccine trial. The researchers explained to the children, ages 9 to 12 years, the nature of the trial and then answered the children's questions about the program. With regard to competence to consent, Lewis and Lewis noted, "They clearly understood that participation would include drawing blood from them on two occasions, a needle stick for the vaccine, and that a certain proportion of them might develop fever and body aches" (p. 65). Still, approximately half of the children indicated their willingness to participate in the study. The authors commented: "To our knowledge, this remains the only reported study of informed consent for children to make the initial decision related to participation in a clinical trial" (p. 65).

Lewis and Lewis (1990) also reported developing a program known as Asthma Care Training for Kids (ACT). They implemented and evaluated the program from 1978 to 1983. Similar curricula were developed and evaluated by other researchers during the same period. These programs significantly affected "the ability of children with asthma to recognize symptoms requiring more aggressive management strategies, including pharmacological therapies" (p. 65). Moreover, the authors found that "[s]everal evaluation trials, including our own, demonstrated in the experimental group a significant reduction in emergency room visits, hospitalizations, and the saving of $200 per child per year as a result" (p. 65). In one program based on these principles— Camp SuperKids, sponsored annually in the state of Nebraska by the American Lung Association—even asthmatic children as young as age 7 or 8 have demonstrated impressive ability to comprehend treatment options and to make appropriate treatment choices (personal communication [to Walker], 1997). Thus, many children who are empowered to participate in their own care clearly are capable of doing so.

Children's Rights in Mental Health Care

Children have also been accorded certain rights in mental health care. In this arena, however, the situation often is even more complicated than it is when

considering medical care. The child who is a candidate for mental health care
may not be competent to give or refuse consent for treatment not only because
of a lack of maturity but because—given the nature of the illness—reasoning
is likely to be impaired as well. Moreover, the interests of child, parents, and
state are especially likely to clash over mental health issues.

Two goals compete in this conflict: (a) the desire to provide mental health
care to minors with genuine need and (b) the necessity of preventing unwarranted commitment (Walding, 1990). Caught in the fray are parents at their
wits' end in dealing with their troubled children and mental health professionals who want to help them—but who, in this age of managed care, also may
be pressured to fill hospital beds. In this regard, Butts and Schwartz (1991)
commented: "Inpatient psychiatric hospitalization offers an attractive combination of treatment and control, a combination that over-stressed parents and
youth services professionals may find hard to resist" (p. 112). Similarly,
Dalton and Forman (1987) noted: "Physicians are pressured in subtle and not
so subtle ways to maintain a maximal census and thus increase profits" (p. 13).

Data from empirical studies provide some disturbing evidence in support
of the assertion made by Butts and Schwartz (1991): The National Institute
of Mental Health reported that only 36% of patients below age 20 years who
had been confined at one psychiatric facility actually required such hospitalization (as cited in *Parham,* 1979). Similarly, a study in Georgia concluded
that more than half of that state's institutionalized children did not need such
stringent confinement (as cited in *Parham,* 1979).

Moreover, appropriate treatment of a disorder requires that the illness has
been properly diagnosed. Unfortunately, diagnosis of mental disorders is an
imprecise science at best (Schwab-Stone, 1989)—especially for child patients. In recent years, the problem of accurate diagnosis has been complicated
by the phenomenon known as "managed health care." As health care costs
have skyrocketed, insurance companies have responded by permitting insurance payments only for certain disorders or conditions. Thus, the reliability
of a child's diagnosis may be suspect because of the tendency to "inflate or
otherwise tamper with the diagnoses to meet the requirements of insurance
coverage" (Mason & Gibbs, 1992, p. 452). Kirk and Kutchins (1988) reported
that, according to survey data, such deliberate misdiagnoses may be widespread.

To complicate matters further, Reisman and Ribordy (1993) estimated
that at least 230 distinct kinds of mental health treatment are used with

children. Thus, it becomes even more important to ensure that mental health consumers understand the nature of the treatments to which they are asked to consent.

What rights, then, can children have to be free from unnecessary confinement for mental health purposes and to participate in their own mental health care? Are children afforded any due process rights in mental health care?

Laws Regarding Institutionalization of Minors

Before 1951, both minors and adults had to consent to treatment before admission into a mental hospital (Walding, 1990). During the 1950s and 1960s, however, most states changed their statutes to conform with the National Institute of Mental Health's (NIMH) *Draft Act for the Hospitalization of the Mentally Ill,* published in 1951 (Ellis, 1996). Under that approach, the institutionalization of minors occurred pursuant to laws enacted at the state rather than the federal level, with most statutes patterned after the NIMH model. The act simplified the process of voluntary mental health treatment for adults, but it also contained provisions that allowed parents to "volunteer" their children for institutional placement. According to the act, children were "voluntary" patients because their *parents* had consented to the children's hospitalization, so neither minors' consent nor their acquiescence (assent) was required (Ellis, 1996). Perhaps not surprisingly, the rate of institutionalization for minors increased substantially in the years following the reduction of procedural protections for children in mental health care (Ellis, 1996).

During the 1970s, a reform movement was mounted to change the laws that had derived from the NIMH Draft Act. Advocates for change argued for precommitment hearings for minors and at least a "need for treatment" commitment standard. Some also advocated for a postcommitment hearing for minors to be held within 2 weeks of admission. Ellis (1996) noted that, in some jurisdictions, these challenges were successful and that a few states changed their laws to provide commitment hearings for children.

During the 1980s, however, the movement to legislate additional procedural protections for children facing commitment wound down. At the same time—not coincidentally—admissions to private psychiatric hospitals more than quadrupled (Weithorn, 1988). Ellis (1996) concluded that studies demonstrated that "private facilities have found it very profitable to treat children

---

Box 7.2

Due Process Health Protections
Afforded Minors in Each U.S. State

Substantial Protections:
   Alabama, Alaska, Connecticut, New Mexico, Wisconsin

Moderate Protections:
   Colorado, Florida, Michigan, Ohio, Pennsylvania, South Dakota, Washington

Few Protections:
   Arizona, Georgia, Idaho, Indiana, Iowa, Kansas, Kentucky, Louisiana,
   Massachusetts, Missouri, Nevada, New Jersey, North Dakota, Oregon,
   Rhode Island, South Carolina, Tennessee, Utah, West Virginia

Silent:
   Arkansas, Delaware, Hawaii, Maine, Maryland, Minnesota, Mississippi, Montana,
   Nebraska, New Hampshire, New York, North Carolina, Oklahoma, Texas,
   Vermont, Virginia, Wyoming

SOURCE: Walding (1990).

---

and adolescents whose care is paid by health insurance and that this profitability has led to serious abuses, including the commitment of children who do not need institutionalization" (pp. 495-496). Moreover, Ellis (1996) warned, institutional staff hardly can be assumed to be neutral fact finders:

> Particularly where the mental health facility stands to profit from the child's admission, whether it is clinically indicated or not, trusting its officials to decide whether a particular child needs to be hospitalized is not a system that can effectively protect children's rights. (p. 498)

Today, states vary widely on the degree to which they afford children procedural rights in mental health care. Walding (1990) developed a list of criteria that he deemed "ideal" with regard to providing juveniles with procedural due process. Using the criteria, he rated existing state statutes as offering either "few," "moderate," or "substantial" protections (see Box 7.2). According to Walding's analysis, only 5 states afford minors substantial protections, 7 states afford moderate protections, and 19 states afford only few protections.

Four Treatment Issues
That Should Be Considered

Four issues are of paramount concern when one considers children's rights in mental health care: (a) What constitutes "voluntary" psychiatric treatment? (b) What are children's rights in the case of involuntary treatment? (c) What rights do children have to consent to treatment on their own behalf? and (d) What rights do children have to refuse the treatments recommended for them?

Voluntary Treatment

What constitutes "voluntary" consent of a minor to psychiatric treatment? If a child requests mental health services (including hospitalization) absent adult influence, it seems reasonable to conclude that the treatment is voluntary. Sometimes that situation occurs, but it is not the norm. If a parent consents to the child's treatment and the child assents (agrees with the parent), then the request also should be considered voluntary. But if the parent consents and the child dissents, then the child's objection negates the voluntariness of the confinement or treatment. In such a case, it seems reasonable to invite a *neutral* third party to adjudicate.

Walding (1990) promoted that idea. He stated:

> If a third party, totally independent of the parents, the hospital, and the child, could be brought into the equation then a formal, adversarial hearing may not be needed. . . . Thus, it seems that with some independent and trained third party playing a role in the decision process, both goals of preventing unwarranted commitment and advancing mental health care to those in genuine need are met. (p. 299)

We agree that this approach is consistent with respecting the rights of children (see U.N. Convention Article 39). Unfortunately, as Melton and Ehrenreich (1992) comment, that is not how informed consent is handled in most cases:

> [W]hen applied to the treatment of children, the informed consent doctrine has been held to give parents, not the child, the right to be informed and consulted. As a matter of law, consent or refusal by the child is considered to be not only insufficient but irrelevant, for once the parent has consented, treatment can be provided even over the child's objection. (p. 1039)

Involuntary Treatment

What happens, then, in the case of a minor who actively resists hospitalization or treatment procedures? Does that child have any due process rights to be heard before the commitment occurs or the treatment is administered— the rights that are accorded adults in the identical situation? The U.S. Supreme Court answered that question in the case of *Parham v. J. R.* (1979).

The *Parham* case, detailed in Chapter 1, involved a Georgia statute that failed to provide hearings for children said to have mental illness—in other words, a statute based on the NIMH Draft Act. Under the statute, no hearing was required if a child's parent consented to the child's placement. If a child had no parents, the statute authorized state social workers to consent to the child's admission.

A federal three-judge district court ruled that all children were entitled to hearings on their need for hospitalization and held, therefore, that the Georgia statute was unconstitutional. But in a split decision, the U.S. Supreme Court reversed the lower court. It applied a balancing test, delineated in *Mathews v. Eldridge* (1976), that weighs individuals' interest in not losing their liberty against the state's interest in not paying for the procedures requested, evaluated in the light of the probability that the procedures requested would produce more equitable outcomes. In applying the *Mathews* balancing test, the *Parham* majority "apparently assigned a lesser weight to the liberty interest of children" (Ellis, 1996, p. 492). The Court held that the due process clause was satisfied so long as the state provided that a medical decision maker interviewed the child and determined that the child needed hospitalization.

The justices who dissented in *Parham* refused to minimize the importance of children's liberty interests, however:

> Indeed, it may well be argued that children are entitled to more protection than are adults. The consequences of an erroneous commitment decision are more tragic where children are involved. Children are, on the average, confined for longer periods than are adults. Moreover, childhood is a particularly vulnerable time of life and children erroneously institutionalized during their formative years may bear the scars for the rest of their lives. (Justice Brennan's dissent in *Parham v. J. R.,* 1979, pp. 627-628)

Justice Brennan further noted: "In my view, a child who has been ousted from his family has even greater need for an independent advocate" (*Parham v. J. R.,* 1979, p. 631). Thus, the dissenting justices concluded:

> The risk of erroneous commitment is simply too great unless there is some form of adversary review. And fairness demands that children abandoned by their supposed protectors to the rigors of institutional confinement be given the help of some separate voice. (*Parham v. J. R.,* 1979, pp. 638-639)

The dissenting view in *Parham* is consistent with the principles of the U.N. Convention. In particular, it supports Article 25, which guarantees the right of children placed by the state for reasons of "care, protection, or treatment" to have all aspects of that placement reviewed regularly. In our opinion, the Supreme Court reached the wrong conclusion in the majority opinion in *Parham.* Apparently, we are not alone in that view. One commentator noted, for example, "No modern U.S. Supreme Court civil case dealing with the rights of the mentally handicapped has been criticized as consistently or as thoroughly" (Perlin, 1994, quoted in Ellis, 1996, p. 492).

The Right to Treatment

Warboys and Wilber (1996) noted that whether juveniles have a constitutional right to affirmative treatment "remains an open question" (p. 516). To date, the Supreme Court has not addressed the question, and decisions from lower courts are inconsistent. Both federal and state courts, however, have held that when a minor is involuntarily confined to a state or local institution, the child is entitled to "basic care and minimally adequate services and training so that the minor does not suffer any harm while in state custody" (Warboys & Wilber, 1996, p. 516). For example, the child is entitled to basic medical and mental health care, as well as basic education.

The U.S. District Court for Rhode Island held, for example, that minors confined to juvenile detention are entitled to receive regular mental health counseling (*Inmates of Boys' Training School v. Affleck,* 1972). That care was defined as including a mental health screening within 24 hours of admission, examination by a psychiatrist within 48 hours (if deemed necessary after initial interview), and ongoing access to a psychiatrist. In the wake of *Affleck,* other courts also required certain services, including (a) individual assessment and treatment planning that includes analysis of the child's history, educational abilities, mental health examinations and testing, and community evaluations and (b) reasonable access to a psychiatrist for consultation and crisis intervention, as well as continuing involvement of psychologists or psychiatrists in long-range treatment planning (*Martarella v. Kelly,* 1973). In addition, courts have restricted the use of certain forms of "control techniques" or aversive therapy. For example, some courts have prohibited locking a child alone in a room or using restraints except in situations where all other alternatives have failed and the child is endangering him- or herself or others (*Gary W. et al. v. State of Louisiana et al.,* 1976).

These measures ensure basic, elemental mental health care for children. But they hardly can be said to guarantee to children the right to the "highest attainable standard of health"—the standard set forth in the U.N. Convention (Article 24). That standard certainly requires more than the "basics." Attaining the highest standard of mental health care also, in our opinion, requires that minors be included in making decisions that affect them. As Tremper and Kelly (1987) noted:

> [P]erceived free choice enhances the effectiveness of treatment. Conversely, lack of choice reduces commitment and may even produce reactance to therapeutic efforts. When minors choose to participate in treatment decision-making, their motivation and performance during the intervention increase substantially, and their progress in treatment is positively related to the degree of perceived choice. (p. 117)

Another issue related to minors' mental health care is their right to seek treatment independently. This issue is particularly relevant to adolescents, who are the major consumers of juvenile mental health care, as Pikunas (1994) discovered in her survey of 23 psychiatric hospitals. She found that the vast majority of minors admitted for care were ages 13 to 17 years.

Professionals face a particularly difficult dilemma when minors independently request mental health services. To deny services to children who need them seems, to us, unethical. But if children request such services against their parents' wishes, whose rights to consent to treatment should prevail? In daily practice, apparently, many counselors side with the children. Apsler, for example, reported that three fourths of mental health professionals in Massachusetts said they had treated children under the age of 16 without parental consent, apparently contrary to state law (cited in Melton & Ehrenreich, 1992).

Hall and Lin (1995) argued that ethical issues related to the rights of children to participate fully in their own mental health treatment have been neglected by mental health professionals. Further, they contended that counselors can inadvertently hurt children in three ways: (a) Mental health counselors may be unaware of their own biases regarding children's competence to make decisions regarding their own welfare, (b) knowledge of what constitutes children's rights in counseling decisions may not be clearly defined, and (c) mental health counselors may be unaware of the ways their current behaviors may violate children's rights.

As a means of overcoming these harms, Hall and Lin (1995) promoted five ethical principles that can serve as a foundation for professionals to involve children in making health decisions:

1. Nonmaleficence is evidenced when we do no harm to our client-children.
2. Beneficence is active when we promote children's psychological growth.
3. Autonomy is shown when we allow children the responsibility of weighing treatment alternatives.
4. Justice is affirmed when children are encouraged to participate in choosing the least intrusive treatment option.
5. Fidelity is protected when counselors respect their bond with children by keeping their promises to them. (p. 70)

The principles outlined by Hall and Lin are consistent with those of the U.N. Convention.

The Right to Refuse Treatment

Not all patients, of course, want to partake in the treatments offered to them as being in their "best interests." Thus, mental patients have been provided some specific rights, either by statute or by court decisions, as a result of increased concern about protecting the civil liberties of people with mental illness. Among those liberties is the right to refuse treatment.

Two federal district courts—one in Massachusetts (*Rogers v. Okin,* 1979) and one in New Jersey (*Rennie v. Klein,* 1978)—held that adult psychiatric patients have the right to refuse medications even if these medications are likely to be beneficial. This right is not absolute, however, and may be overridden if one or more of the following conditions exist: (a) if the patient's conduct is dangerous toward self or others, (b) if the patient is so ill as to be unable to make a competent decision about treatment, and (c) if there is an emergency that, according to a physician, makes forced medication necessary (Wrightsman, Nietzel, & Fortune, 1994).

Similarly, the U.S. Supreme Court has employed the doctrine of deferring to the professional judgment of physicians who treat the adult patient. In

Youngberg v. Romeo (1982), the Court held that honoring the rights of patients cannot be used to restrict unnecessarily the professional judgment of treating physicians. Today, therefore, "the availability of numerous ways to override a patient's refusal converts this right into more of a right to object to treatment and have the medical necessity of the treatment reviewed" (Wrightsman et al., 1994, p. 411).

But does the same right to refuse treatment accrue to juveniles as well? Pikunas (1994) surveyed judges and hospital administrators in Michigan regarding a child's right to object to psychiatric hospitalization. According to Pikunas, the judges expressed a shared belief that a child should have the right to object to treatment. Although they varied as to what age that right should apply, the responses "clustered around the age of 13 [years]" (p. 4). The majority of judges (83%) believed that judicial hearings should not be mandatory in *all* cases—that is, whether the minor has chosen to object or not—but 96% responded that if a minor has chosen to object, the appropriateness of hospitalization should be determined by a court of law. Most (76%) also said that minors who object to hospitalization should have a right to an attorney.

Pikunas's (1994) survey of 19 psychiatric hospitals regarding 169 juvenile admissions revealed that in only 30% of the cases had the minor been asked to sign a written informed consent for hospitalization. In 3% of those cases, the child refused. Similarly, aggregate data for 13 hospitals in 1990 showed that 31 (1.4%) of 2,161 minors had formally objected to hospitalization.

When asked whether they would admit minors who objected to hospitalization, 23 hospitals agreed that they would admit children ages 8 to 11 years solely on the basis of parental consent. All hospitals reported that, if after a week of hospitalization, minors ages 8 to 15 years decided that they wanted to leave, they would keep the children confined. Most, however, said that they would allow such children to present objection statements for the purpose of a judicial hearing. Only 1 hospital out of 23 answered that it would seek a 15-year-old's consent and, if not obtained, would either deny admission or refer the minor elsewhere.

Thus, whereas most judges surveyed expressed the opinion that minors should be consulted about treatment, most hospitals indicated that children and adolescents were not, in fact, consulted as a matter of course. According to Article 12 of the U.N. Convention, children have the right to express their own views—a principle with which we agree. Therefore, we support recommendations offered by Melton and Ehrenreich (1992):

Children should be viewed as active partners in child mental health services with heavy weight placed on protection of their liberty and privacy. . . . Mental health services for children should be respectful of parents and supportive of family integrity. . . . When out-of-home placement is necessary for the protection or treatment of the child, it should be in the most family-like setting consistent with those objectives. (p. 1050)

Recommendations Regarding the Rights of Children in the Health Care System

The World Health Organization (WHO) defines *health* as "a state of complete physical, mental, and social well-being" (Van Bueren, 1995, p. 297). Thus, according to WHO, health no longer is defined simply as the absence of disease; rather, health involves the maximization of individuals' physical and mental potential. In most countries, the primary responsibility for preventing children from pursuing activities harmful to their health rests with the family, whereas the duty to provide adequate health care lies with the state (Van Bueren, 1995).

In the United States, as noted above, medical decisions concerning children require a delicate balancing act involving the sometimes competing rights of children, their parents, and the state. Who should decide whose interests prevail in a given case?

Goldstein (1977), adopting the nurturance orientation, argued that children need continuous protection, which is best provided by the parents in most instances. According to Goldstein, state intervention could be justified only if the state were to order a "proven, non-experimental medical procedure, when its denial would mean death for a child who would otherwise have an opportunity for either a life worth living or a life of relatively normal healthy growth toward adulthood" (p. 651). With regard to children's competence to make their own medical decisions, Goldstein recommended standards for establishing emancipation status that are objective (e.g., chronological age). According to Goldstein, determinations should not be made on a case-by-case basis with "some body of wise persons" being satisfied that the child is "mature enough" (p. 662).

Brian-Mark (1983) offered a contrasting view that supports the self-determination orientation and is more in concert with the U.N. Convention principle that children should have the right to express their own views

(Article 12). According to Brian-Mark, when a medical condition affects a child, the court should determine whether the child is of "sufficient general capacity to express a mature, intelligent and informed preference regarding a course of treatment" (p. 54). The determination should consider the child's preference, the parents' preferences, the conventional treatment according to expert testimony, the risks involved, and the interest of the state. With regard to assessment of the child's competence, Brian-Mark offered the following specifics:

> (a) The court may appoint independent counsel to represent the child. (b) No finding of incapacity should be reached without first interviewing the child. (c) The court shall consider all relevant evidence including (i) the child's education and level of intelligence, (ii) the child's awareness of the treatment and potential outcomes, (iii) any psychological and educational evaluations that are submitted, and (iv) the length of time the child has to cope with the medical condition. (d) In no case shall the lack of capacity be found solely on the basis of the child's age, unless the child is too young to express any communication. (p. 54)

According to Brian-Mark, the competent child's preference should be given at least equal weight with all other factors.

We agree with Brian-Mark (1983), believing that this approach is consistent with the principles set forth in the United Nations Convention on the Rights of the Child. It also is consistent with the Juvenile Justice Standards of the American Bar Association (1980), which state that a minor of at least age 16 may receive medical care without prior parental consent if the individual has sufficient capacity to understand the nature and consequences of the treatment (§ 4.6). Indeed, according to that criterion, even 8-year-old "Alice" who elected not to undergo a second organ transplant was competent to make a critical medical decision.

But what are the consequences of empowering such young children to participate in their own medical and mental health care? Lewis and Lewis (1990) identified physicians' resistance and parents' fear of losing control as the major barriers to meaningful participation by children. They found, for example, that the primary obstacles to "the dissemination of a proven strategy to empower children to manage their asthma and seizure disorders were not the children but the adults—particularly the physicians who cared for these patients" (p. 65). Similarly, Lewis and Lewis found that parents feared that their children would learn more than the parents themselves had about the illness the child had experienced; the parents feared losing control, therefore, over the health management of their children.

These barriers are surmountable, however. Programs that encourage children to participate in their own health care could include education for the parents, as well as opportunities for parents to express and resolve their fears. Similarly, medical school curricula could include education on child development and strategies for communicating with children of various ages, as well as opportunities to interact directly with children as consumers of medical and mental health information and services. Lewis and Lewis (1990) noted that "direct interaction with children as though they were adults requires a set of skills that are seldom taught or learned in medical school or residency" (p. 66). But emphasizing those skills would be entirely consistent with the principles of the U.N. Convention, particularly Articles 12 and 13. We agree with Erlen (1987) that that approach is "an idea whose time has come" (p. 156).

8

Lessons Learned

The Rights of Children in the Educational System

> Young people should be involved, according to their
> capacities and interests, at all stages in the formulation
> and pursuit of their rights and education.
>
> Stuart N. Hart and Zoran Pavlovic,
> Researchers (1991)

Theresa, a junior high school student, enters the school building and goes to her locker. There, she observes the vice principal with a police officer who is leading a German shepherd alongside the rows of lockers that line the corridor. Theresa overhears another student saying that they are searching for marijuana and other forms of contraband. In homeroom, Theresa watches her teacher attempt to break up a fight between two students. The teacher pushes one of them to the side of the corridor, banging his head several times against a locker. During English class, the teacher informs students that she wants them to read a book that involves the role of sexuality in defining a person's sense of self; they are to choose the book, but she warns that the students may have to go to the public library to find one because the school board recently completed an investigation of the contents of the school library and ordered several books concerning this topic removed from the shelves. After lunch, Theresa goes to the student newspaper office, where she is assistant editor and a reporter. She and some friends have proposed that the school newspaper run a series of articles covering such topics as unwed mothers, birth control, pregnancy and family planning resources, date rape, and AIDS. The newspaper's faculty adviser has threatened to shut down the paper and suspend anyone involved if any articles on these topics appear in the newspaper. After school, Theresa returns to the cafeteria to attend a prayer and Bible study meeting. The group had distributed posters around the school, inviting anyone interested to attend. Soon after the meeting begins, the principal enters the room, apologizes for the interruption, and tells the group that they will have to find a place off school grounds to hold their meeting. As she leaves the building, Theresa is surprised to see two of her classmates sitting on the sidelines during football practice. Jim tells her that he has been suspended from the team until he shaves off his beard. Tim says that he's not playing because he has refused to submit to a mandatory urinalysis required of all members of school sports teams in the district. Theresa goes home, wondering why she has to attend school at all.

This series of scenarios depicting a day in the school life of Theresa (Peach, 1988) raises intriguing questions about the rights of children in the educational system. Do children have the right to an education? Or to refuse an education? Do teachers have the right to use corporal punishment of students? What are students' rights in school building searches and seizures? Do students have rights to free expression of ideas and religious beliefs? Must students submit to drug testing?

Two articles of the U.N. Convention pertain directly to the rights of children in education. Article 28 guarantees children the right to a primary school education that is free and compulsory. That article also guarantees children equal access to secondary and higher education and requires the state to ensure that school discipline does not threaten the child's human dignity. Article 29 guarantees children the right to an education that includes (a) the development of the child's personality, talents, and mental and physical abilities to their fullest potential, (b) the preparation of the child for responsible life in a free society, and (c) the development of respect for the child's parents, basic human rights, the natural environment, and the child's own cultural and national values and those of others—that is, respect for human rights and fundamental freedoms enshrined in the Charter of the United Nations.

Other articles also are pertinent but less directly so. Article 15 guarantees the right to freedom of association and freedom of peaceful assembly, and Article 16 protects the right to privacy—relevant to school searches and seizures. In addition, Article 13 guarantees children permission to seek and receive information and ideas, and Article 12 ensures the right to freely express those ideas.

In this chapter, we explore U.S. case law regarding the rights of children in education. As will be demonstrated, education-related decisions in the United States do not always support the principles advanced by the U.N. Convention.

The Purpose of Education

What is the purpose of educating children? Answering that question requires reexamining the interface of parents' and children's rights. Is the purpose of educating children "to normalize, discipline, and synchronize them" or to help them attain "high levels of capacity and contribution" to society (Hart & Pavlovic, 1991, p. 350)? One's answer, of course, reflects one's alignment with one of two divergent schools of thought. The first suggests that children are not yet persons and, as such, they must be "firmly directed by authority toward common general goals" (Hart & Pavlovic, 1991, p. 349). According to that line of thought, achieving support for common cultural goals requires civilizing children. Thus, children need to be subjected to physical or psychological discipline or both—even including harsh punishments—for the good of the community and thus "for their own good."

In contrast, the second line of reasoning posits that children need not earn personhood status—that children are persons in their own right. As such, the educational system must respect their inherent value and instill socially responsible self-determination. According to that approach, an inherent trust in the dignity and potential of young people underlies the belief that children can learn to direct their own destiny. Furthermore, that goal can be strengthened through education.

Over the years, those two attitudes have clashed repeatedly in a variety of educational areas. The following questions provide a sampling of such issues: Are all children entitled to an education? Should children be permitted to refuse to be educated? Should children be permitted freedom of speech at school? Should children be party to their own disciplinary hearings at school? Should school administrators be allowed to use corporal punishment when disciplining children? If so, which forms of punishment should be permitted?

Do children surrender their due process rights when they enter the school-house door? May children's possessions be searched on school grounds? If so, by whom?

Answers to those questions depend in large measure on whether one believes that children have personhood status. Our discussion of issues in this chapter is founded on the belief that children are persons and that the purpose of their education should be to guide them toward autonomous decision making. This view is consistent with the principles of the U.N. Convention.

Why Is Education Important?

Many lofty reasons exist for valuing education. For example, as the Learnfare program—first established in Wisconsin—illustrates in its goals, education prepares individuals to become informed citizens, critical thinkers, good decision makers, and skilled workers (Gerber, 1993). Perhaps the most compelling reasons for valuing education are seen in its absence—namely, the effects of receiving inadequate schooling as a result of chronic truancy.

Hibbett and Fogelman (1990) conducted a study of the long-term effects of truancy. They surveyed approximately 15,000 people born in Great Britain from March 3 to 9, 1958. Participant data were collected at birth and at ages 7, 11, 16, and 23. Results of their National Child Development Study suggested important reasons for encouraging school attendance.

After controlling for such factors as social background, prior educational attainment, and qualifications obtained, the authors concluded that truants experienced many more difficulties in early adulthood than nontruants. As compared with nontruants, truants were more likely to have experienced marital breakdown by the age of 23, to have had more children (and at younger ages), to be more prone to heavy smoking, and to be more likely to have experienced depression. Specifically, male truants were two times more likely than nontruants to have a broken marriage by the age of 23; female truants were three times more likely. Female truants also were six to seven times more likely than nontruants to be single mothers. Truants were three times more likely to be depressed. Moreover, those differences were more pronounced for children who had been truant for longer periods of time before age 11.

Hibbett and Fogelman (1990) concluded that "truancy is a predictor of multiple problems in early adulthood" (p. 179). Thus, a variety of factors—

some positive, others negative—argue for encouraging children to become active and sustained participants in the educational process.

What Constitutes an Education?

Although conventional wisdom seldom questions the importance of children's education, there is less agreement about what education should provide and what its outcomes should be. One reason for the disagreement about the purposes and goals of education is that the term *educate* has multiple connotations. For example, the Merriam-Webster dictionary (1993) defines the word in the following ways:

> **1 a :** to provide schooling for b: to train by formal instruction and supervised practice esp. in a skill, trade, or profession **2 a :** to develop mentally, morally, or aesthetically esp. by instruction **b :** to provide with information . . . **3 :** to persuade or condition to feel, believe, or act in a desired way or to accept something as desirable (p. 367)

Another reason for lack of concordance regarding educational goals and outcomes is that the schools serve a variety of constituents, and the interests of those diverse groups may conflict. In this regard, Brassard et al. (1991) raise the following question:

> Who are schools most obligated to serve—children, parents, or society? If parents disagree with something being taught, which is the greater right, the parents' right to control their child's education, the state's need for informed citizens, or the child's right to know? From a balancing perspective, the immediate right of a parent needs to be balanced against the long-term right of the child to be informed, and against the right of the state to educate children. (p. 376)

For the purposes of this chapter, we define *education* as the encouragement of physical, mental, moral, and aesthetic development through student-centered instruction designed to lead to informed and increasingly autonomous student decision making. Moreover, we contend that, to achieve those ends, in most cases the child's right to know and the state's need for informed citizens should take precedence over the parents' right to control their child's education. Again, this view is consistent with the principles of the U.N. Convention.

Do Children Have a Right to Be Educated?

Wringe (1981) strongly stated the case for education: "Failure to receive an education is not simply to be left with a restricted view and distorted understanding of the universe and our place in it. It is to have no understanding at all" (p. 371). Article 28 of the U.N. Convention endorses Wringe's position by guaranteeing children the right to "free and compulsory" education. At first glance, the article appears to introduce an oxymoron, for it suggests that children have the right to be forced to comply. Hart and Pavlovic (1991) offered an explanation for this apparent contradiction:

> The concept of the "best interests of the child" is at work here, in short-term opposition to and long-term support of self-determination. If the child were free to make a wrong decision in an area so important to the development of knowledge and skills to be applied in future decision-making, his or her best interests might not be served. As Veerman (1986) put it, we should not seriously question whether compulsory education is a right, but rather what are the rights of children *in the school*. Again, the answer to this question should respect the child as both "being" and "becoming" a person. (p. 353)

Despite the strength of those arguments for compulsory education, neither the U.S. Constitution nor the U.S. Supreme Court has asserted a fundamental right to education for all citizens in the United States. Indeed, in *Craig v. Selma City School Board* (1992) and in *Hill by and through Hill v. Rankin County, Mississippi School District* (1993), the Court noted that because there is no constitutionally protected fundamental right to an education, preventing someone from attending school is not unconstitutional if it is related to a legitimate purpose (e.g., disciplinary suspension).

Despite the lack of a fundamental right to an education, in 1922 the U.S. Congress passed the Compulsory Education Act of 1922 (cf. Virginia [1922]), which requires the state to ensure that every parent or guardian in custody of a child aged 8 to 16 years sends that child to public school for the time the school is in session each year. Failure to comply with the Compulsory Education Act is a misdemeanor punishable by fines or jail time or both.

Shane (1987) suggested that any attempt at compulsory education raises the tension between parents' liberty interests and children's rights to equality, a controversy that commonly takes the form of the public versus private school debate:

A critical aspect of this choice for any society would be the determination whether parents may bid freely for control over the upbringing of their children, or whether a society committed to equal resources could justifiably limit parental choices in this respect. (p. 97)

That tension was the subject of the Supreme Court's decision in *Pierce v. Society of Sisters* (1925). In that decision, the Supreme Court repudiated an Oregon law that required parents to educate their children in the public schools, rather than in private ones. In *Pierce,* the Court held that public education is not required; however, the Court held that private schools must ensure that their teachers have been certified by the state and that they have adopted a specific core curriculum. Nearly half a century later, the Court revisited the state-control versus parent-control debate in *Wisconsin v. Yoder* (1972). In that case, it upheld the First and Fourteenth Amendment rights of Amish parents to withdraw their children from the public schools after the eighth grade, in recognition of their claim of religious freedom and their traditions in raising their children.

Thus, the Court has expressed a preference for equality, at least before the age of adolescence. After that point, however, liberty interests of the parents may hold sway. We find this trend curious, given the fact that, as Chapter 4 documented, the cognitive abilities and competencies of adolescents essentially are indistinguishable from those of adults. Moreover, this trend seems to contradict the U.N. Convention's emphasis on permitting children to express their own views and to seek information (Articles 12 and 13, respectively).

Do Children Have a Right Not to Be Educated?

Initially, public schools in the United States were established for the benefit of poor children whose families could not afford to provide private instruction (Areen, 1992). In 1874, New York passed legislation specifying that children between the ages of 8 and 14 years were required to attend some public or private school for at least 14 weeks per year or to be instructed at home for the same period of time. Thirty-five years later, in 1909, New York began to require children aged 7 to 16 years to either attend public school or receive instruction from a competent teacher. Today, all states except Mississippi require children to attend school for 9 or more years (Areen, 1992). For all intents and purposes, therefore, U.S. children do not have a right to refuse education.

The particular form that compulsory education takes in the United States, however, varies by state. Generally, compulsory education statutes can be grouped into three categories, depending on the type of schools children are required to attend (Caput, 1985). The *no exception statutes* (e.g., Georgia) require children to attend either a public or a private school, with no other exceptions. The *explicit exception statutes* (e.g., Missouri) allow attendance at a public, private, or other school, including an approved home education program. The *equivalency statutes* (e.g., Oklahoma) allow for children to attend public, private, or other schools or to receive other means of education. The latter set of statutes may be further subdivided into two categories. *Explicit equivalence statutes* (e.g., Wisconsin) specify the equivalency requirement, whereas *implied equivalence statutes* (e.g., Oklahoma) fail to outline the equivalency requirement. Thus, the requirements of implied equivalence statutes usually are imposed by attorney general opinions or case law and consequently may result in a patchwork of statutory interpretations (Caput, 1985).

Regardless of the specific form of compulsory education laws, statutory noncompliance results in sanctions. Failure to comply with the Compulsory Education Act is a misdemeanor. Thus, parents who allow their children to be truant risk fines or jail time or both, as well as charges of child neglect under many state statutes. In some states, other sanctions for truancy also may be imposed against parents.

For example, Wisconsin pioneered the statutory enactment of a program known as Learnfare that was intended to keep pregnant teenagers in school; other states followed suit. According to Gerber (1993), Wisconsin claimed to have two goals for Learnfare: First, the state wanted more teenagers whose families received Aid to Families with Dependent Children (AFDC, now known as Temporary Assistance to Needy Families, or TANF) to finish high school (or its equivalent) so that they could become productive members of society. Second, Wisconsin wanted to establish a mutual responsibility between the state (providing benefits) and welfare recipients (self-improvement).

In practice, Learnfare is a controversial social program in which a needy family loses AFDC benefits if a teenager from that family misses a certain number of days in school or fails to attain a certain grade point average. According to Gerber (1993), "Learnfare burdens the poor in an effort to make them conform to 'middle class values' without imposing a similar burden on the middle class. This unequal treatment implicates the Equal Protection Clause [of the U.S. Constitution]" (p. 2173).

Whether just or not, Learnfare is one example of the fact that U.S. children do not have the right to refuse an education. The decision in *Battles v. Board* (1996) provides another example. In *Battles*, the U.S. District Court for Maryland held that a state statute requiring children to attend school and setting standards for home education does not violate either the First Amendment or the Religious Freedom Restoration Act of 1993.

Cheryl Anne Battles told the court that she chose to educate her daughter at home because she believed the public school system indoctrinated children in teachings contrary to her religious beliefs. To ensure compliance with home-schooling regulations, parents who educate children at home must sign a consent form indicating they have read and understand the regulations. Ms. Battles refused to sign the form and would not allow the school system to monitor the child's education as required by law. Ms. Battles filed suit in federal district court, alleging the compulsory education law was unconstitutional. The court ruled that Ms. Battles's assertion that the public schools indoctrinate children in an anti-Christian worldview was not sufficient to show that the educational laws were designed to suppress her religion. This decision reaffirmed the view that children in the United States do not have a right to refuse education.

Children's Rights Regarding Specific Educational Issues

Veerman (1986) argued that the focus should not be on the right to compulsory education, but rather on the rights of children who are in the school. Given that education in the United States is compulsory, the rights of students seem of paramount importance in the general discussion of children's rights. In the sections below, we address issues in several educational areas: First Amendment freedoms (speech and religion, disciplinary hearings, corporal punishment), Fourth Amendment freedoms (from unreasonable searches and seizures), and education of students with disabilities.

The U.S. Supreme Court has recognized that minors, as well as adults, are protected by the U.S. Constitution and thus possess constitutionally protected rights (see Chapter 1 for a description of those rights; see, e.g., *Goss v. Lopez*, 1975; *In re Gault*, 1967; *Tinker v. Des Moines Independent Community School District*, 1969). By 1970, the Court had established that school-children have the right to equal protection of the law (*Brown v. Board of Education*, 1954), to procedural due process in the context of juvenile justice (*In re Gault*, 1967), and to freedom of speech (*Tinker v. Des Moines Independent Community School District*, 1969; *West Virginia State Board of Education v. Barnette*, 1943). In *Tinker* (1969), for example, the Court stated: "It can hardly be argued that either students or teachers shed their constitutional rights to freedom of speech or expression at the schoolhouse gate" (p. 506), a sentiment echoed two decades later in *Carey on Behalf of Carey v. Maine School Administrative Dist. No. 17* (1990).

The Court also has made clear, however, that the constitutional rights of children cannot be equated with those of adults (see, e.g., *Bellotti v. Baird*, 1979). Generally, the Court has favored protecting the students' nurturant interests (the "best interests of the child") over ensuring their self-determinative interests, in large part because of the peculiar vulnerability of the child. In *Bellotti v. Baird* (1979), for example, Justice Lewis Powell noted: "During the formative years of childhood and adolescence, minors often lack the experience, perspective, and judgment to recognize and avoid choices that could be detrimental to them" (p. 635).

Thus, Goetz (1985) concluded:

> When the child's interests clash with those of the parent, the Court will defer to parental authority only to the extent that parents maintain control over the child's errant impulses. If they do not, the Court will defer to the state to control the child.
> Thus, the Court has not significantly increased children's rights. It has merely decided who can best control or protect the child: the parent or the state. . . . While the concerns of the child will be recognized, the Court, in the end, will defer to the authority of either the parent or the state. (pp. 1231-1232)

First Amendment

The free speech and free press rights guaranteed to citizens by the First Amendment have an ambiguous status when applied to schoolchildren. Students may not be required to salute the U.S. flag (*West Virginia State Board of Education v. Barnette,* 1943), nor may they be prohibited from wearing armbands in protest of war (*Tinker v. Des Moines Independent Community School District,* 1969). Thus, court decisions have recognized the rights of schoolchildren to express opinions and to engage in activities not condoned by school officials. The Court has not tolerated, however, raucous student behavior or "vulgar and offensive" language used by students (*Bethel School District No. 403 v. Fraser,* 1986).

In *Hazelwood School District v. Kuhlmeier* (1988), the Supreme Court affirmed the constitutional right of school authorities to control the expression of students "so long as their actions are reasonably related to legitimate pedagogical concerns" (p. 273). Writing for the majority in *Hazelwood,* Justice Byron White argued that educators have the authority to suppress or censor "school-sponsored publications, theatrical publications, and other expressive activities that students, parents, and members of the public might reasonably perceive to bear the imprimatur of the school" (p. 273).

It is important to note that the nature of the Supreme Court decisions regarding children's educational rights has changed over the years. During the late 1960s and 1970s, children were acknowledged as people (see, e.g., *In re Gault* [1967]), a recognition that carried with it an assumption of their natural rights. During the 1980s and 1990s, however, when the Court's composition was more conservative, children's First Amendment rights in education have been restricted.

Our position is that only when a person is given the freedom to make wrong choices does the opportunity for learning how to make responsible choices develop. In that perspective, both schools and courts should encourage the right of the child to make informed—even if unpopular—choices unless those choices violate society's compelling interest in protecting its citizens from harm.

School Discipline

Disciplinary Hearings

The Supreme Court's general view of children as "equal, but not quite" is well illustrated by its decisions regarding school discipline. In *Goss v. Lopez* (1975), the Court held that a student must be given notice and an informal hearing before being suspended from school, a position advocating the treatment of children as persons equal before the law. It is noteworthy, however, that the ruling was based on a 5-to-4 split in votes. Goetz (1985) summarized the dissenting opinions:

> [T]he four dissenting Justices argued that the child's interests were not sufficiently important to require an informal proceeding. Chief Justice Burger, and Justices Blackmun, Powell, and Rehnquist felt that schools need broad discretionary authority to maintain discipline and good order. In their opinion, providing due process in "routine" disciplinary problems would interfere with the daily functioning of schools, thus actually disserving the student in the long run. (p. 1224)

What is missed in this approach is the reality that students learn through all of their experiences. When they experience procedural and substantive due process, they learn it. When they experience punishment without the legitimating due process that determines whether punishment is justified, they learn the lessons implicit in that experience as well. If the U.S. Constitution is not worthy of educators' respect, from what internalized experience should the student draw in later life—for example, as a workplace supervisor—when confronted with due process issues?

In today's more conservative Court, it is likely that the *Goss* dissenting opinion would be the basis for the majority ruling. Evidence for that speculation is provided by the Court's decision 2 years later in *Ingraham v. Wright* (1977). In that case, the Court held that due process did not require a school to use procedural safeguards before it could administer corporal punishments to a child. Thus, children in school have been afforded the right to protect themselves against suspension, but not beatings!

In our opinion, the Supreme Court has been less than straightforward in advocating procedural due process rights for children involved in disciplinary proceedings at school. We cannot agree with the Court's record on procedural due process for schoolchildren. Article 12 of the U.N. Convention provides clear guidance in this matter. It states that children have the right to express opinions in matters affecting them and to have their opinions heard. We agree.

Corporal Punishment

Corporal punishment—that is, penalties affecting the body—has been associated with the American educational system since colonial times (Benz, 1992). For example, the first headmaster of Harvard College (est. 1636), one Master Eaton, was dismissed from his position for beating a junior assistant with a "walnut log big enough to kill a horse" (Moore, 1976, p. 339). Two centuries later, Horace Mann, generally considered to be the founder of American education, reported that "in one week 328 floggings were meted out in a school with only 250 scholars" (Maurer, 1990, p. 33) and that, in another district, "18 boys [were] flogged within two hours" (Maurer, 1990, p. 33). Mann protested such treatment, but his words fell on deaf ears.

Despite the current outrage over child abuse occurring in homes, the use of corporal punishment by parents has not waned significantly; school officials and teachers, as they stand *in loco parentis* (in the place of the parent), thus have not had much encouragement (other than civil litigation defense) to change. For two decades, the Office of Civil Rights (OCR) of the Department of Education has gathered statistics on corporal punishment. The OCR surveyed all 50 states during academic year 1975-76 and found that more than 1.5 million children had been subjected to corporal punishment as a means of discipline in the school setting (Maurer, 1981). By 1980, the OCR reported that well over one million children had been hit by their teachers and principals, representing a decline of approximately one third during the 4-year period. But, as Maurer (1990) aptly points out, those statistics are grossly underestimated:

> The statistics were flawed in that they were self reports and were full of gaps and inconsistencies. Omitted were all school districts with an enrollment under 1500 where fully a third of all children attend, and where much more corporal punishment is used than in the larger cities. Budget tightening by the Reagan administration required that figures from sample schools be extrapolated to cover whole states. Informal slaps and slams given on a spur of the moment basis were not to be counted. (p. 31)

Newspaper reports provide additional statistics. For example, the January 17, 1982, edition of the *Columbus Dispatch* reported that 30,660 incidents of paddling had been reported among the 73,698 students enrolled in the district (Maurer, 1990). According to the *Nashville Tennessean,* just after Christmas in 1987, Nashville school officials and teachers reportedly hit students 18,885 times, yet the total enrollment was only 8,768 students (Maurer, 1990)!

More recently, Shaw and Braden (1990) reviewed 6,244 discipline files from 16 Florida schools during one academic year. Judges rated the severity of each infraction on a 35-point scale and coded punishments as either corporal or noncorporal. The overall corporal punishment rate was 24.7%, although wide variations existed in the groups receiving that form of discipline (e.g., 11% for white females vs. 41% for black males). Shaw and Braden also found that younger children were more likely to receive corporal punishment than were older students and that males were significantly more likely to be corporally punished than were females.

Shaw and Braden's (1990) results mirrored those obtained by the OCR (1984). According to the OCR, 24.5% of U.S. students are black, yet 37.3% of corporal punishment cases involve black children. Moreover, whereas males comprise 51.3% of the nation's schoolchildren, more than 80% of corporal punishment cases involve males. Shaw and Braden concluded that gender and race accounted for 22% of the overall variance in the administration of corporal punishment.

Use of corporal punishment has resulted in a variety of brutalities. One teacher required a student with uneven legs and an unhealthy heart to run 350 yards in less than 2 minutes (*Waechter v. School Dist. No. 14-030 of Cassopolis, Mich.,* 1991). One child was partially deafened after a whistle had been blown directly into her ear, and another child's head was held in the toilet bowl while the toilet repeatedly was flushed (Maurer, 1990). A child with Down's syndrome came home from school with adult-size, handprint-shaped bruises on her arms and legs. When the girl's mother complained to the police, they replied, "Look, Lady. It's legal" (Maurer, 1990, p. 38). It is difficult to imagine that such abuses could be committed in the name of educating children.

Such practices clearly violate the spirit of the U.N. Convention. Article 19 requires the state to protect children from all forms of abuse, neglect, and exploitation by parents or others, and Article 28 guarantees children a right to school discipline that does not threaten their human dignity.

Newspaper columnist Stephanie Salter (1996) stated the case compellingly:

> If hitting a troubled kid is so good for him, why didn't Charlie Manson turn into a model citizen? Or Hitler? Or Stalin? If there is "no harm in a swat on the butt" for a child, why is it against the law to do the same thing to an adult? If a state-authorized beating is a desirable method of punishment and deterrence for a school child, why did the U.S. military outlaw it for soldiers in the late 1800s? And why has it been two generations (Delaware abolished it in 1952) since corporal punishment for adults was on the books in any state? . . . Study after study (not to mention the majority of locked cells in every prison) prove that children who are "disciplined" with physical violence and humiliation don't become line-toeing little Gandhis; they become adults who equate power with violence and humiliation.[1]

Table 8.1 States' Positions on Corporal Punishment in the Schools

---

States Whose Statutes Specifically Prohibit Corporal Punishment (21)
California, Connecticut, Hawaii, Illinois, Iowa, Maine, Maryland, Massachusetts,
Michigan, Minnesota, Montana, Nebraska, Nevada, New Jersey, North Dakota,
Oregon, Vermont, Virginia, Washington, West Virginia, Wisconsin

States Whose State Regulations Prohibit Corporal Punishment (4)
Alaska, New Hampshire, New York, Utah

States Whose Statewide School Board Policies Prohibit Corporal Punishment (2)
Rhode Island, South Dakota

States Permitting Corporal Punishment (23)
Alabama, Arizona, Arkansas, Colorado, Delaware, Florida, Georgia, Idaho, Indiana,
Kansas, Kentucky, Louisiana, Mississippi, Missouri, New Mexico, North Carolina,
Ohio, Oklahoma, Pennsylvania, South Carolina, Tennessee, Texas, Wyoming

---

SOURCE: Weiss (1996). For more information, contact the National Coalition to Abolish Corporal
Punishment in Schools, 155 West Main Street, Suite 100-B, Columbus, OH 43215, (614) 991-8829.

Why, then, are so many schoolchildren subjected to physical punishments?
Benz (1992) commented:

> Curiously, even though there is heightened awareness and concern over child
> abuse and the possibility of the misuse of corporal punishment, courts
> steadfastly hold that unless no state remedies are available, no substantive
> due process claim under 42 U.S.C. 1983 exists. This is true even when the
> corporal punishment is inspired by malice, is excessive or is shocking to the
> conscience. (pp. 13-14)

Thus, unless statutes specifically prohibit the use of corporal punishment,
school administrators are free to spank, paddle, strike, and otherwise inflict
pain on the bodies of students.

Nationwide, 23 states currently permit corporal punishment in the
schools (Monaghan, 1997); 27 states have statewide bans on corporal punishment, by statute, by state regulation, or by school board policies (Weiss, 1996;
see Table 8.1). It should be noted, however, that some states that currently ban
corporal punishment are considering repealing those bans (e.g., California,
Michigan). In addition, according to Weiss (1996), some states listed as having
bans on corporal punishment by statute have either amended the relevant
statutes or construed the term *corporal punishment* narrowly (e.g., Alaska,
Michigan, Montana, Vermont, Virginia). A narrow construction distinguishes

the use of force to maintain control and order in the classroom from the use of force to punish.

Although a 1989 Harris poll indicated that a slight majority of citizens were opposed to corporal punishment (Shaw & Braden, 1990), the U.S. Supreme Court has upheld the school's right to use corporal punishment despite parental objections (*Baker v. Owen*, 1975). Indeed, even when mental and physical harm resulting from corporal punishment have been documented, the Court has ruled in favor of the procedure (*Ingraham v. Wright*, 1977).

Ingraham v. Wright (1977) is the leading case regarding corporal punishment and substantive due process rights in the schools. The case involved two students, James Ingraham and Roosevelt Andrews, each of whom was corporally punished on separate occasions in their Florida junior high school. *Ingraham* summarized Dade County School Board Policy 5144 as authorizing

> paddling the recalcitrant student on the buttocks with a flat wooden paddle measuring less than two feet long, three to four inches wide, and about one-half inch thick. The normal punishment was limited to one to five "licks" or blows with the paddle. (pp. 656-657)

Ingraham was struck by the paddle more than 20 times in the principal's office. As a result, Ingraham required medical attention that prevented him from attending school for several days. Andrews was paddled on repeated occasions and "[o]n two occasions . . . [was] struck on his arms, once depriving him of the full use of his arm for a week" (*Ingraham v. Wright*, 1977, p. 657).

Although the Court found that the paddlings were "exceptionally harsh" (p. 657), it ruled against both the Eighth Amendment (cruel and unusual punishment) and Fourteenth Amendment (procedural and substantive due process) claims offered by the complainants. The Court held that the Eighth Amendment's protection against cruel and unusual punishment was designed for application to criminal punishment and therefore was not relevant to corporal punishment in the schools. In other words, the Court ruled that persons who are convicted criminals are constitutionally protected from the unrestrained anger and retribution of their designated punishers but schoolchildren are not. Moreover, the Court held that "the due process requirements of notice and hearing were not necessary before effectuating school-administered corporal punishment because Florida's common law permitted such punishment" (Benz, 1992, p. 16). Thus, children and adolescents daily confined for the purpose of education are denied the opportunity to learn, by the powerful lesson of experience, the basic principles of a law-based society.

Corporal punishment cases decided since *Ingraham* have not resulted in a coherent pattern of findings. In *Hall v. Tawney* (1980), the Fourth Circuit Court of Appeals ruled that a sixth grader's beating with a rubber paddle (which resulted in a 10-day hospitalization and possible permanent injuries) was not in accordance with state law and policy, but instead was "based on episodic application of force" (p. 613). Thus, the child-victim was entitled to bring his cause of action. In other words, the appeals court ruled that the child's due process rights indeed had been violated. The court noted that, in the public school context, corporal punishment violates *substantive* due process if

> the force applied caused injury so severe, was so disproportionate to the need presented, and was so inspired by malice or sadism rather than a merely careless or unwise excess of zeal that it amounted to a brutal and inhumane abuse of official power literally shocking to the conscience. (p. 613)

Woodard v. Los Fresnos Independent School District (1984) addressed the question of conflicting school and parental rights in the administration of corporal punishment. In that case, a Los Fresnos student had used abusive language with a school bus driver. The school district's policy allowed parents the option of allowing or declining discipline in the form of corporal punishment. The student's parents and the principal agreed that a 3-day suspension would be administered instead of corporal punishment. The student claimed that the principal later called her to the office and required that she choose which form of punishment would be employed. Because her scholarship standing would have been jeopardized by suspension, the student chose corporal punishment (three spanks). The Ninth Circuit Court of Appeals for the District of California ruled that the minor's constitutional rights had not been violated because corporal punishment is a deprivation of substantive due process only when "it is arbitrary, capricious, or wholly unrelated to the legitimate state goal of maintaining an atmosphere conducive to learning" (*Woodard v. Los Fresnos Indep. School Dist.*, 1984, p. 1246).

Garcia v. Miera (1987) provides an example of a slight shift away from the *Ingraham* standard. Teresa Garcia, a 9-year-old student, was called to the principal's office after she hit a boy who had kicked her. When the principal, Miera, could not enlist Garcia's cooperation in the administration of corporal punishment, a teacher was called in to assist in the process. The teacher "held Garcia upside down by her ankles while Miera struck Garcia with a wooden paddle" (p. 653), which had a split in the center, "making it clap and grab upon impact" (Benz, 1992, p. 21). After she had been hit five times, a cut appeared on Garcia's leg, which resulted in a permanent scar. In a subsequent conference with Garcia's parents, Miera agreed not to paddle the child again without notifying them. However, Miera again paddled the child without parental consent, resulting in a struggle between Garcia and an administrative assistant:

> During the skirmish, Garcia injured her back on the principal's desk. Garcia was then given the three blows which resulted in severe bruising and back pain for several weeks, due to the impact with Miera's desk. (Benz, 1992, pp. 21-22)

The United States District Court for New Mexico held that qualified immunity protected the school officials against any due process violations resulting from the imposition of corporal punishment against Garcia. The Tenth Circuit Court of Appeals, however, concluded that corporal punishments that are "so grossly excessive as to be shocking to the conscience implicate a liberty interest and violate substantive due process rights" (p. 656). The question yet to be resolved is whether *Garcia* is distinguished from *Ingraham* as a matter of kind (permanent injury) or degree (e.g., the level of restraint).

Benz (1992) argued that *Ingraham* and its progeny have left the issue of corporal punishment in the schools in a state of flux, with different circuit courts expressing divergent views. According to Benz (1992), the Fourth, Sixth, and Tenth Circuits believe that excessive corporal punishment violates due process, whereas the Fifth Circuit follows *Ingraham*. The Third and Eighth Circuits have devised their own tests for due process violation, whereas the Seventh Circuit has not created an official position, but rather uses a mixture of the Fourth and Eighth Circuit standards.

Benz (1992) concluded:

> The position of the Circuit Courts regarding the violation of substantive due process rights in public school corporal punishment settings is apparently in a state of turbulence. Seemingly, the United States Supreme Court left this issue open to let the matter simmer in the Circuit Courts before it is forced to decide the issue. Unfortunately, the Circuit Courts have promulgated incom-

patible standards and the question of whether a child is protected from excessive corporal punishment seems to rest solely on the forum state.

Case law does not define precisely what punishment will shock the conscience of our courts. This is startling because much of the corporal punishment now administered would probably be deemed excessive by the general public, especially in light of this nation's heightened awareness of child abuse.

It seems imperative that this issue be clarified once and for all in order to stop abuses which stem from ill-defined and ambiguous verbiage. This nation's children should not have to suffer because the legal system cannot decide what is and what is not excessive punishment in its school systems. Children depend on those with more maturity, knowledge, and wisdom, those who are less vulnerable than they are, to keep them from being legally abused. (pp. 25-26)

A similar view was espoused by Justices White, Brennan, Marshall, and Stevens in the dissent to *Ingraham* (1977): "Where corporal punishment becomes so severe as to be unacceptable in a civilized society, I can see no reason that it should become any more acceptable just because it is inflicted on children in the public schools" (p. 692).

We agree. In our view, corporal punishment creates a host of difficulties, not the least of which is diminution of human dignity. Maurer (1990) provided evidence that use of corporal punishment is associated with increases in vandalism, school dropout rates, violence against teachers, and juvenile crime. Cryan (1987) noted that many researchers have found that corporal punishment is not particularly effective in changing behavior. Instead, its use tends to lead to decreased self-esteem, as well as increases in fear, anxiety, aggression, and self-destructive behavior.

The use of corporal punishment teaches children that hitting is permissible so long as the punisher has authority and physical control over the recipient. That approach is totally inconsistent with both the nurturance and self-determination views of children's rights, as well as the U.N. Convention (specifically, Articles 19 and 28). Therefore, we cannot defend the use of corporal punishment in U.S. schools; instead, we advocate for nationwide abolition of corporal punishment. In its place, schools may substitute such alternatives as the use of "time-outs," in-school suspensions, and disciplinary practices designed to instill internal controls in children.

In 1971, a task force of the National Education Association (NEA) proposed eliminating corporal punishment, but the NEA did not take a formal stand against the practice for another 16 years (Maurer, 1990). Similarly, in

Nebraska, a bill to abolish corporal punishment first was introduced in 1971 but was defeated by a 3:1 margin after colorful debate. Not until 1988 did the bill finally pass the state's unicameral legislature. Another indication of reluctance to take action against corporal punishment was that a bill to prohibit the practice in state-licensed day care settings did not pass in the Nebraska legislature. Thus, successfully advocating for nationwide abolition of corporal punishment likely will be a lengthy process.

Searches and Seizures

The Fourth Amendment to the Constitution protects citizens against unreasonable searches or seizures of their person or property. Most Americans greatly value this right. But does the right to privacy guaranteed to all adult U.S. citizens extend to children in the schoolhouse?

Some individuals argue that school searches should be exempt from court scrutiny because school officials are private citizens acting *in loco parentis,* as opposed to government officials, who are subject to the constraints of the Fourth Amendment (see McLaughlin, 1985). McLaughlin (1985) refuted that line of reasoning on several grounds: (a) The Fourth Amendment covers all unreasonable searches, not just those conducted by police officers, (b) the state confers legal rights on school officials to act on behalf of parents, which in turn makes them government officials (see *People v. Scott D.,* 1974; *State v. Baccino,* 1971), and (c) the tendency of school officials to seek criminal prosecution for severe rules infractions differentiates them from parents. McLaughlin (1985) concluded, "To be sure, when fruits of a search may be used to expel or suspend a student, the search can hardly be characterized *in loco parentis*—for the child's welfare" (p. 528).

In *New Jersey v. T.L.O.* (1985), first discussed in Chapter 1, the U.S. Supreme Court considered whether Fourth Amendment rights apply to children in school. In *T.L.O.,* the Court held that competing interests require some relaxation of the restrictions normally applied to searches by public officials. The Court noted that schoolchildren have legitimate expectations of privacy but also recognized the school's need to maintain an environment conducive to learning. Specifically, the *T.L.O.* Court removed the requirement of a search warrant and lowered the probable cause threshold for searching students and their property in school. Thus, according to Goetz (1985), the Court's willingness to favor the school's authority to discipline children serves to erode children's Fourth Amendment search and seizure rights.

More recent decisions have clarified the Court's ruling in *T.L.O.* In *Widener v. Frye* (1992), a federal court held that school searches must be justified at their inception. In *Burnham v. West* (1987), a Virginia federal district court decided that school officials must have "individualized suspicion" before searching students' backpacks, purses, and/or pockets, a position reaffirmed in *Cornfield by Lewis v. Consolidated High School Dist. No. 230* (1993). *Cornfield* specified that a school administrator must base a search on conduct by a student that creates a reasonable suspicion that a specific law or regulation has been broken and that the search must be designed to garner evidence of that infraction. Thus, generalized suspicious actions by a student are not sufficient to allow search. In *New Mexico v. Michael G.* (1987), the state appeals court ruled that lockers may be searched under the *T.L.O.* "reasonable grounds" standard. One year later, the Colorado Supreme Court ruled that searching a student's car is a task that must be left to the police (*In re P.E.A.*, 1988), whereas in 1993, *Cornfield* held that school officials—even those of a different gender from the student—may conduct strip-searches. In addition, according to *Webb v. McCullough* (1987), school officials are permitted to conduct searches away from school grounds because, in supervising such excursions, the officials are acting *in loco parentis*. Finally, in *Schaill v. Tippecanoe County School Corp.* (1988), a court upheld the school's right to require high school athletes to consent to random urinalysis for the purpose of testing for drug use. This view was challenged and upheld by the U.S. Supreme Court in *Vernonia School Dist. 47J v. Acton* (1995).

Collectively, inspection of the case law suggests that factors such as age, history of disciplinary problems, and reliability of the information prompting the search are important in determining whether reasonable grounds exist. The lack of one or more of those factors, however, does not necessarily render a search unconstitutional.

Particularly in this day and age, school searches may be based on the need to protect other students, faculty, and administrators from dangers involving drugs or weapons or both. Indeed, juvenile crime statistics are alarming.

A landmark study by the U.S. Centers for Disease Control and Prevention (cited in Shogren, 1993), for example, found that nearly one fourth of high school students surveyed during a 1-month period in 1993 carried weapons; 12% of them brought those weapons to school. The 1987 National Adolescent Student Health Survey (cited in Wallace, 1994) found that, nationally, as many as 100,000 students carried guns to school every day. Shogren (1993) reported that a study (funded by the National Institute of Justice and the Office of Juvenile Justice and Delinquency Prevention of the U.S. Department of Justice) found that more than 20% of male high school students surveyed in high-crime urban neighborhoods acknowledged owning a gun and that 45% said they had been shot at or threatened with a gun on their way to school. According to FBI statistics (Chapman, 1994), the number of juveniles arrested for violent crimes in the United States rose during a recent 5-year period from 62,530 to 92,188—almost a 50% increase.

As these statistics demonstrate, violence in U.S. schools is increasing dramatically and is more likely to threaten the lives of others than in any previous time. Therefore, the benefit of protecting an individual student's right to procedural due process must be weighed against the risk of failing to protect the common good. Thus, we conclude that protecting the safety of all persons in the school building should carry great weight in school search decisions. Of course, it is important to safeguard the procedural due process rights of children to the greatest extent possible, but the safety of others must not be the price paid. (See Chapter 9 for further discussion of children's rights in the context of searches and seizures.)

Education of Children With Disabilities

The Education for All Handicapped Children Act of 1975 created provisions for federal money to assist state and local agencies in educating handicapped children. The act defined *handicapped* as encompassing physical, mental, emotional, and learning disabilities and required that each state provide programs for children with those conditions. The act required that disbursement of funds be conditioned on a state's compliance with certain goals and procedures. For example, to qualify for federal assistance under the act, a state must demonstrate that it "has in effect a policy that assures all handicapped children the right to a free appropriate public education" (1412[1]). That "free appropriate public education" must be tailored to the unique needs of the child with the handicap by means of an "individualized educational program" (IEP) (1401[18]). Moreover, the act gave parents the right to be notified about all programs, the right to attend all meetings pertaining to their children, and the right to challenge any decision about their children made by the school district. Thus, the Education for All Handicapped Children Act empowered parents to advocate for the rights of their children with disabilities. It did not, however, directly authorize the participation of children with disabilities themselves.

Section 504 of the Rehabilitation Act of 1973 also has been invoked to protect the educational rights of children with disabilities. It states, in part: "No handicapped individual . . . shall, solely by reason of his handicap, be excluded from the participation in, be denied the benefits of, or be subject to discrimination under any program or activity receiving financial assistance" (pp. 529-530).

The passage of the Americans with Disabilities Act of 1990 also served to protect the educational rights of the disabled. The act mandated that children with disabilities have equal access to education.

Case law repeatedly has held that children with disabilities have the right to enjoy equal opportunity to free, public education in the least restrictive environment possible. This right accrues to individuals with life-threatening, communicable diseases (*Ray v. School Dist. of DeSoto County*, 1987; *Thomas v. Atascadero Unified School District*, 1986), mental disabilities (*Martinez v. School Dist. Board Hillsborough County, Fla.*, 1987), physical challenges (*Ramon, et al. v. Illinois State Board of Education, et al.*, 1992), and emotional problems (*Joey T., et al. v. Azcoitia, et al.*, 1994).

The rights of those with disabilities are not absolute, however, as *Petersen v. Hastings Public Schools* (1993) illustrated. Nicholas Petersen and other severely hearing-impaired students required sign-language interpreters in the classroom. They used Signing Exact English in their homes and requested that the school district use that system. The request was denied, and Nicholas's parents sued. They argued that the Individuals with Disabilities Education Act (1997) and the Americans with Disabilities Act (1990) required the school district to provide classroom instruction in the signing system the children chose, rather than the school district's choice. The circuit court acknowledged that the plaintiffs were raising legitimate concerns but held that it was prevented from displacing the sound educational policy judgments of the school district.

Certainly, children with disabilities—like all other children—should be entitled to educational opportunities. Article 23 of the U.N. Convention guarantees the right of disabled children to special care and training designed to help them achieve self-reliance and full and decent lives in society. But not all accommodations requested of school districts can be considered reasonable, as the *Petersen* case aptly illustrates.

Children's Capacity to Make Decisions
Regarding Their Educational Rights

Kaufman (1990) has asserted that, by the age of 14 years, most children have attained full adult cognitive development. Several empirical studies support Kaufman's claim (see Chapter 4).

Thus, adolescents have the potential to demonstrate adult cognitive skills. As evidence in previous chapters has demonstrated, even younger children can make rational, informed decisions (see Chapter 7). However, children typically lack adult life experiences in decision making. In this regard, Brassard et al. (1991) noted:

> This lack of experience, which leaves them vulnerable to exploitation by others and to poor judgment on their part, makes adult guidance desirable. However, their cognitive capacities entitle them to have their opinion solicited and valued as part of the decision-making process. While this is sometimes being done in child-custody cases in divorce agreements and in some medical and psychiatric treatment decisions, it occurs less often in individual education plans (IEP) or out-of-home placements and interventions. (p. 373)

It is time, we believe, for children to be included in the educational decisions that affect them.

Recommendations Regarding the Rights
of Children in the Educational System

Hart and Pavlovic (1991) suggested that the children's rights movement and educational improvements must dovetail to serve the long-term best interests of children. According to Hart and Pavlovic, reaching that goal requires that certain objectives be attained:

> (a) a vision for the long-term development of children; (b) an empirically supported developmental perspective to guide educational expectations and practices; (c) involvement of young people in the children's rights movement and in directing their education; (d) organizational structures, planning, and processes within education which assure respect for children's rights; and

(e) the application of psychology, in this case particularly school psychology, to serve these purposes. (p. 353)

Toward those ends, we offer the following recommendations: First, schools should develop detailed, well-articulated, and empirically evaluated educational programs designed to ensure both protection and nurturance rights for children, as well as steady progress toward participation and self-determination in educational decision making. Children should be involved, according to their developing capacities and interests, in planning and pursuing their education.

Second, students should be involved in determining the expectations, guidelines, and rules to be applied to their classroom behavior. In addition, students should be represented on all major school decision-making, goal-setting, and policy committees, and their input should involve increasing levels of participation as developmental capacity and experience increase.

Students should be protected from a violent school atmosphere, whether that environment is created and maintained by other students or by school officials. Specifically, in accordance with Article 28 of the U.N. Convention, corporal punishment in the schools should be abolished.

Of course, achieving those objectives will involve struggle. Hart and Pavlovic (1991) note:

> In the initial periods, if not on a continuing basis, advances in the empowerment of children are likely to be viewed by their parents and teachers as a threat to their authority and power. Children will be granted as much autonomy as adults can tolerate. (p. 355)

The time has come to recognize children's personhood and to empower children in age-appropriate ways. Empowerment through developmentally appropriate educational participation is one important step. Eliminating institutionally condoned abuse of children is another.

Note

1. From "The Movement to Make Child Abuse Official," by S. Salter, January 14, 1996, *The San Francisco Examiner.* © The San Francisco Examiner. Used with permission.

9

On Guilt and *Gault*

The Rights of Children in the Juvenile Justice System

> [I]t would be extraordinary if our Constitution did not require
> the procedural regularity and the exercise of care implied
> in the phrase "due process." Under our Constitution, the
> condition of being a boy does not justify a kangaroo court.
>
> *In re Gault* (1967, pp. 27-28)

Michael, a 16-year-old boy, was taken into police custody and questioned about a man's murder (*Fare v. Michael C.,* 1979). The boy had a long record of being in trouble with the law, and the juvenile court had placed him on probation 4 years earlier. Michael was given his *Miranda* warnings (*Miranda v. Arizona,* 1966) by the police before they attempted to question him, but they refused to allow his probation officer to be present during the questioning although Michael had made that request.

What role should a probation officer play in such a situation? Should he or she be allowed to serve as the probationer's "counsel"? It would be very interesting to know what role the probation officer played in Michael's life, how long Michael had been reporting to him, and how Michael viewed him. Had that probation officer achieved what many believe to be the hallmark goal of the juvenile court—an interpersonal relationship of trust? What difference would there have been in the outcome of the murder investigation if the answers the police sought had come directly to them during their interrogation of Michael, as opposed to those answers from Michael coming through his probation officer? The murder victim was apparently already known to be dead; a few hours' delay may not have been harmful to the investigation. But then, what difference would it have made to Michael had his plea for his probation officer's assistance been honored?

During his police interrogation, after having been denied access to his probation officer, Michael became quite upset and began crying. Eventually, he agreed to talk with the police without a lawyer present. In fact, he made statements and drew pictures that incriminated him in the murder.

The Supreme Court held that Michael had knowingly and voluntarily waived the privilege against self-incrimination, his rights under *Miranda,* and that his statements and drawings could be used in court against him. Because Michael had had an extensive police record, the Court held that he had a sufficient understanding and knowledge of police procedures to have been competent to waive his rights. The Court did not agree with the defendant that his request to speak with his probation officer was an invocation of his right to counsel. Such an invocation, had the Court recognized Michael's desire to talk with the probation officer as a request for counsel, would have made all statements to, and drawings for, the police—without counsel present—inadmissible in court under what is known as the "exclusionary rule." The Court explained its reasoning by stating that the justices did not believe that a probation officer was in a position to represent Michael in the way that the *Miranda* decision had intended.

What matters, though, is what Michael thought. If Michael's understanding of his *Miranda* rights included a right to be counseled by someone he trusted, then Michael was not competent, by the Court's own reasoning, to waive his rights; he did not understand what his rights were. Similarly, if he said he did understand but then evidenced his misunderstanding by asking for his probation officer's help instead of the help of a different kind of law officer (an attorney), then the police took advantage of his misunderstanding and the Supreme Court approved of the police officers' actions. What has Michael learned? What effect did the interrogation experience have on his prospects for rehabilitation? Had Michael already been written off as disposable?

The Child Is a Person Before the Constitution—Almost

The further we move from 1967 and the work of the U.S. Supreme Court that year, the more we can appreciate the radical nature of what it accomplished for children. In requiring the same procedural safeguards for children that were provided to criminally charged adults, *In re Gault* (1967) became the landmark decision in juvenile law establishing children themselves as worthy of constitutional recognition. The decision marked the distance U.S. society had traveled from its belief that children were the property of their fathers and, in the father's or his delegate's absence, subject without recourse to the will of the state exercising its *parens patriae* power.

American mothers and fathers today, without actually owning their children, are acknowledged by the Supreme Court to rule over most aspects of their children's lives with little check from the state (see Chapter 5; see also *Parham v. J. R.,* 1979; *Wisconsin v. Yoder,* 1972). Although no longer considered to be property, children are yet to be fully acknowledged in the United States as possessing rights beyond those of criminal procedural due process and of freedom from serious physical, mental, or emotional endangerment (see Chapter 8). Provided a child is not unreasonably absent from school or working for a wage in some way that contravenes state or federal law (see Chapter 10) and provided a parent does not put the child's life or health at serious risk (see Chapters 6 and 7), the Supreme Court has found that the state has no right to interfere with the choices a parent makes for his or her child (see *Meyer v. Nebraska,* 1923; *Pierce v. Society of Sisters,* 1925; *Stanley v. Illinois,* 1972).

When the state itself acts to exert disciplinary control over a child, however, the U.S. Supreme Court, in *In re Gault,* held that the state has far less power than a parent exercising his or her right to discipline that child. The state's power, according to the *Gault* Court, is limited by the very tool that limits state action against adults—the U.S. Constitution.

Through the 1960s and 1970s, while the Supreme Court was examining closely the Constitution's first 14 amendments and the limiting effect of those amendments on governmental action against the individual citizen, it seems logical—from today's vantage point—that the Court's focus on the protections of the Constitution for the criminally accused adult then would be turned to encompass the criminally accused juvenile. The two groups of alleged offenders, however, had been treated not only as separate but also as dissimilar for over a century.

Differences Between Juveniles and Adults in the Justice System

The dissimilarity between the child or adolescent offender and the adult offender was recognized early in the 19th century. Delinquent children were housed with those who were abandoned and impoverished (DiFonzo, 1995; Kane, 1994), whereas the convicted adult was imprisoned with other criminals.

By the mid-1800s, it was clear that the states were failing in their efforts at housing all unwanted children together—unwanted, that is, through either their wrongdoing or their orphaned or impoverished status. Congregating all children together in institutions led more often than not to the education of one child by the young felon with whom he or she lived throughout childhood (Fox, 1996; Kane, 1994).

By 1857, Illinois had enacted legislation requiring a finding of the child's fitness for treatment before he or she could be confined in the Chicago Reform School (Kane, 1994). Little if any attention by the court was to be paid to whether the youth had been charged with wrongdoing, let alone to factual findings of guilt or innocence (DiFonzo, 1995; Kane, 1994).

Illinois, however, which is considered to have been at the forefront with Colorado in the juvenile law reform movement (Fox, 1996), found the lack of appropriate court procedures to be unconstitutional, and so criminally charged young persons were tried thereafter in criminal court. Not until 1899 did Illinois develop a new set of rules for the adjudication of criminally charged youths' guilt or innocence, allowing for the disposition of their persons by private agencies. "Children don't stop being children just because they commit a crime," noted the Honorable William Hibbler, Cook County (Illinois) Juvenile Court.[1]

In essence, the 1899 legislation created the potential for Solomonic decision making—a summary disposition by a wise man after affording a hearing to the defendant youth. Indeed, three juvenile court judges have found a place in history for their acceptance of a "jurisprudence of caring" (Allegretti, 1996)—Richard S. Tuthill and Julian W. Mack of the Cook County Juvenile Court, and Ben B. Lindsay of the Denver County Court (Fox, 1996).

The goals of the juvenile court as a rehabilitative influence on wayward youths do survive, but those goals have been called into serious question. For example, Bart Lubow of the Annie E. Casey Foundation noted, "Now there is a crisis of confidence, since the very notion that has been [the juvenile court's] cornerstone, that children are different from adults and therefore need to be treated differently, is in question."[2]

Echoing John Locke's (1690/1980) theory of the child as a citizen-in-development, social scientists in the United States have evaluated the young offender as one who could be educated in good citizenship, rehabilitated to fit within society, and therefore saved from the influences that brought him or her to the attention of the juvenile court. In fact, most U.S. juvenile courts provide their services to those criminally charged youths who appear to be capable of rehabilitation. Only one state, New Jersey, requires that a youth be capable of rehabilitation before achieving adulthood, arbitrarily set at 19 years of age (*N.J.S.A.,* 1987).

Today, professionals eschew the development of an interpersonal dialogue between a judge and an accused youth to coax admissions from the youth as a procedure worthy of sustaining. Judges Mack and Lindsay, though, both brought a style of parental caring to their interactions (Fox, 1996) that, if coupled with sound due process safeguards, could serve as a model for today's juvenile court officers.

> The problem for determination by the judge is not, Has this boy or girl committed a specific wrong, but What is he, how has he become what he is, and what had best be done in his interest and in the interest of the state to save him from a downward career. . . . The child who must be brought into court should, of course, be made to know that he is face to face with the power of the state, but he should at the same time, and more emphatically, be made to feel that he is the object of its care and solicitude. . . . Seated at his desk, with the child at his side, where he can on occasion put his arm around his shoulder and draw the lad to him, the judge, while losing none of his judicial dignity, will gain immensely in the effectiveness of his work. (Mack, 1909, pp. 119-120)

These kind words have proved insufficient to regulate the conduct of juvenile court judges as those judges developed their craft over the decades. But even in reforming the more damaging of those developments, the Supreme Court specifically stated that it did not seek to replace "the kindly juvenile court judge . . . by its opposite" (*In re Gault,* 1967, p. 26). Indeed, the Honorable Walter Beckham's advice to juvenile court judges in 1949 retains a valuable authenticity today: "In my opinion, the greatest qualification a juvenile court judge can have is a genuine love of people, interest in their problems, and an understanding and sympathetic heart" (p. 14). This view is consistent with the spirit of the U.N. Convention (1989).

Addressing the safeguards needed to ensure fairness has become the hallmark of judicial review of juvenile court cases in the latter half of the 20th century. But marrying those safeguards to the rehabilitative goals of the juvenile court has proved more difficult than perhaps even the U.S. Supreme Court could have forecast back in 1967.

Trial judges in the U.S. legal system are charged with neutral governance of the conduct of adversaries, the rendering of legal decisions designed to allow a court action to proceed without favoring either of the parties to the action unfairly, and the instruction of the deciders of the facts of the case—the jury. Challenges to the conduct of the trial or the instruction of the jurors are available in the form of appeals to a higher court, either for an error in law made by the trial judge or for an abuse of discretion in the few areas where trial judges are allowed to invoke their own judgment. In the blueprint of the juvenile court, trial judges were recast as wise, caring dispensers of rehabilitation, deciding both legal and factual aspects of a child's case as there were no juries to interfere with the judge's dispensing of fatherly kindness, education, and punishment.

The Juvenile Court After Gerald Gault

Much can be said about young Gerald Gault's punishment decided by the judge of the local juvenile court—confinement for 6 years in a state training school—as compared with the maximum sentence an adult would have received: a fine ranging from $5 to $50 or not more than a 2-month jail sentence (*In re Gault,* 1967; see Chapter 1). However, the disparity in procedural protections won the Supreme Court's considerable attention.

When 15-year-old Gerald Gault was taken into state custody on the charge of making an obscene telephone call to a neighbor, he was removed from his parents' care without any of the procedural protections available to an adult under similar circumstances. Recognizing the Fourteenth Amendment's application of the Bill of Rights to the states, the Court found that "neither the Fourteenth Amendment nor the Bill of Rights is for adults alone" (*In re Gault,* 1967, p. 12). Endorsing the view that "loose procedures, high-handed methods and crowded court calendars, either singly or in combination, all too often have resulted in depriving some juveniles of fundamental rights that have resulted in a denial of due process" (p. 18), the Court went on to require that the procedural due process protections of the Constitution be made a part of juvenile court actions. The Supreme Court's decision in *In re Gault* is founded on a child's right to *fair and accurate* findings of fact, for which the U.S. system requires the careful observation of procedural due process (p. 18).

Finally, the Court's recognition of the juvenile's potential loss of liberty, as opposed to a mere restraint for educational or other childhood benefits, serves as an important affirmation of the juvenile as a person with a right to liberty. The Court recognized the Fifth Amendment language as encompassing all testimony, in any forum, that would tend to be inculpatory; such forums and testimony would, of course, include the juvenile court and the juvenile's words to the judge who seeks the child's trust and admissions of guilt.

The Court acknowledged a juvenile's right to notice, a right to counsel, and a right to confront one's accuser and cross-examine witnesses brought by the state, as well as the privilege to refrain from self-incrimination. Most important, the *Gault* Court determined the accused juvenile to be a person—a person whose liberty was at risk and whose liberty was protected by the Constitution.

Other Protections Accorded Juvenile Offenders

Standard of Proof. The right to decisions based on proof beyond a reasonable doubt was resolved in the juvenile's favor 3 years later in *In re Winship* (1970). Justice Harlan's concurrence offers a succinct statement of the need for a high proof standard:

> [A] factual error [in a juvenile court case], as in a criminal case, exposes the accused to a complete loss of his personal liberty through a state-imposed confinement away from his home, family, and friends. And . . . a delinquency determination . . . stigmatizes a youth in that it is by definition bottomed on a finding that the accused committed a crime. . . . [I]t is far worse to declare an innocent youth a delinquent [than to let a guilty youth go free]. . . . [A] juvenile court judge should be no less convinced of the factual conclusion that the accused committed the criminal act with which he is charged than would be required in a criminal trial. (p. 374)

Trial Process. Protections against double jeopardy—that is to say, being at risk for punishment for the same offense arising out of a single set of events—were made applicable in juvenile cases in the Supreme Court's decision in *Breed v. Jones* (1975) and affirmed in *Swisher v. Brady* (1978). The right to a speedy trial was acknowledged in *United States v. Calloway* (1974). The Court has found no absolute right to jury trial, leaving the matter to the states, as it decided in *McKeiver v. Pennsylvania* (1971). Some states permit jury trials under specified circumstances, as Table 9.1 describes.

Table 9.1 States Permitting Jury Trials for Juveniles

State	Special Conditions
Colorado	No jury if the juvenile is charged with a Class 2 or 3 misdemeanor, a petty offense, or a violation of a city ordinance
Idaho	Available for murder or attempted murder, robbery, rape, controlled substance violation near school, mayhem, assault or battery with intent to commit any of above
Illinois, Kansas	Available for third offense, if juvenile would have been prosecuted as an adult felon
Montana	If youth denies all offenses
New Mexico, Virginia	If offense would be triable by jury if juvenile was charged as adult, except in probation revocations
Texas	If child is in jeopardy of a determinate sentence
Wisconsin	If requested pursuant to timeliness statutes
Wyoming	In all adjudications except probation revocations

Searches and Seizures. The Fourth Amendment's protection against unreasonable searches and seizures implies a right to be safe in one's person and to have the privacy of one's belongings respected by the state (see Chapter 8). Nowhere else, perhaps, is the child's status as a person under the control of his or her parents and thus under the control of those who stand *in loco parentis* made more obvious.

In the critical case of *New Jersey v. T.L.O.* (1985), the Supreme Court made clear that "[s]chool children have legitimate expectations of privacy. They may find it necessary to carry with them a variety of legitimate, noncontraband items, and there is no reason to conclude that they have necessarily waived all rights to privacy in such items by bringing them onto school grounds" (p. 362). But the balance must be struck. Children are required by state law to be in school, and as the Court pointed out, the school has the legitimate need to "maintain an environment in which learning takes place [which] requires some easing of the restrictions to which searches by public authorities are ordinarily subject" (p. 326). Thus, the school does not have to obtain a warrant under which to conduct a search of a student's possessions, nor does the school need to demonstrate probable cause as the condition for the search. The totality of the circumstances that show the reasonableness of the search is sufficient. *T.L.O.* proves an exemplar case of the "scaled-down version" of the Bill of Rights for children: Balancing two competing interests of the child—to be educated and to be free from privacy intrusions where probable cause is insufficient to support a warrant being issued—yields a weaker Fourth Amendment right to be free from state searches and seizures of one's property that are unreasonable and without probable cause.

Self-Incrimination. A child's ability to waive his or her Fifth Amendment right is similarly subject to the balancing of interests. Parents seek to raise their children to be truthful and to be compliant with authority. They want their children who err to acknowledge their actions, endure the penalty for them, and return to society with the lessons of the experience learned and internalized. The principle of the Fifth Amendment offers safe silence to the accused, from which no negative inference may be drawn. And yet the application of that principle is complicated. Although no adult or youth in the United States who has watched a "cops and robbers" television show should be able to claim ignorance of the *Miranda* rights, research has demonstrated again and again the apparent inability of a juvenile to comprehend, let alone to invoke, those rights properly (Flin, Davies, & Stevenson, 1987; Grisso, 1981, Saywitz, 1989; Warren-Leubecker, Bradley, Hinton, & Ozbek, 1989). *Fare v. Michael C.* (1979), described in the introduction to this chapter, is a case in point.

In fact, Macaulay (1987) suggested that television tends to "misrepresent the nature and amount of crime . . . , the roles of actors in the legal system . . . and present important issues of civil liberties in distorted ways" (pp. 197-198). Perry and Wrightsman (1991) noted:

> For example, how often does the actual culprit break down and confess on the witness stand (as *Perry Mason* would have us believe)? Or, if the child's source of knowledge is *People's Court,* why would he or she think that attorneys ever appear in court? Or if *Night Court* is more familiar, why would he or she understand the true roles of (or feel a modicum of respect for) any of the players? (pp. 100-101)

If children have firsthand experience with the legal system, one might expect them to have more useful knowledge. Saywitz (1989), however, argued to the contrary—that direct experience with court may, in fact, *reduce* comprehension of the legal system because it presents more complex information in a more confusing context. In other words, it may be difficult for children to understand the legal proceedings and the roles of the various players

because the system does not operate in a straightforward, textbooklike fashion. Instead, the process is fraught with motions, delays, continuances, objections, and other obfuscations. Thus, Perry and Wrightsman (1991) concluded:

> It is safe to assume, then, that most youngsters know precious little about
> courtroom personnel and procedures. Moreover, they do not always develop
> legal concepts in a logical fashion. Rather, they may move from complete
> lack of knowledge to incorrect perceptions and assumptions before they
> finally achieve accurate comprehension. (p. 101)

Empirical Evidence Regarding
Juveniles' Comprehension of Waiver

Grisso (1981) assessed the ability of child and adolescent subjects (ranging in age from 10 to 16 years) and adults to comprehend the *Miranda*
warnings and their implications. Juvenile subjects were residents of a boys'
town, residents of a correctional school, and recently arrested juveniles. The
two samples of adults included offenders on parole and custodial/maintenance
crews.

Grisso (1981) developed three measures of vocabulary and phrase comprehension: (a) a 12-item true-false test, (b) a set of questions requiring
subjects to paraphrase important *Miranda* concepts, and (c) a test requiring
subjects to define six crucial words in the warnings (*consult, attorney, interrogation, appoint, entitled,* and *right*). In addition, subjects' perceptions of the
function and significance of the warnings were assessed through a structured
interview in which they described their understanding of three drawings:
(a) police questioning a suspect, (b) a suspect consulting with an attorney, and
(c) a courtroom.

Grisso (1981) found that the majority of the 600 wards of the juvenile
court whom he assessed could not fully comprehend the *Miranda* warnings
and their implications. Comprehension (or lack of it) was not related to the
children's amount of prior experience with the courts or police or to their race
or their socioeconomic status. The specific findings included the following:

- At least one of the four crucial elements of the *Miranda* warnings was inade-
  quately paraphrased by 55% of juveniles, as compared with 23% of adults.
- At least one of the six crucial vocabulary words was completely misunderstood
  by 64% of minors and 37% of adults.

- The majority of those juveniles below 15 years of age had significantly poorer comprehension of the significance or function of the warnings than did the adults.
- Prior court experience was not related to an understanding of the vocabulary and phrases in the warnings, but those juveniles with more court experience had a better appreciation of the significance of *Miranda* rights.

Grisso (1981) concluded that children and adolescents younger than 15 years of age do not understand all of their *Miranda* rights and that they therefore require assistance to waive these rights knowingly. He recommended a *per se* approach that would capitalize on at least one of four special protections: (a) using a simplified *Miranda* warning appropriate for juveniles, (b) requiring a preinterrogation screening of the juvenile to assess whether he or she comprehends the warnings adequately, (c) requiring the presence of an interested adult during the interrogation to advise the juvenile, and (d) requiring that an attorney for the juvenile be present during interrogation. Grisso favored the last alternative, suggesting that it was "probably . . . one of the most direct and effective remedies" (p. 200). Even for those juveniles beyond the age of 15 years, a *per se* approach may be justified because older juveniles also showed gaps in their understanding of the *Miranda* warnings.

To us, it seems counterrational to require assistance of counsel for adults during questioning but to deny children the same safeguard. Adults may waive that right. Rather than risk an invalid waiver—given an adolescent's genuine inability to appreciate the consequences of the waiver—being upheld, however, we believe that all juveniles are better served in the legal process by the presence, advice, and counsel of a skilled lawyer. If nothing else, the juvenile will experience and perhaps learn the importance of legal procedure and the value of due process and other constitutional protections.

Balancing Privileges and Realities

When working with a juvenile offender, the court must attempt to balance the privilege of preventing self-incrimination with the reality of the child's developmental status and the rehabilitation goals of the juvenile justice system. The *Fare v. Michael C.* (1979) decision stands as a precedent on whether an adolescent defendant is competent to waive his or her constitutional rights. In that case, the U.S. Supreme Court endorsed the "totality of circumstances" rationale when the legitimacy of a child's waiver of the Fifth

Amendment privilege is raised. The *totality of the circumstances approach* prevails in the vast majority of U.S. courts, but some states follow the *per se approach,* and jurisdictions are free to choose between these two approaches in evaluating juveniles' competence.

In the totality of the circumstances approach, the child's age, intelligence, physical condition, conduct, and prior experience in the courts, as well as the methods used by the police to interrogate the suspect and gain a waiver of rights, are used to determine the validity of the child's waiver of rights (*West v. United States,* 1968). In the "totality of circumstances," however, one does not read about the potential or realized impact on the child or adolescent of the police interrogation. Just as the social reformers of the 19th century decried the education of the innocent by the young felon in the almshouses where they lived together, should people today not be as concerned about the education given accused juveniles about the legitimacy of governmental power when that power has no regard for the accused's need for assistance—particularly assistance in the decision about self-incrimination? People do want accused youths to come clean, to confess wrongs, to endure the penalties, and to come back into society, willingly adopting its rules and moral code. When those who hold power in society show no respect for the spirit of the Bill of Rights, though, how can young offenders learn to respect it themselves? How can young offenders learn to come back into society, willingly adopting its rules and moral code?

In contrast, the *per se* approach makes the assumption that children and adolescents are limited in their understanding of criminal justice issues. The *per se* approach requires that young people be provided assistance from an interested adult to help them grasp the meaning of rights and the implications of waiving them. If such assistance is not given, the waiver would be judged incompetent, and any subsequent confession would be ruled inadmissible.

The more protective approach of the *per se* rule may have two or more versions: (a) requiring the presence of an "interested" adult who has some ongoing relationship of trust with the interrogated juvenile or who can develop that rapport quickly and (2) requiring a skilled lawyer to be present to advise the juvenile prior to and during the interrogation. Under each model, the supportive, advising adult would be free to intervene in the interrogation at a point he or she believes is necessary and to instruct the youth to invoke the Fifth Amendment privilege. This approach is consistent with the spirit of the U.N. Convention.

More likely than not, the lawyer to be called for this service would be one employed in public defense and fully able to advise his or her young client well. If the lawyer called is not so experienced, but rather is from the local *pro bono* list, the juvenile's interest may not be served at all if the lawyer believes that his or her task is to substitute his or her judgment for the child's or to be a parental disciplinary force in the child's life. In such instances, a lawyer may counsel a young client to cooperate without regard to any interests the client may possess in raising his or her constitutional rights, especially if that lawyer is inexperienced in criminal defense (see O'Connor, 1991, cited in Arcia, 1995). And, again, what does the youth learn when he or she sees "criminal justice" require a lawyer who does not know juvenile offender law to advise a youth about his or her rights to due process and liberty? Does the juvenile learn that the law does not value the youths of the society to which it claims to give order and liberty?

The Transfer to Adult Court

The Decision to Transfer

Waiver refers to the process of moving an accused youth from the juvenile court setting to the adult criminal court. Almost without exception, the waiver procedure is initiated by the prosecutor asking the juvenile court to transfer the case to the criminal court. The prosecutor typically succeeds in such an action when he or she can demonstrate that the juvenile is beyond the rehabilitative assistance of the juvenile court by virtue of the nature of the crime charged or the delinquency/criminal history of the accused.

Nebraska serves as an interesting, if singular, example of the reverse process—that is, of "waiver down" to juvenile court, as opposed to the more typical "waiver up" to adult court. In Nebraska, any juvenile charged with a certain crime or who is between the ages of 16 and 18 years bears the burden of proof to show that the case properly belongs before the juvenile court, as he or she will be charged criminally first and then moved to juvenile court on a charge of delinquency if successful at the waiver hearing (Neb. Rev. Stat., 1993).

The prosecutor's request to transfer the youth to adult court is based on an assessment of the type of treatment to which the juvenile is most amenable.

Box 9.1

Elements Considered in the Decision to Transfer
Youths From Juvenile to Adult (Criminal) Court

- Evidence that the offense was violent or premeditated
- The alleged motivation for the commission of the offense
- The age of the accused juvenile and the ages and circumstances of any others who might have been involved in the alleged offense
- Any previous history of juvenile offenses, antisocial behavior, or patterns of physical violence
- The accused juvenile's sophistication and maturity as they may be determined by his or her home life and school activities
- The accused juvenile's emotional attitude toward the alleged offense
- The accused juvenile's prior contacts with law enforcement agencies
- The competing requirements of the best interests of the accused juvenile and the security of the public
- The juvenile's desire to be treated as an adult

The request depends on variables. Usually, several variables are considered. Box 9.1 lists typical elements considered in the decision to transfer.

Of some note is the condition that is set by New Jersey to allow an accused juvenile to remain in the juvenile court process—namely, that the accused juvenile demonstrate that he or she will benefit from the juvenile court's aim of rehabilitation by the age of 19 years (*State of New Jersey in the Interest of S.M.,* 1986). Other states explicitly require only that the accused juvenile be able to benefit from the rehabilitative goal. The factors considered by the prosecutor and the court in making the decision to transfer are not well understood, however, and constitute a worthy issue for future research.

Given the number of factors considered by the prosecution in its decision to ask for a transfer to criminal court, it is not hard to see the difficulty confronting the juvenile in the waiver hearing. To go forward without representation for the juvenile seems to amount to an obvious win for even the minimally skilled prosecutor. In most instances, the juvenile may not return to the juvenile court for charges made after a conviction in criminal court, thus closing off the benefits of juvenile court forever. In addition, the twin goals of the criminal court—punishment and retribution—leave no room for reha-bilitation and treatment. Equally important, though, can be the full-scale (adult) constitutional rights accorded a defendant in criminal court.

Thus, it is not hard to see the need for legal representation for the juvenile facing such serious and complex issues. In *Kent v. United States* (1966), the right to counsel at waiver hearings was extended to juveniles—a major departure from the history of the juvenile court as a paternal incarnation of the state in the form of a judge who acted out of regard for the child's need to develop into a good citizen and without much regard for legal process that was due any adult in a similar (criminal court) circumstance. In *Kent,* the U.S. Supreme Court

> ruled that the child was entitled to legal representation at the waiver stage, an opportunity for a hearing prior to waiver, and access to records upon which the [c]ourt might decide to waive. Significantly the Court held that the child was entitled to these protections despite the fact that the case was civil in nature. The core concept in *Kent* is its rejection of an unfettered *parens patriae* approach to juvenile justice matters. (Dale, 1992, pp. 205-206)

Losses Experienced by the Accused Juvenile in Transfer

Transfer to adult court involves the loss for the accused juvenile of several key benefits, aside from the rehabilitative disposition of the court. For exam-ple, criminal court allows for no consideration of the juvenile's best interests. Another loss is the right not to be confined with adults. Once tried and convicted as an adult, the youth is subject to the punitive and retributive actions of the court, which may result in confinement with adults being similarly punished.

Thus, transfer to adult court violates the U.N. Convention. Article 3 generally requires that the state give serious consideration to the child's best interests. More specifically, Article 37 forbids the incarceration of juveniles with adults, and Article 40 is violated in any court result that does not accommodate the rehabilitative needs of the juvenile (Tinkler, 1992).

Recommendations

We believe that, at a minimum, no juvenile under any circumstance should be subjected to punishment and retribution to the exclusion of rehabilitation.

Regardless of the offense for which he or she is convicted, no juvenile should be denied rehabilitative services.

We further believe that no juvenile should be incarcerated with adult offenders; as the social welfare researchers learned in the 19th century, no good can come from imprisoning younger persons with those who are more criminally experienced and less caring and who can teach by example and by continuing offensive behavior. Such incarceration does nothing for the best interests of the young person, who by the U.N. Convention is entitled to have his or her best interests taken into account in all actions by the state.

Juvenile Crime and the Death Penalty

What are the rights of juveniles convicted of committing serious crimes? Should youths be subjected to the same range of penalties as adults—including execution? According to Davis (1997):

> The issue of capital punishment of juvenile offenders raises constitutional and moral questions of the profoundest order, mirroring in many respects the debate over capital punishment in general. At the same time, putting a teenager to death is viewed with a special significance, quite apart from the debate over the moral and constitutional validity of the death penalty generally. It has been viewed as a human rights violation under the terms of three major international agreements, to which the United States is a signatory, condemning execution of persons under the age eighteen [years]. It has been abolished by other nations that share our Anglo-American heritage and by leading nations of the western European community. It is opposed by the American Bar Association and the American Law Institute. It is banned by the statutory or decisional law of thirty-two states. (pp. 6-59 to 6-60)

The three international agreements referred to are (a) the International Covenant on Civil and Political Rights (1966), Article 6(5), which has been ratified by the United States; (b) the American Convention on Human Rights (1970), Article 4(5), signed but not ratified by the United States; and (c) the Geneva Convention Relative to the Protection of Civilian Persons in Time of War (August 12, 1949), Article 68 (ratified by the United States) (Davis, 1997, p. 5-59, footnote 201). Capital punishment of juveniles under the age of 18 years also violates Article 47 of the U.N. Convention on the Rights of the Child.

Table 9.2 Jurisdictions Banning the Death Penalty

Jurisdictions Banning the Death Penalty for All Persons as Provided by State Statute	Jurisdictions Banning the Death Penalty for Juveniles as Identified by State Statute
District of Columbia	Connecticut
Alaska	Georgia
Hawaii	Illinois
Iowa	Indiana
Maine	Kentucky
Massachusetts	Maryland
Michigan	Nebraska
Minnesota	Nevada
North Dakota	New Hampshire
Rhode Island	New Jersey
West Virginia	New Mexico
Wisconsin	North Carolina
	Ohio
	Oregon
	Tennessee
	Texas

SOURCE: Davis (1997, p. 6-60, footnote 205).

In fact, the number of jurisdictions banning the death penalty has declined since the publication of the case Davis cited—*Thompson v. Oklahoma* (1988, pp. 826, 829; footnotes 25 and 30 of the case). The remaining states banning capital punishment, and particularly for persons who were juveniles at the time of the offense for which they have been convicted, are noted in Table 9.2.

As Davis pointed out, though, one flaw in grouping states under the label "banning the death penalty for juveniles" is the varying ages at which states identify an offender as a juvenile. Most states use 18 years as the point at which teenagers become adults, some use 17 years, and others use 16 years (see Table 9.3).

The age of majority is significant because it is unlikely that a state legislature—which both permits the imposition of the death penalty and defines a juvenile as a person under 16 or 17 years—will exempt a person from the death penalty after a capital offense conviction when that person was over the legislated age of majority (but under 18 years of age) when the offense was found to have been committed. The U.S. Supreme Court, examining this

Table 9.3 Jurisdictional Age of the Juvenile Court

---

16 Years
   Connecticut, Nebraska,* New York, North Carolina, Vermont

17 Years
   Georgia, Illinois, Louisiana, Massachusetts, Michigan, Missouri, South Carolina, Texas

18 Years
   District of Columbia, Alabama, Alaska, Arizona, Arkansas, California, Colorado,
   Delaware, Florida, Hawaii, Idaho, Indiana, Iowa, Kansas, Kentucky, Maine, Maryland,
   Minnesota, Mississippi, Montana, Nevada, New Hampshire, New Jersey, New Mexico,
   North Dakota, Ohio, Oklahoma, Oregon, Pennsylvania, Rhode Island, South Dakota,
   Tennessee, Utah, Virginia, Washington State, West Virginia, Wisconsin, Wyoming

---

SOURCE: Davis (1997, p. 6-60 and Appendix B generally).
NOTE: *Nebraska law provides the juvenile court with jurisdiction for all those persons 16 years
and younger, although the age of majority is 19 years. Nebraska further provides for the waiver
from district court down to juvenile court for persons under 18 years of age.

issue in *Stanford v. Kentucky* (1989) and *Wilkins v. Missouri* (1989), found by
a 5-to-4 vote that requiring the death penalty for teenagers aged 16 years and
17 years was not unconstitutional, thus supporting those states that impose
death on teenagers who were between the ages of 16 and 18 years at the time
of their crimes. Specifically, the majority of the Court found that the Eighth
Amendment prohibition against cruel and unusual punishment was not violated in either case: Stanford was a 17-year-old at the time of his crime;
Wilkins was a 16-year-old. Kentucky's law allowed execution for convicted
teenagers who were 16 and older at the time of the crime; Missouri's law did
not set a minimum age for execution. Justice Brennan authored the dissent;
Justices Blackmun, Marshall, and Stevens concurred in his argument that any
imposition of the death penalty on a person who was not an adult at the time
of the crime (18 years or older) amounted to cruel and unusual punishment,
thus violating the constitutional provision prohibiting it (*Stanford v. Kentucky,*
1989; *Wilkins v. Missouri,* 1989, p. 382).

Davis (1997) suggested, as noted above, that the debate surrounding the
execution of adolescents between the age of 16 years and the commonly
accepted age of majority, 18 years, will continue "for some time to come"
(p. 6-69), reflecting the larger debate in U.S. society regarding the death
penalty generally. However, there is a difference of kind—and not just of
degree—between the execution of adults and adolescents that requires us to
resolve the issue of executing adolescents.

Leaving aside the issue of Article 68 of the 1949 Geneva Convention, a treaty that was ratified by the United States, we face the issue of the death penalty itself, framed by the Supreme Court as one based on "evolving standards of decency that mark the progress of a maturing society" (*Trop v. Dulles,* 1958, p. 101). Looking for signs of a maturing society, we see that every nation but two has signed and ratified the U.N. Convention on the Rights of the Child, which by its Article 47 outlaws the execution of persons under 18 years. Of course, the two in noncompliance are remarkably dissimilar. Somalia has no government at this time that could serve as a ratifying force for a Somali representative's signature to the Convention. The other, the United States, has not ratified the Convention despite the existence of a stable government body, the U.S. Senate, authorized to ratify treaties.

The United States has recognized itself, in the words of its high court, as a society in progress. But unlike other entities that seek objective standards for measuring its progress, the United States looks to itself for measures of its maturing process while it is surrounded by nations by which it might accurately appraise itself. Should it do so, the United States must find itself quite lacking in maturity and quite slow in its evolution toward its maturity. For example, the United States might acknowledge that its neighbors around the globe have declared the execution of persons below the age of 18 years, an accepted date of adulthood, to be unlawful.

Chief Justice Warren's words in 1958 were written in a very different society—one of state government apartheid, one where the oppression of minorities was accepted and the repression of women was the norm. In his time, Chief Justice Warren led the U.S. Supreme Court to many moral victories; some of its finest were for children: *Brown v. the Board of Education* (1954 and 1955), *Kent v. United States* (1966), *In re Gault* (1967).

With an increasingly conservative Court, it seems unlikely that such moral victories will soon be realized again: The Court's willingness to understand the impact of the laws of the several states and of its own decisions on the lives of young people seems to recede with each appointee. Most notably, Justice Scalia's dissent in *Thompson v. Oklahoma* (1988) appears to be the uncompromising foundation on which the conservative Court is building its interpretation of the Constitution. In his dissent, Justice Scalia was unwilling to recognize any limitation in age on the imposition of the death penalty other than that found at common law: Criminal responsibility under the common law began at the so-called age of reason, 7 years. Below 7 years of age, there was no criminal responsibility; hence, there could be no imposition of criminal penalties (e.g., execution) under the law (Davis, 1997).

Justice Scalia's assertion in *Thompson v. Oklahoma* (1988) was that no national consensus against the death penalty for persons younger than 16 years existed. That view was reflected in the majority opinion in *Stanford v. Kentucky* (1989) and *Wilkins v. Missouri* (1989), just 1 year after *Thompson* (Davis, 1997). Thus, Kentucky, a state with an explicit provision for the execution of 16-year-old juveniles, provided support for Scalia's view that no national consensus against the death penalty for juveniles exists. Without a national consensus against it, Scalia found that execution of juveniles could not be cruel and unusual. If U.S. society does consider the execution of a child under the age of 16 years to be acceptable, then surely evolution of the United States will be the slowest maturation process imaginable.

Children as Legal Witnesses

Introducing children into the criminal justice system as key witnesses n criminal and civil procedures has been fraught with difficulties because that system was designed for adults. In cases involving children as witnesses, legal procedures must be examined in the light of balancing three important objectives: "(a) protecting children from traumatization, (b) protecting defendants from false charges, and (c) protecting defendants' constitutional rights" (Perry & Wrightsman, 1991, pp. 134-135). Perry and Wrightsman (1991) noted:

> In this process, courts have been required to tackle a number of questions: Who has the right to be present at the proceedings, to observe the witnesses, and to hear the testimony offered? How should child witnesses be questioned under both direct and cross-examination? What are the parameters of confrontation in cases involving children as witnesses? What forms of confrontation are legally acceptable, and how vigorous may the confrontation be? What specific procedures should the court allow to protect those most likely to be harmed by the experience of testifying—the child witness? (p. 133)

In attempting to address these issues, many courts have instituted innovative procedures to protect children from undue traumatization—that is, to protect their nurturance rights. For example, courts have used child-size witness chairs, permitted children to testify while sitting on the floor, used dolls or drawings to supplement or supplant the child's oral testimony, permitted exceptions to the hearsay rule, used a screen to shield the child witness from the defendant, and permitted the child to testify via videotape or closed circuit television.

Some of those innovations have withstood judicial scrutiny; others have not. In this regard, Perry and Wrightsman (1991) concluded:

> Courts generally have been sympathetic to courtroom and procedural changes that make the experience of testifying less traumatic for children, so long as defendants' constitutional rights are not unduly compromised in the process. Recent decisions by the Supreme Court suggest that the essence of the right to confrontation must be maintained, including physical presence of the child, administration of the oath, cross-examination by defense counsel, and observation of the child's demeanor by the trier of fact. Moreover, the Court has stated clearly that there must be an individualized finding of need when alteration of standard procedures is requested. (p. 173)

For example, in *Coy v. Iowa* (1988), the U.S. Supreme Court ruled that placing a barrier (a semitransparent screen) between defendant and accuser directly defied the Sixth Amendment confrontation clause of the Constitution. That decision was consistent with other rulings, spanning nearly a century, rejecting prosecutors' attempts to shield alleged victims from defendants at trial.

Two years later, however, in *Maryland v. Craig* (1990), the Court ruled that *in camera* testimony, broadcast via videotape to the courtroom where the trial is occurring, is permissible when it has been demonstrated to the court that the particular child witness would be unduly traumatized by giving testimony publicly. The Court held that the Constitution allows for exceptions to potentially traumatic confrontations when competing interests of the state are overriding. It is important to note that, in *Craig,* the reliability of child witness testimony was ensured by maintaining the essential elements of physical presence of the child in the courthouse, administration of the oath to the child witness, cross-examination of the child by defense counsel, and observation of the child witness' demeanor by the trier of fact. Although the child could not see the defendant (Craig), Sandra Craig could see the child and remained in electronic communication with her attorney. Objections could be made and ruled on as if the witness were in the courtroom. Thus, two elements—retaining the essence of the right to confrontation and individualized findings of traumatization—distinguished *Craig* from *Coy.* Perry and Wrightsman (1991) concluded that "[t]hese two elements are essential to withstanding judicial scrutiny in child witness cases that involve nonstandard procedures" (pp. 167-168). We believe that this approach is sound.

Recommendations Regarding the Rights of Children in the Juvenile Justice System

Article 40 of the U.N. Convention clearly states that accused children have a right to be treated with dignity. The article requires that every accused child be informed promptly of the charges, be presumed innocent until proved guilty in a prompt and fair trial, receives legal assistance, and not be compelled to give testimony or to confess guilt. We believe that, to meet these requirements, all children who have been accused of serious crimes should be provided meaningful assistance of counsel from an attorney trained in juvenile law.

In addition, we strongly recommend that the several states of the United States, in accordance with the U.N. Convention, reconsider their rules regarding the waiver of juvenile court process for accused juveniles; specifically, we urge the states to disallow any waiver to adult court (and for Nebraska, charging in adult court) unless such waiver is requested by the competent juvenile after the advice of skilled legal counsel. By virtue of their youth alone, juveniles under the age of majority require us to consider their rehabilitation, best interests, and education within the "jailhouse" in all we do to prevent the risk of reoffending and reinjuring the society in which juveniles themselves have a crucial interest.

Moreover, the U.N. Convention provides evidence that a global consensus exists regarding prohibition against execution of juveniles—that is, persons under 18 years of age. Surely, the United States, composed of peoples from around the globe, should demonstrate no less maturity than those nations from which its people have come. Therefore, we recommend that the United States ratify the U.N. Convention with its important prohibition against the execution of juveniles. Having agreed to abide by Article 68 of the Geneva Convention Relative to the Protection of Civilian Persons in Time of War, the United States has committed itself already to the evolutionary process identified by Chief Justice Warren in *Trop v. Dulles* (1958). It is time for the country to take the next step.

Notes

1. From "With Juvenile Courts in Chaos, Critics Propose Their Demise," by F. Butterfield, July 21, 1997, *New York Times,* p. A13. Copyright © 1997 by The New York Times Co. Reprinted by permission.

2. From "With Juvenile Courts in Chaos, Critics Propose Their Demise," by F. Butterfield, July 21, 1997, *New York Times,* p. A13. Copyright © 1997 by The New York Times Co. Reprinted by permission.

10

Working It Out

The Rights of Children in Employment

> Oppressive child labor is a problem that, having been ignored
> and denied, has grown at an astonishing rate. Through a
> combination of lax enforcement, underfunding, societal apathy,
> and an influx of immigration, child labor abuse is as bad—
> and in some areas, worse—than it was in the 1920s.
>
> Michael A. Pignatella, Law Journal Editor (1995)

When Charles Dickens wrote the novel *Little Dorrit* in 1857, his goal
was to dramatize the horrors and injustices of child labor in England
at that time. In the 19th century and the early part of the 20th century, U.S.
employers seeking to cut their costs took advantage of young workers desperate for money, often replicating the conditions described by Dickens. One
writer provided the following description of children working in the United
States in 1842:

> Chained, belted, harnessed like dogs in a go-cart, black, saturated with wet
> and more than half-naked—crawling upon their hands and feet, and dragging
> their heavy loads behind them—they present an appearance undescribably
> disgusting and unnatural. (author unknown, quoted in deMause, 1975)

In those days, restrictions against the use of children as workers were virtually
nonexistent.

216

How much have matters changed in more recent times? Certainly, advances have been made in the treatment of child workers in the United States, but the improvements have not been as great as might be expected. Pignatella (1995) commented:

> Despite anti-child labor legislation by Congress and affirmation of that legislation by the Supreme Court, child labor abuse is flourishing on farms [which generally are exempt from child labor laws] and in the garment districts, grocery stores, and restaurants of the United States—injuring and killing children, and locking them into a lifelong cycle of poverty. (p. 171)

Nature and Scope of the Problem Today

Facts from a report written by the National Safe Workplace Institute, an independent group that monitors workplace safety, support Pignatella's claim. The Institute reported that, of the 5.5 million workers in the United States age 12 to 17 years, more than 70,000 had been hurt and 300 killed during 1 year as a result of their jobs (as cited in Pignatella, 1995, p. 172). The report was particularly critical of the restaurant industry, noting that approximately 20,000 children are injured annually in that industry—primarily in fast-food restaurants—as a result of slips and falls, cuts, burns, electrical shocks, vehicle accidents, heavy lifting, chemical exposure, and loss of sleep.

The National Safe Workplace Institute report echoed earlier federal reports that uncovered thousands of violations every year. In 1990, for example, the U.S. Department of Labor conducted a series of four unannounced 3-day child labor "sweeps" known as Operation Child Watch. In that initiative, 500 investigators launched more than 9,500 child labor investigations. They discovered more than 29,000 child labor violations and cited approximately 41% of the businesses investigated for violations of child labor laws (Lantos, 1992). Deviations from the hours limitation for 14- and 15-year-olds were the most common of the various irregularities reported. But one sixth of the reported violations involved children *under* age 14. "Unfortunately," commented Pignatella (1995), "aside from these sweeps, it was business as usual at the Department of Labor, with only 13,000 or so violations reported for the remainder of the year" (p. 201).

The General Accounting Office (GAO) provided even more staggering data (Pignatella, 1995). During 1988, the GAO conservatively estimated that about 18% of all employed 15-year-olds—166,000 of them—were working in violation of federal child labor laws. This number is more than 10 times higher than the approximately 14,000 children the Department of Labor found to be illegally employed in that year.

According to the American News Service (1997), government statistics show that 210,000 teens are hurt on the job each year, with one third of them needing emergency medical care. "Every week, at least one teen-ager on average dies as a result of a work-related injury."[1]

These troubling statistics raise some difficult questions: What rights do children have to engage in or refuse employment? What rights do children have when deciding how much work they choose to do or how much they are required to do? What rights do they have to choose the conditions under which they will work, the tasks they will perform, or the compensation they will receive? And at what age should children be permitted to work?

Article 32 of the U.N. Convention on the Rights of the Child (1989) speaks directly to those questions. The article gives children the right to be protected from economic exploitation and from engaging in work that constitutes a threat to health, education, and development. It further directs the state to set minimum ages for employment, to regulate conditions of employment, and to provide sanctions for effective enforcement. Article 31 is relevant as well, as it ensures children the right to leisure, play, and participation in cultural and artistic activities—pursuits that may be precluded by children's work.

Children Who Work:
Answers to Some Important Questions

Is Work Good or Bad for Children?

The place of work in the lives of children is a two-edged sword. Work can be good if it protects children from harm, helps them develop useful skills, and fosters positive relations with adult role models. When it exploits children, prevents them from being involved in making decisions that affect them, or hinders them from developing useful skills, work's positive values are lost.

Positive Effects of Children Working

Some individuals argue that work is good for children, not just because of the financial benefits, but because of work's contributions to the development of responsibility and self-esteem. Senator Charles S. Thomas unabashedly espoused this view during the 1920s:

> The real problem in America is not child labor, but child idleness. You cannot convince me that it hurts a child either physically or morally to make him work. Where one child, in my experience, has been injured from work, ten thousand have gone to the devil because of lack of occupation. (as cited in Pignatella, 1995, p. 199)

According to this view, children who want to work should be encouraged to do so (Lumpkin & Douglas, 1937)—and even children who do not want to work may be required to do so.

According to John Croyle, author of *Bringing Out the Winner in Your Child,* self-esteem "skyrockets" when children start earning and saving their own money (as cited in Johnson, 1997). According to an article in the July 20, 1997, edition of the *Omaha World Herald,* Barbara McLaughlin—mother of three children (Kyle, age 11; Brett, age 10; and Jessie, age 7) and supervisor of the children's company, "KBJ All the Way Lawn Maintenance Co."—agrees: "It teaches them how to be responsible," she said. Her son Kyle noted, "We pay half to the bank each Saturday and give 10 percent to the church."[2]

In their survey of 4,000 15- to 18-year-olds, Steinberg and Dornbusch (1991) reported positive effects of work, including the accumulation of practical knowledge about the business world and the development of personal (but not social) responsibility. Steinberg, Greenberger, Garduque, Ruggiero, and Vaux (1982) reported an increase in autonomy associated with work, at least for girls. According to D'Amico (1984), fewer work hours (but some) lead to increased rates of completing high school, although very extensive work involvement leads to a greater dropout rate from school. Thus, work can provide important benefits and foster positive outcomes for children. For these reasons—among others—many adults favor permitting children to work.

Negative Effects of Children Working

The nature of some positive outcomes and benefits of child labor has been questioned by researchers in the field. Greenberger and Steinberg (1986) noted:

> The kind of responsibility that working adolescents seem to be developing has a somewhat egocentric flavor. They obtain jobs more to earn spending

money than to gain experience or to explore an area of work that might interest
them in the future. They view themselves as good workers, and they get to
work dependably . . . and do what is required of them—but seldom more.
They control a substantial amount of money, but they spend it largely on
themselves to support a higher level of consumption than their parents would,
or could, provide. (p. 106)

In this regard, Giampetro-Meyer and Brown (1992) noted that "children
who work extensive hours to purchase luxury items are hurting themselves
and society by spending less time on school work and demonstrating an
insatiable desire for money and the goods money provides" (p. 548). Furthermore, these authors expressed the view that current laws and regulations are
oblivious to the problems created by teen consumption. They also acknowledged that society is not as concerned by this issue, commenting "[T]he
picture of the child laborer as a spoiled, self-centered teenager does not trigger
the same emotions as the picture of the child laborer as a poor, overworked
waif" (Giampetro-Meyer & Brown, 1992, pp. 549-550). They also noted that
the type of work that children primarily do today (e.g., working in fast-food
restaurants) does not prepare them for their future careers, a fact that appears
not to concern most adults. Instead, parents are eager to encourage such work
for their children to accommodate the children's luxury spending (p. 554).

Those who generally oppose children's work also express concerns that
work interferes with children's education (cf. Greenberger, 1983). Studies
performed in the 1980s (reviewed by Steinberg & Dornbusch, 1991) concluded that students who work extensive hours (more than 15 or 20 per week
during the school year) were less involved in school and earned poorer grades.
They also used significantly more drugs and alcohol, were more distant from
their parents, and had more cynical attitudes toward work than students who
worked less than 15 or 20 hours per week (Steinberg & Dornbusch, 1991).
Similarly, a study by the state of Washington, published in 1992 (as cited in
Pignatella, 1995), concluded that students who worked more than 20 hours
per week during the school year were at risk of failing the most rudimentary
levels of English, mathematics, and reading.

In their survey of 15- to 18-year-olds, Steinberg and Dornbusch (1991)
concluded that the negative correlates of school-year employment—lowered
academic performance, greater psychological maladjustment, increased drug
and alcohol use, premature autonomy from parents, and delinquency—were
closely linked with the number of hours worked per week. Moreover, studies
show that intensive employment during the 10th and 11th grades is associated

with higher dropout rates. A 1980 study conducted by Ohio State University, for example, revealed that approximately 15% of male high school dropouts reported they had left school because they "chose to work" or "were offered a good job" (Pignatella, 1995). Interestingly, the United States is unique among industrialized nations in the percentage of teens who work. In the United States, more than two thirds of teenagers work, whereas in Japan that figure is only 2% (Pignatella, 1995).

The negative effects of children's work on educational outcomes are very worrisome. The research described clearly indicates that working several hours per week—certainly more than 20—is associated with a variety of significant negative outcomes and thus tends to violate the intent of Article 32 of the U.N. Convention. Because of their negative consequences, such long work hours therefore should be prohibited for youths in school or of school age.

Although the number of work hours certainly is of concern, working conditions are even more troublesome. Society expects children to be protected in the workplace from hazards that threaten their lives, limbs, and well-being (Coens, 1982). But, as Box 10.1 illustrates, children in contemporary society continue to be placed in work environments that can lead to adverse—and even life-threatening—consequences.

Which Industries Are the Worst Offenders of Child Labor Laws?

Pignatella (1995) noted that four areas of industry seem to be most egregious in their violations of child labor law: (a) the garment industry, (b) agricultural occupations (particularly migrant farm work), (c) fast-food and grocery industries, and—surprisingly—(d) door-to-door candy selling. Interestingly, farm work, once generally considered to be a wholesome and worthwhile occupation for children, now is known to be the most lethal employment situation for children. Pignatella (1995) noted:

> Whereas the family farm once may have been a good place to raise a child, today it is unfortunately frequently an equally good place for a child to be maimed or killed. . . . Although estimates vary widely, between one and two million children labor in the fields of this country. They begin work before dawn, and finish after dusk. They spend their days stooped in fields, with little time off to rest. They miss school. They are sprayed with pesticides. In general, theirs is a life of misery. (p. 190)

Box 10.1

The Risks of Work

In July 1982, while participating in a movie filming, a helicopter lost power and plunged into the Santa Clara River. The helicopter's rotors struck and killed three actors in the movie. One was an adult, Victor Morrow; the other two were children, ages 6 and 7. The accident occurred at 2:30 a.m. Questions were immediately raised: Should the children have been working during a predawn filming session? Should the children have been working under such potentially hazardous conditions?

Further investigation revealed that the director of the film had misled the children's parents about the potential dangers to them and had failed to obtain the work permits required when children were hired as actors. The director, John Landis, was brought to trial; he was charged with 15 counts of criminal negligence with respect to his handling of the matter, but a jury found him not guilty on all counts, apparently concluding that Landis was genuinely unaware of (and therefore not responsible for) the dangers.

SOURCE: Farber and Green (1988).

Similarly, in the food industry:

> America's children are . . . illegally employed, in dangerous occupations, risking everything from simple exhaustion to death and dismemberment, while the restaurant industry justifies its practices with claims that "it's not like . . . [child employees] need to get home and bring the cows in anymore." (p. 194)

Oddly, one high-risk industry for children is door-to-door candy sales. Pignatella (1995) suggested that candy selling today is a scam bearing little resemblance to the childhood experience many of us remember of selling candy bars to neighbors to assist our sports clubs and youth groups:

> Instead, small fly-by-night operations recruit inner-city children, some as young as seven, to sell door-to-door for them. The children are taken into suburbs after school, usually in vans in which it is not uncommon for drugs and alcohol to be used. The children begin to work immediately after school, often until as late as 10:00 p.m. on weekdays and midnight on weekends. In addition, the children often wait hours to be picked up by the vans, if they get picked up at all. (pp. 194-195)

Such child labor violations are appalling and obviously violate Article 32 of the U.N. Convention. (See Box 10.2 for examples of abuses that abound in the four highest-risk industries named by Pignatella [1995].)

Employers have come under increasing attack in the past few years as reports of abusive child labor practices in those industries have escalated. One campaign that attracted national attention targeted popular entertainer and talk show hostess Kathie Lee Gifford, as described in Box 10.3.

Children's Wages: Who Owns Them?

When a child or adolescent works and is paid for the work, do the wages become his or her property? One version of a "Bill of Rights" for children has unequivocally answered yes; "A child has a moral right and should have a legal right to earn and keep his (or her) own earnings" (as cited in McGovern, 1983, p. 301). But the law does not always agree; the conflict between children's rights and parents' rights surfaces again.

In most cases, common law pertains in this area. When a child still is under parental "control," the parents have the right to the child's wages. In some jurisdictions, however, statutes state that unless the parent or parents give notice to the employer that they are to receive the minor's wages, those wages go to the child and become the property of the child. Furthermore, children may make an agreement with their parents that the money they earn is to be their own; this "partial emancipation" of the child does not affect other aspects of the parent-child relationship. Also, some states permit child "prodigies" and children who earn substantial amounts as entertainers or models to keep their earnings in a special fund until they reach the age of maturity (Sussman, 1977).

As consideration of the questions in this section has revealed, the rights of children, their parents, and the state all must be balanced when children are employed. Consequently, both the individual states and the federal government have enacted legislation that attempts to provide guidance in the area of child labor.

Development of Child Labor Laws

Early (But Unsuccessful) Efforts

The current regulations regarding child labor evolved in response to the sweatshop conditions and exploitation of children that characterized the

---

Box 10.2

Child Labor Abuses in Four Major Industries:
Some Alarming Facts

Garment Industry

- In New York City alone, approximately 1,500 garment sweatshops are illegally employing approximately 7,000 children, some as young as 8 years old.

- A 1991 sting operation in San Francisco found 70 of 200 garment factories to be in violation of child labor laws, providing no heat or air conditioning, providing no fire safety equipment or exits, and requiring long hours at subminimum pay.

- In New York City, a 15-year-old immigrant boy worked at a table sewing pleats into cheap white chiffon skirts for $1 per hour; the temperature in the room was 8° Fahrenheit.

Agriculture

- The death rate for child laborers on farms is the highest for any occupation in the nation: More than 300 children under the age of 16 are killed on farms each year, and more than 23,500 are injured.

- The Food and Drug Administration (FDA) estimates that more than 1,000 deaths and 9,000 injuries occur annually because of pesticides, yet children as young as 12 are allowed to work on farms that regularly use these toxins.

- The school dropout rate among migrant farm children is about 80% in Florida and 90% in Texas.

- Twelve-year-old Shaun Petersen climbed into a cement silo to help his father finish the day's chores using a sweep auger. Minutes later, the powerful screwlike device sliced through and crushed his arms, chest, and leg. An hour

---

United States especially during the first quarter of the 20th century (Coens, 1982)—conditions disturbingly depicted in Dickens's *Little Dorrit* (1857). Prior to the advent of factory work, children mostly worked on nearby farms or in jobs in close association with their parents. They were socialized to work responsibly; close supervision was part of the nature of such work. Children worked long hours, but few people thought they were placed in jeopardy (Giampetro-Meyer & Brown, 1992), although recent statistics regarding children laboring on today's mechanized farms bespeak a different reality for children (see Box 10.2).

later, he died, his body so shattered that the attending physician recalled struggling to find a single unruptured vein in which to insert an intravenous line.

Food Industries

- Late in 1992, Burger King—while denying any wrongdoing—agreed to pay $500,000 to the U.S. Department of Labor to settle claims that it had been requiring minors to work longer hours than legally allowed, 2 years after the restaurant chain had stopped employing 14- and 15-year-olds.

- On July 28, 1993, the A&P grocery stores paid $490,000 in fines for more than 900 child labor violations, including employing 14- and 15-year-olds for excessive hours per week and during prohibited times, as well as allowing children under the age of 18 to use equipment deemed hazardous by the Department of Labor.

- On August 3, 1993, Food Lion, Inc., a southern grocery store chain, paid a settlement sum of $16.2 million, $1 million of which was for child labor violations.

- Jennifer Forshee, age 15, cut off the top of her right middle finger while illegally using a power slicing machine.

- In Exeter, New Hampshire, 15-year-old Justin Lowell split his hand while attempting to cut 54 blocks of cheese in 20 minutes while illegally using a power slicer.

- Bobby Lee Cantley, age 15, slipped on the floor at a beef processing plant in Cincinnati and fell into the meat grinder. It cut off his arm.

Door-to-Door Candy Selling

- In Washington, an 11-year-old girl was killed by a car at 10:00 p.m. on a school night while she was selling candy to raise money—160 miles from her home.

The 19th century's shift to factory work brought not only oppressive conditions but also work that gave children little contact with adults who could provide mentoring. The U.S. Department of Labor described one example of working conditions in a glass factory circa 1910:

Into the work of the snapping-up boy there enters the hardship of looking into the bright glaring light of the glory-hold. . . . Not only is constant walking necessary, but also constant arm movement, some bending, and in general, an incessant activity of the whole body. . . . In a Pennsylvania establishment, where the temperature on the outside was 88 degrees, the temperature at the

---

Box 10.3

The Kathie Lee Gifford Story

The devotion of entertainer and talk show hostess Kathie Lee Gifford to needy children has been well publicized. She has donated large sums of money to programs that help children, established two centers that assist children, and developed her own line of clothes at Wal-Mart—with proceeds to benefit children in need.

But in April 1996, Kathie Lee and her clothing line came under attack for alleged child labor abuses. It was charged that Honduran children were producing her clothing line and earning about 31 cents an hour. Then, in New York City, a reporter discovered that "Kathie Lee" blouses were being made in a local sweatshop where workers had not been paid for a period of time.

After being informed of the abuses, Kathie Lee and husband Frank Gifford gave $300 to each blouse laborer they could locate in New York City. Then they joined New York's governor and the U.S. Secretary of Labor to press for reforms to protect garment workers and to abolish sweatshops. She said:

> I don't want my name attached to anything that involves the exploitation of any worker, child or not. But I'm now convinced that withdrawing won't solve anything except possibly getting me off the burner. I'm in a very unique and privileged position to be able to change things. I'm going to stay with the clothing line as long as I can feel like we're changing laws, making people aware, and making things that were wrong, right. (cited in Hanover, 1996, p. 68)

Although Kathie Lee Gifford took strong, positive steps to curb the abuses that had been discovered, the personal hurt she felt remained:

> When I first heard that children were being exploited making my clothes, it was like a kick in the gut. But the most painful moment came that night at home when the news shows were on. Cody [her son] came up to me and said, "Mommy, why are they saying that you're such a bad lady?" That devastated me. I've spent every day since he was born teaching him how to live his life, trying to be a role model for him. I know I'm not perfect. But it hit me hard. He said, "Mommy, just take everybody to Cody House, let them see. Then they'll know that you love children." That's when I cried. And that's when I got angry. (p. 68)

---

point where the snap-up rubs off the excess glass was 100 degrees; in front of the glory-hold, it was 140 degrees. . . . The speed rate of the snapping-up boy is fixed by the output of the shop, and in case of such small objects as one ounce and under he must work with great rapidity. (as cited in Giampetro-Meyer & Brown, 1992, p. 551)

As early as 1872, the Prohibition Party—whose *raison d'être* was the abolition of alcoholic beverages—included in its platform a clause condemning oppressive child labor (Trattner, 1970). Five years later, the American Federation of Labor (AFL) proposed a constitutional amendment that would have empowered the federal government to regulate child labor; that attempt was unsuccessful (Trattner, 1970).

The first effort to restrain such abuses was a series of statutes passed by state legislatures; even by the end of the first decade of the 20th century, most states had restrictions on the employment of children, although many of those laws were narrowly drawn and riddled with loopholes. Progress during the next few decades was erratic.

Federal Efforts

The federal government took over when Congress passed the Keating-Owen Act of 1916, banning certain types of child labor. But 2 years later, in the *Hammer v. Dagenhart* (1918) decision, the U.S. Supreme Court nullified the act, concluding that Congress had exceeded its authority to regulate interstate commerce. In 1919, Congress passed a law (the Child Labor Tax Act of 1919) that put an excise tax on any goods manufactured with child labor, but 3 years later the Supreme Court found this law to be an unconstitutional intrusion on states' rights (*Bailey v. Drexel Furniture Co.,* 1922). Thus, in the early part of the 20th century, no clear direction emerged regarding child labor.

A later approach by Congress, in 1924, was the proposal of a constitutional amendment to establish the protection of child labor. Despite widespread popular approval, however, only 20 of the required 36 states approved the proposal. Later, as a result of the economic depression in the 1930s—recognizing the need to protect adult workers from lower-waged child labor—Congress again adopted restrictions on children's work as part of the National Industrial Recovery Act (1933). Again, however, the Supreme Court intervened. In a highly unpopular decision, *Schechter Poultry Corporation v. United States* (1935), the Court ruled that Congress had again exceeded its authority to regulate business within a state's borders.

The first real federal-level breakthrough was passage of the Fair Labor Standards Act (FLSA) in 1938, including child labor protections among the multitude of wage and hour provisions. "The FLSA was broad in scope, addressing minimum wages, maximum hours, overtime pay, and oppressive child labor" (Pignatella, 1995, p. 175). Finally, children were protected by the law's prohibition against manufacturers, producers, and dealers shipping goods that were the product of "oppressive" child labor (see Box 10.4).

Three years later, the newly reconstituted Supreme Court, in *United States v. F.W. Darby Lumber Co.* (1941), expressly overruled *Hammer v. Dagenhart* and decided that the FLSA was a valid exercise of Congress's authority to regulate commerce. With several major amendments since 1949 (see Box 10.5), Congress extended child labor protection to the majority of the U.S. workforce, to virtually every employer except for certain small "mom and pop" operations.

Today, the FLSA, as amended, establishes a basic minimum age of 16 years for employment in the United States. The act defines as hazardous all those activities associated with mining, roofing, and excavation; in other jobs, more specific activities—such as use of power saws and metal presses—are prohibited.

The act provides exceptions for the minimum working age: 14- and 15-year-olds may be employed in a variety of occupations, particularly in retail work and service jobs, but they are not allowed in construction, laundry work, and work involving machinery or hazardous materials. Specific exemptions permit children of any age to deliver newspapers, to serve as baby-sitters or golf caddies, and to be employed as actors and performers. Work on a farm receives even more extended exemptions: Children at the ages of 12 and 13 are allowed to perform nonhazardous work on any farm outside school hours, provided they have parental consent or their parents are working on the same farm. But children under age 12 may be employed only on their parents' farm or, with their parents' consent, on small farms not covered by the FLSA. In addition, 10- and 11-year-olds may work as local "harvest laborers" during the urgent need for harvesting short-season crops such as strawberries in Washington and Oregon and potatoes in Maine.

States' Efforts

Regulation of child labor occurs not just at the federal level, but at the state level, too. Today, all 50 states and the District of Columbia enforce child

Box 10.4

The Fair Labor Standards Act of 1938

The principal federal law governing the employment of children is found within the Fair Labor Standards Act. Section 212 of the act, as amended, provides:

(a) No producer, manufacturer, or dealer shall ship or deliver for shipment in commerce any goods produced in an establishment situated in the United States in or about which within 30 days prior to the removal of such goods therefrom any oppressive child labor has been employed. . . .

(b) No employer shall employ any oppressive child labor in commerce or in the production of goods for commerce or any enterprise engaged in commerce or in the production of goods for commerce.

Oppressive child labor is defined in the act as follows:

"Oppressive child labor" means a condition of employment under which (1) any employee under the age of sixteen years is employed by an employer (other than a parent or a person standing in place of a parent employing his own child or a child in his custody under the age of sixteen years in an occupation other than manufacturing or mining or an occupation found by the Secretary of Labor to be particularly hazardous for the employment of children between the ages of sixteen and eighteen years or detrimental to their health or well-being) in any occupation, or (2) any employee between the ages of sixteen and eighteen years is employed by an employer in any occupation which the Secretary of Labor shall find and by order declare to be particularly hazardous for the employment of children between such ages or detrimental to their health or well-being; but oppressive child labor shall not be deemed to exist by virtue of the employment in any occupation of any person with respect to whom the employer shall have on file an unexpired certificate issued and held pursuant to regulations of the Secretary of Labor certifying that such person is above the oppressive child-labor age.

The act further provides:

The Secretary of Labor shall provide by regulation or by order that the employment of employees between the ages of fourteen and sixteen years in occupations other than manufacturing and mining shall not be deemed to constitute oppressive child labor if and to the extent that the Secretary of Labor determines that such employment is confined to periods which will not interfere with their schooling and to conditions which will not interfere with their health and well-being.

Box 10.5

Amendments to the Fair Labor Standards Act of 1938

1949: Amendments altered almost every provision of the original legislation, giving the child labor provisions of the FLSA the general structure they possess today, including:

- a change in the definition of the term *oppressive child labor* such that it became more inclusive
- prohibition against the use of oppressive child labor both in commerce and in the production of goods for commerce
- a change in the child labor exemption used in agriculture such that it applied only 'outside of school hours for the school district where such employee is living while he is so employed'
- expansion of the exemption for actors and performers in motion pictures and theatrical performances to include child performers in radio and television
- exemption for any employee engaged in the home delivery of newspapers

1961: Extended the protection of the child labor provisions to retail establishments, the construction industry, and gas stations—but curiously exempted from minimum wage, maximum hours, and child labor provisions 'any homeworker engaged in the making of wreaths composed principally of natural holly, pine, cedar, or other evergreens.'

1966: Prohibited the employment of children under age 16 in agricultural occupations that the secretary of labor finds to be particularly hazardous, although the provision does not protect children employed on family farms.

1974: Substantially limited the use of child labor in agriculture, barring children under the age of 12 from working on any but family farms; children ages 12 to 14 were permitted employment on farms other than family farms, but only if their parents work on the same farm. Also established a civil penalty of up to $1,000 for any violation of the child labor provisions of the FLSA.

1990: The Omnibus Budget Reconciliation Act of 1990 raised the civil penalty provisions of the FLSA from a ceiling of $1,000 to a floor of $1,000 and a ceiling of $10,000 per violation. It also provided for penalties to be deposited in the general treasury, as opposed to being applied to the Department of Labor's Wages and Hours Division (which investigates child labor violations).

1996: The Minimum Wage Increase Act of 1996 set the minimum wage for all employees (including children) at not less than $5.15 per hour beginning September 1, 1997.

labor standards (McGovern, 1983), and some have even more stringent provisions than the federal law.

For example, several states limit 16- and 17-year-olds to 30 hours per week, thus establishing more restrictive rules than the federal regulations. In 1991, the New York legislature went even further when it reduced the limit on the school-year work week for 16- and 17-year-olds from 48 hours to 28 hours (Brown, 1997). In addition, New York prohibits 16- and 17-year-olds from working after 10 p.m. on school nights unless they have written permission from school officials and their parents (Brown, 1997). Washington State proposed changes in its regulations to restrict youths ages 16 and 17 to a 20-hour work week (rather than 40 hours) during the school year and to restrict 14- and 15-year-olds to 15 hours per week (rather than 18) ("Legislature 1997," 1997). In 1991, the New Hampshire legislature amended its Youth Employment Law to require a student to show a satisfactory level of school achievement before she or he could be issued a work certificate. Indiana, Ohio, Florida, and Hawaii are among the states in the 1990s that have been reconsidering their child labor laws in order to make a commitment to quality education. Some observers still see the general state of things, though, as reflecting a "dearth of restrictions on 16 and 17 year-old workers" (Giampetro-Meyer & Brown, 1992, p. 563).

Thus, some states are more restrictive than the federal standards; some less. Currently, federal regulations place no limits on how many hours 16- and 17-year-olds can work, but they do restrict 14- and 15-year-olds to 18-hour work weeks during the school year ("What the Laws Say," 1996). Under these rules, the latter children may work no more than 3 hours on a school day and 8 hours at other times and may not work between 7 p.m. and 7 a.m. except during the summer ("What the Laws Say," 1996). When federal and state standards conflict, the FLSA provides that the "higher standards"—that is, the ones offering the child greater protection—should apply.

Shortcomings of the FLSA

The amended FLSA constitutes an important step toward protecting the rights of employed children. But concerns with the legislation's imperfections remain. One of those concerns centers on the perceived toothlessness of the FLSA regulations. At issue is the effectiveness of the Wage-Hour Division (a unit of the Employment Standards Administration in the U.S. Department of

Labor) in its monitoring and enforcement of child labor regulations. In 1980, 1,053 people served as compliance officers (Pignatella, 1995)—a number that permitted no more than 4% of the nation's business establishments to be reviewed each year (Coens, 1982). Today, the situation is even worse. Lack of funding has forced the Department of Labor to cut back investigators; only 833 remained in 1993 (Pignatella, 1995).

Another concern involves the fact that children have no recourse when they are injured while illegally employed. The *Breitwieser v. KMS Industries, Inc.* (1972) decision that children have no rights when they have participated in the violation of federal child labor laws has been called "an unfortunate landmark decision in child labor law advocacy" (McGovern, 1983, p. 304). In that case, a 16-year-old employee was killed in an on-the-job accident while operating a forklift truck—an action clearly in violation of federal regulations. The Fifth Circuit Court of Appeals decided that a violation of the child labor laws did not give the victim's family a right to seek damages and that the sole remedy was under the state (Georgia) worker compensation statutes. The U.S. Supreme Court refused to review the appeal.

Pignatella (1995) delineated other shortcomings of the FLSA: (a) Children under age 18 years are not prohibited from employment in agricultural occupations that are found to be particularly hazardous; (b) children are not prohibited from being employed in hazardous conditions by their parents; (c) there is no federal restriction on the number of hours children over age 16 may work per week; (d) fines collected for child labor violations now go to the U.S. Department of the Treasury instead of the Wages and Hours Division of the Department of Labor, where the funds previously were used to investigate child labor violations. Correcting these weaknesses in the federal legislation would help the United States comply with Article 32 of the U.N. Convention.

Using Empirical Research to Guide Governmental Policy on Child Labor

Do psychological research findings ever affect the passage of legislation involving children's rights? The case of Ellen Greenberger's (1983) testimony before the Subcommittee on Labor Standards of the U.S. House of Representatives is illustrative.

In mid-1982, during the Reagan administration, the U.S. Department of Labor proposed regulatory changes that would increase the permissible number of hours that younger adolescents could work while school was in session; these hours were to be increased from 18 to 24 per week. Also, the curfew on school-night employment was to be extended from 7 p.m. to 9 p.m. In recommending these alterations, the Department of Labor rather cavalierly asserted that the proposed changes "will not interfere with [the] health or well-being" of children (as cited in Greenberger, 1983, p. 104). Speculation on the source of the proposed changes centered on the restaurant and amusement park industries—employers who sought to increase their access to a pool of cheap labor and who sought advantages in the Reagan administration's laissez-faire attitude toward the regulation of business.

Ellen Greenberger, a psychologist at the University of California, Irvine, whose research is described in this chapter, was asked to testify by Representative George Miller, chair of the subcommittee. A portion of her testimony is included in Box 10.6. The testimony of Dr. Greenberger and other witnesses generated a great deal of publicity, much of which was critical of the Department of Labor's proposal. In fact, the proposal was withdrawn before a second day of hearings was held, and child labor regulations were not relaxed.

Promising Trends in Child Labor Practices

Everyone has attitudes about child labor. For some, attitudes may stem from the desire to be relieved of some financial responsibility for their children; for others, they may reflect assumptions about the qualities of work—either positive or negative. The evolution of laws about child labor reflects these conflicting values.

We sense that, compared with the other types of rights examined in this book, society currently expresses relatively little concern about abuses of children's rights in the workplace. Some exceptions do exist, however, and evidence suggests that a groundswell may be building. In 1997, for example, a diverse coalition launched a nationwide campaign called "Work Safe This Summer" to publicize the hazards of child labor and to promote ways to keep youth employees safe on the job (American News Service, 1997). According to the American News Service (1997), Kmart Corporation distributed 37 million shopping bags featuring the Work Safe This Summer logo along with information on how to learn more about teen safety at the workplace. Each of

Box 10.6

Testimony on Proposed Changes in Child Labor Regulations

On July 28, 1982, Ellen Greenberger presented testimony reflecting a statement that she and L. D. Steinberg prepared for the House Subcommittee on Labor Standards. Their arguments against the proposed regulatory changes—including increased work hours for adolescents—are summarized as follows:

1. Although working is associated with some benefits to youngsters' development, it is also associated with certain costs. Research studies show that these costs are related to the amount of time youngsters spend in the workplace. Working long hours has a negative impact on schooling and family life and leads to increased use of cigarettes, alcohol, and marijuana. [Thus] the proposed increase in maximum permissible hours of work during the school year runs counter to teenagers' best interests.

2. The employment of in-school 14- and 15-year-olds has increased substantially over the past 40 years, without benefit of the proposed new regulations. Employment of students is far more extensive in this country than in other industrialized nations. Any proposal that would encourage more youngsters to work still more hours during the school year will exacerbate serious national problems. These problems include the declining educational attainment of our students and the quality of family life. [Thus] the proposed expansion of opportunities for young teenagers must be weighed against alternative policies that might ameliorate long-standing educational and social problems.

3. Expansion of job opportunities for 14- and 15-year-olds is not likely to have favorable policy consequences. Poor minority children will not be the major "beneficiaries" of the new jobs. The greatest proportion of new jobs will go to the children of middle classes: They live where the jobs are. Moreover, "unemployment" among 14- and 15-year-old school-going children is a pseudo-problem. The real problem the administration needs to address is unemployment among out-of-school youths, ages 16 to 19, and among older adults. These are the people who need expanded job opportunities, at living wages. [Thus] the proposed new legislation is at cross-purposes with efforts to supply employment, at a living wage, to those individuals who must "make it" on their own.

4. The history of child labor repeats itself. The demand for child labor is nearly always driven by market demand for cheap, unskilled labor, which translates into larger profit margins for employers. Put the other way around, we do not propose increased job opportunities for youngsters because we have identified jobs that are eminently well suited to their abilities, interests, or long-run prospects in life. The proposed new regulations are a throwback to a historical era that we do not look back on with pride.

SOURCE: Greenberger and Steinberg (1982).

Kmart's 2,100 stores also posted the Department of Labor's "Teen Worker's Bill of Rights" describing criteria for safe working conditions for young employees.

According to the American News Service (1997), other promising campaigns also have been initiated. In Virginia, a chain of 31 pizza restaurants posted signs offering $100 rewards to workers under age 18 who reported that they had been asked to perform hazardous jobs, such as operating a dough-flattening machine. Wawa convenience stores in Pennsylvania, New Jersey, Maryland, and Delaware issued different-colored smocks to workers under age 18 so that supervisors would know on sight who was not allowed to operate the electric meat slicer. In Texas, Whataburger restaurants developed a computer tracking system to ensure that their 8,000 young employees in nine states were not scheduled for too many hours per week or for work too late in the evening.

Recommendations Regarding the Rights of Children in Employment

These trends are promising, to be sure, and we agree with such efforts. But other problems remain to be righted. For example, children's labor rights generally have been neglected by researchers. Social scientists need to provide empirical evidence about children's decision-making abilities and competencies with regard to work-related issues. What types of jobs are children capable of performing? Does the opportunity to work induce the development of social as well as personal responsibility? Can we further illuminate the conclusion that "some work is good but too much is bad" for children?

Decisions regarding child labor should take the results of such studies into consideration. If a certain number of hours of work per week leads to greater responsibility and maturity without infringing on the child's right to leisure, play, education, and participation in cultural and artistic activities— rights guaranteed by Articles 28 and 31 of the U.N. Convention—then such work should be encouraged. Indeed, encouraging the development of such skills fits well with U.N. Convention Article 29, which states that education should be directed at developing the child's personality and talents, as well as at preparing the child for responsible life in a free society.

At the same time, Article 32 should serve as the primary guide. The article cautions that children have the right to be protected from economic exploita-

---

Box 10.7

When Child Labor Laws Are Ludicrous

For good reasons, laws restrict the amount of work that minors are allowed to do. Sometimes, however, such laws seem overly restrictive or self-defeating. For example, in 1993 it came to light that the 14-year-old batboy for the Savannah (Georgia) Cardinals' minor-league baseball team was in violation of local child labor laws, which stated that 14- and 15-year-olds could not work past 7 p.m. on school nights or 9 p.m. during the summer. The baseball club reluctantly released the youth, Tommy McCoy, and hired a 16-year-old as his replacement.

The definition of *school day* served to complicate the issue. Because children in the United States attend school Monday through Friday, those days are referred to as "school days." Thus, when a state specifies that a child may not work later hours on a "school day," that child may not be permitted to work later than 7:00 p.m. on Friday night (although Saturday is *not* a school day) but may be allowed to work later on Sunday night (although Monday *is* a school day). Sometimes rules don't make sense.

National publicity led to strong reactions to Tommy McCoy's situation. U.S. Secretary of Labor Robert Reich termed the application of child labor laws to batboys as "silly," saying that "it is not the intent of the law to deny young teenagers employment opportunities so long as their health and well-being are not impaired." After the Department of Labor announced that it would not enforce any such work restraints for batboys, the Labor Commission for the state of Georgia granted a waiver of state laws and—happily—Tommy McCoy was rehired.

SOURCE: From "Batboy Is Called Out: U.S. Is Reviewing Law," May 28, 1993, *New York Times,* p. A7. Copyright © 1993 by The New York Times Co. Reprinted by permission.

---

tion and from engaging in work that constitutes a threat to health, education, and development.

Thus, whenever a particular child seeks employment, certain questions should be addressed: What is the age of the child? What is the maturity level of the child? Is the work necessary to the economic well-being of the child and her or his family? What opportunities will the working child have for education, play, leisure, and cultural pursuits? Will the work contribute positively to the development of the child's life or professional skills? In what ways will the work develop the child's personality and talents? How will the child be protected from harm at work? How will the child be protected from economic exploitation by employers—or even by parents? Does the work constitute a threat to the child's health or welfare? (See Box 10.7 for one example of a law gone awry.) Does the child want to work? Answers to these questions—based on reliable research—should help in deciding whether a particular employment opportunity is appropriate for a given child.

Notes

1. "'Work Safe' Targets Teens Nationwide," by American News Service, July 20, 1997, *Omaha World Herald,* p. 1G. Used by permission of the American News Service.

2. Quotes from "No Jobs for Kids? Try Baby-Sitting or Mowing Grass," by S. J. Johnson, July 20, 1997, *Omaha World Herald,* p. 17-G. Copyright 1997 by *The Macon Telegraph.* Published with permission from *The Macon Telegraph.*

Concluding Comments

Children Are *Persons!*

The United Nations Convention on the Rights of the Child (1989) is a historic document that forcefully advocates every child's rights to identity, protection, nurturance, and self-determination. As noted in Chapter 3, the U.N. Convention has gained nearly universal ratification; to date, only the United States and Somalia have failed to comply with the international consensus on ratification.

Our view is that this document provides the appropriate guidance for nations worldwide to be able to protect the various rights to which children—as persons—are entitled. The United Nations Convention on the Rights of the Child can and should serve as the model for U.S. policy. In most cases, U.S. statutes already conform to the tenets of the Convention. In those cases where the U.N. principles and U.S. laws conflict, the United States may choose either to change federal and state laws (e.g., as we should with corporal punishment and juvenile death penalty) or to ratify and implement the document with specified Reservations, Understandings, and Declarations (see Chapter 3).

Of course, the U.N. Convention is no panacea. Ratification of the document alone will not ensure a better life for children in the United States. But ratification will require the United States to monitor compliance; in other words, the United States—like other nations—will be held accountable by the international community for the welfare and development of its children. As any psychologist can attest, when behavior is observed, it is more likely that conduct will conform to the standards set.

We see no good reason, therefore, for the United States to delay any longer ratification of the United Nations Convention on the Rights of the Child. It can and should ratify and implement this historic human rights treaty.

As this country implements the Convention, it undoubtedly will face dilemmas that appear to place children, parents, and the state in opposition to one another. But such struggles are not new; indeed, this nation's history is replete with Supreme Court decisions requiring that a balance be reached among the competing interests of these constituents. How can such dilemmas be resolved in an orderly way with due consideration of both the U.N. Convention and the U.S. Constitution?

Proper resolution, we believe, rests on the assumption that children should be included in making the decisions that affect their lives, both keeping in mind their limitations as maturing citizens and according respect to their evolving capacities. In implementing the U.N. Convention, it will be incumbent upon adults to teach children how to make good decisions. In this regard, Brassard et al. (1991) commented:

> it is in adults' best interests to prepare children to make decisions, take responsibility for their actions, develop an internal moral standard, and learn other tasks necessary for successful life as an adult. Children who don't develop these skills, which must be taught or modeled as they are not an automatic outcome of general development, do not magically come to possess them once they turn 18 [years]. It seems prudent to prepare children, in a developmentally responsive way, to learn to handle some constitutional rights and consequent responsibilities.
>
> How do children develop the ability to handle constitutionally supported rights of decision-making, privacy and confidentiality, . . . legal representation, self-determination, and so on? How can adults find the balance of providing adequate guidance and support while allowing independent development? Both parents and educators have the difficult task of preparing young people for competency, while simultaneously ensuring that they are not endangering themselves or others. This entails a close monitoring of developmental ability, both from a general and individual perspective, and a tailoring of responsibilities and tasks to this assessment. (p. 376)

A Developmental Model
of Children's Rights

We believe that the participation in treatment decisions model proposed by
Erlen (1987) and the Billick (1986) model of children's competency to make
decisions provide particularly useful frameworks for completing this task.
Erlen's model (described in Chapter 7) assumes that, with increasing age and
competence, children should take increased responsibility for decisions. Thus,
over time, a child moves from the capacity to *assent* to decisions, to the ability
to *dissent* from decisions, and finally to the competence to provide informed
consent. Like Erlen's model, Billick's model (also described in Chapter 7) is
founded on the assumption that informed consent requires judgment and
wisdom, factors that typically increase with age.

By combining the two models, we arrive at a recommendation for guidelines for children's participation in decision making:

Ages	Children's Participation in Decision Making
0-6	Children's guardians (whether parents, other adults, or the state) generally should make important decisions for children.
7-11	Children should have the right to *assent* to important decisions. Their guardians should provide informed consent, but children should be given ample opportunities to provide assent. Children's dissent should be weighed but usually should not be the determining factor in decision making.
12-14	Children should have the right to *dissent* from decisions. Whereas their guardians should provide informed consent, children's dissent should be taken very seriously.
14+	Children, assuming they can demonstrate the requisite competence, should have the right to *consent* to important decisions affecting their lives and well-being.

In implementing these guidelines, we also recommend that the capacities
of individual children be assessed. Certainly, wide variations in developmental competency exist, particularly as minors reach adolescence. As we have
documented, some minors are capable of making important—even life-or-
death—decisions at quite young ages, whereas some adults cannot make even
the most rudimentary decisions. Thus, although it is expedient to use an
objective criterion (e.g., chronological age) as a guidepost, we believe that use
of such an approach is not in the best interests of children.

Tasks for the Future

We believe that the United States should embrace the tasks implicit in implementing the aims of the U.N. Convention. Thus, we see three tasks before us:

U.S. Ratification of the U.N. Convention

First, the United States must ratify the United Nations Convention on the Rights of the Child. During the past decade, many nations—as they emerged from totalitarian governments—have looked to the United States as the model of "how to be" as a nation-state. Now the United States should look to the world and accept the consensus, in the form of this Convention, about "how to be" as a state that fully values both adult and child citizens.

Research on Children's Competencies in Decision Making

Second, the United States should seek out, encourage, and support valid, reliable research that explores the developing competencies of children as decision makers. Some groundbreaking studies from the 1970s and 1980s can serve as guides in this area (see Chapter 4), but we should not continue to rely on those studies alone. It is time to expand on that early work. In particular, we encourage empirical research in the contexts described in both the U.N. Convention and this book—that is, within the family; under the umbrella of state social services; in health care, education, and employment; and with the meaningful assistance of legal counsel in resolving questions of juvenile justice. Research is needed to understand better a given child's competence to make decisions within each specific context.

Refinement of National Policies on the Rights of Children

Finally, we believe that much important work is yet to be done in the refinement of national policies once ratification of the U.N. Convention has been accomplished and the results of research into children's competencies have been reviewed and validated. That work, of course, will require professionals to engage in a time-consuming and, at times, difficult process of balancing potentially competing needs.

We believe that, until children's competencies at decision points in specific areas of consequence are known, it is incumbent on professionals to endorse a nurturance orientation regarding a child's rights in a specific area. As professionals become familiar with a given child's competence in a decision-making area, they should provide that child with self-determinative responsibility as his or her capacity warrants. In all, though, professionals should be most careful that the use of self-determinative decision making is based on *demonstrated* competencies within a particular area, and not on an ideal criterion, such as chronological age.

In all cases, refinement of national, state, and local policies must be guided by the principles and articles of the U.N. Convention and illuminated by relevant research findings. By implementing the United Nations Convention on the Rights of the Child and guiding children toward increasingly independent decision making with increasing age, the United States will provide a climate in which the interests of children, parents, and the state all can be adequately protected. Under this approach, children always can be considered persons—as they should be.

References

42 U.S.C.A. 606 (1962, July 25); Pub. L. 87-543 104(a)(2); Title I, 104(a)(3)(D).

42 U.S.C.A. 651 *et seq.* (1967; 1968, January 2, 1968); Pub. L. 90-248 402.

42 U.S.C.A. 671(a)(15) *et seq.*

42 U.S.C.A. 675(5)(B).

Adoption Assistance and Child Welfare Law of 1980, 42 U.S.C.A. 671 *et seq.* (1980).

Africa News Service. (1997, June 6). Amnesty opposes execution of South African youth in Miss Amnesty International. *Africa News Service,* [page unavailable]. Available at Westlaw cite WL 11109208.

Albiston, C. R., Maccoby, E. E., & Mnookin, R. H. (1990, Spring). Does joint legal custody matter? *Stanford Law and Policy Review, 2,* 167-179.

Allegretti, J. G. (1996). *The lawyer's calling: Christian faith and legal practice.* Mahwah, NJ: Paulist Press.

American Bar Association. (1980). *Standards relating to rights of minors/recommended by IJA-ABA Joint Commission on Juvenile Justice.* Cambridge, MA: Ballinger.

American Convention on Human Rights, art. 4(5), O.A.S. Official Records, OEA/Ser. K/XVI/1.1, Doc. 65, Rev. 1, Corr. 2 (1970).

American News Service. (1997, July 20). "Work Safe" targets teens nationwide. *Omaha World Herald,* p. 1G.

Americans with Disabilities Act of 1990 (ADA), 3 U.S.C. § 421 (1990).

Andell, E. G. (1973). A minor has an absolute right to sue his parent for a negligent tort. In A. E. Wilkerson (Ed.), *The rights of children: Emergent concepts of law and society* (pp. 98-105). Philadelphia: Temple University Press.

Andersen, J. J. (1993). Capital punishment of kids: When courts permit parents to act on their religious beliefs at the expense of their children's lives. *Vanderbilt Law Review, 46,* 755-777.

Arcia, O. J. (1995, Winter). Comment: Objections, administrative difficulties, and alternatives to mandatory *pro bono* legal services in Florida. *Florida State University Law Review, 22,* 771-798.

Areen, J. (1992). *Cases and materials on family law* (3rd ed.). New York: Foundation Press.

243

Associated Press. (1991, August 30). Blind, deaf teen found locked in car. *The Record* (Northern New Jersey), p. A04.

Aumend, S. A., & Barrett, M. C. (1984). Self-concept and attitudes toward adoption: A comparison of searching and nonsearching adult adoptees. *Child Welfare, 53,* 251-259.

Bailey v. Drexel Furniture Co., 259 U.S. 20 (1922).

Baker v. Owen, 96 S.Ct. 210, 395 F.Supp. 294 (1975).

Baltimore City Department of Social Services v. Bouknight, 110 S.Ct. 900 (1990).

Baran, A., Sorosky, A. D., & Pannoz, R. (1975). Secret adoption records: The dilemma of our adoptees. *Psychology Today, 9,* 38-42, 96-99.

Batboy is called out: U.S. is reviewing law. (1993, May 28). *New York Times,* p. A7.

Battles v. Board, 95 F.3d 41 (4th Cir. 1996).

Baum, L. F. (1900). *The wonderful wizard of Oz.* Chicago: George M. Hill.

Beckham, W. H. (1949, June). Helpful practices in juvenile court hearings. *Federal Probation, 13,* 10-14.

Bellotti v. Baird, 443 U.S. 622 (1979).

Benz, V. N. (1992). Corporal punishment in today's public schools: Child discipline or legal abuse? *Journal of Juvenile Law, 13,* 13-26.

Bethel School District No. 403 v. Fraser, 478 U.S. 675 (1986).

Beyer, H. A. (1974, September). *The child's right to refuse mental health treatment.* Paper presented at the annual meeting of the American Psychological Association, New Orleans.

Billick, S. B. (1986). Developmental competency. *Bulletin of the American Academy of Psychiatry and Law, 14,* 301-308.

Blank, S. W., & Blum, B. B. (1997, Spring). A brief history of work expectations for welfare mothers. In R. E. Behrman (Ed.), *The future of children: Vol. 7. Welfare to work* (pp. 28-38). Los Altos, CA: Center for the Future of Children.

Blissets Case, 98 Eng.Rep. 899 (K.B. 1774) (Mansfield, C.J.).

Brassard, M. R., Hyman, I., & Dimmitt, C. (1991). What can children expect? Protecting and nurturing children in a school and community context. *School Psychology Review, 20,* 369-381.

Breed v. Jones, 421 U.S. 519 (1975).

Breitwieser v. KMS Industries, Inc., 467 F.2d 1391 (5th Cir. 1972), *cert. denied,* 410 U.S. 969 (1973).

Brian-Mark, L. (1983). The competent child's preference in critical medical decisions: A proposal for its consideration. *Western State Law Review, 11,* 25-58.

Brody, L. (1997, August 6). Foster child sacrifices for her own child, girl 2 ½, at center of custody case. *The Record* (Bergen Co., NJ), p. L01.

Bronfenbrenner, U. (1990). Who cares for children? *Research and Clinical Center for Child Development, 12,* 27-40.

Brooks, C. M. (1994). Overview and introduction. In C. M. Brooks & R. S. Stick (Eds.), *Nebraska juvenile court procedures manual* (2d ed., pp. I-1 through I-10). Lincoln: Nebraska Continuing Legal Education.

Brooks, C. M., Perry [now Walker], N. W., Starr, S. D., & Teply, L. L. (1994). Child abuse and neglect reporting laws: Understanding interests, understanding policy. *Behavioral Sciences and the Law, 12,* 49-64.

Brooks, C. M., & Stick, R. S. (1994). *Nebraska juvenile court procedures manual* (2nd ed.). Lincoln: Nebraska Continuing Legal Education.

Brosig, C., & Kalichman, S. (1992, August). *To report or not to report: Child maltreatment reporting decisions.* Paper presented at the annual meeting of the American Psychological Association, Washington, DC.

Bross, D. C. (1991). The rights of children and national development: Five models. *Child Abuse & Neglect, 15*(Suppl. 1), 89-97.

Brown, P. (1997, November 30). For state's teens, a work break: New child labor law called toughest in the nation, *Newsday*, p. 5.

Brown v. the Board of Education, 347 U.S. 483 (1954) [*Brown I*].

Brown v. the Board of Education, 349 U.S. 294 (1955) [*Brown II*].

Burnham v. West, 681 F.Supp. 1160 (E.D. Va. 1987).

Burton, L. M., & Bengston, V. L. (1985). Black grandmothers: Issues of timing and continuity of roles. In V. L. Bengston & J. F. Robertson (Eds.), *Grandparenting* (pp. 61-77). Newbury Park, CA: Sage.

Butterfield, F. (1997, July 21). With juvenile courts in chaos, critics propose their demise. *New York Times*, pp. A01, A13.

Butts, J., & Schwartz, I. (1991). Access to insurance and length of psychiatric stay among adolescents and young adults discharged from general hospitals. *Journal of Health and Social Policy, 3*, 91-116.

Camara, K. A., & Resnick, G. (1989). Styles of conflict resolution and cooperation between divorced parents: Effects on child behavior and adjustment. *American Journal of Orthopsychiatry, 59*, 560-575.

Caput, R. B. (1985). *Roemhild v. State* and *State v. Popanz:* Their effect on the constitutionality of Oklahoma's compulsory education statute. *Oklahoma Law Review, 38*, 741-752.

Carey on Behalf of Carey v. Maine School Administrative Dist. No. 17, 754 F.Supp. 906 (1990).

Carter, P. I., & St. Lawrence, J. S. (1985). Adolescents' competency to make informed consent birth control and pregnancy decisions: An interface for psychology and the law. *Behavioral Sciences and the Law, 3*, 309-319.

Cevallos, D. (1996, March 27). Children: International tribunal condemns child labor. *International Press Service* [page unavailable].

Chapman, A. (1994, June 26). Old statutes and young lawbreakers: Legislators and police officials say antiquated laws are inadequate to cope with the current juvenile crime explosion in Texas. *Fort Worth Star-Telegram* [page unavailable].

Charen, M. (1993, February 7). Children's Defense Fund not the savior that it seems. *Kansas City Star,* p. K-4.

Chasnoff, I. J., Landress, H. J., & Barrett, M. E. (1990). The prevalence of illicit drug or alcohol use during pregnancy and discrepancies in mandatory reporting in Pinellas County, Florida. *New England Journal of Medicine, 322*, 1202-1206.

Cherlin, A. J., & Furstenberg, F. F., Jr. (1986). *The new American grandparent: A place in the family, a life apart.* New York: Basic Books.

Cherney, I., & Perry [now Walker], N. W. (1996). Children's attitudes toward their rights: An international perspective. In E. Verhellen (Ed.), *Monitoring children's rights* (pp. 241-250). The Netherlands: Kluwer Law International.

Child Health Forum. (1997, May 15). *Windows, worries, and welfare reform: Assuring a safety net for children's health.* Presentation at the CityMatch/University of Nebraska Medical Center conference, Omaha, NE.

Child Labor Tax Act of 1919, 40 Stat. 1138 (1919).

Children's Defense Fund (CDF). (1994). *Wasting America's future.* Boston: Beacon.

Children's Defense Fund (CDF). (1997). *The state of America's children: Yearbook 1997.* Washington, DC: Author.

Clark, H. H., Jr. (1987). *The law of domestic relations in the United States* (2d, ed.). St. Paul, MN: West.

Clingempeel, W. G., & Reppucci, N. D. (1982). Joint custody after divorce: Major issues and goals for research. *Psychological Bulletin, 91,* 102-127.

Coens, T. A. (1982, October). Child labor laws: A viable legacy for the 1980s. *Labor Law Journal,* pp. 668-683.

Cohen, C. P. (1990). United Nations Convention on the Rights of the Child: Overview. In D. Nurske & K. Castelle (Eds.), *Children's rights: Crisis and challenge* (pp. A1-A5). New York: Defense for Children International-USA.

Cohen, C. P., & Davidson, H. A. (Eds.). (1990). *Children's rights in America: U.N. Convention on the Rights of the Child compared with United States law.* Chicago: American Bar Association in Cooperation with Defense for Children International-USA.

Cohen, C. P., & Miljeteig-Olssen, P. (1991). Status report: United Nations Convention on the Rights of the Child. *Journal of Human Rights, 8,* 367-382.

Cohen, H. (1980). *Equal rights for children.* Totowa, NJ: Rowman and Littlefield.

Commonwealth of PA v. Addicks I, 5 Binn. 520 (Pa. 1813).

Commonwealth of PA v. Addicks & Lee (Addicks II), 2 Serg. & Rawle 174 (Pa. 1815).

Compulsory Education Act of 1922, Va. Const. Art. 8, 3 (1922).

Connecticut General Statutes, Section 17a-101e, Subsection (c) (1997).

Cornfield by Lewis v. Consolidated High School Dist. No. 230, 991 F.2d 1316 (1993).

Coy v. Iowa, 108 S.Ct. 1798, 487 U.S. 1012 (1988).

Coyne, A. (1992). *On bonding and attachment* [Videotape]. Washington, DC: National Council of Family and Juvenile Court Judges.

Cozic, C. P. (Ed.). (1997). *Welfare reform.* San Diego, CA: Greenhaven.

Craig v. Selma City School Board, 801 F.Supp. 585 (1992).

Cramer, D. (1986). Gay parents and their children: A review of research and practical implications. *Journal of Counseling and Development, 64,* 504-507.

Cross, H. J., & Kawash, G. F. (1968). A short form of PARI to assess authoritarian attitudes. *Psychological Reports, 23,* 91-98.

Cryan, J. R. (1987). The banning of corporal punishment. *Childhood Education, 63,* 146-153.

Custody of a Minor, 375 Mass. 733 (1978).

Czajkowski, E., & Koocher, G. B. (1987). Medical compliance and coping with cystic phybrosis. *Journal of Child Psychology & Allied Disciplines, 28,* 311-319.

Dale, M. J. (1992, Summer). The Supreme Court and the minimization of children's constitutional rights: Implications for the juvenile justice system. *Hamline Journal of Public Law and Policy, 13,* 199-228.

Dalton, R., & Forman, M. (1987). Conflict of interest associated with psychiatric hospitalization of children. *American Journal of Orthopsychiatry, 56,* 12-14.

D'Amico, R. (1984). Does employment during high school impair academic progress? *Sociology of Education, 57,* 152-164.

Danelen, R. F. (1991). Statutory immunity under the Child Abuse and Neglect Reporting Act: From first impression to present day. *Journal of Juvenile Law, 12,* 16-25.

Davis, S. M. (1997). *Rights of juveniles: The juvenile justice system* (2d. ed.). Deerfield, IL: Clark, Boardman, Callaghan.

Davis v. Davis, 842 S.W.2d 588 (1990), affirming Tenn. Ct. App. (1990).

deMause, L. (1975). Our forebears made childhood a nightmare. *Psychology Today, 8,* 85-88.

Demos, J. (1979). Images of the American family, then and now. In V. Tufte & B. Myerhoff (Eds.), *Changing images of the family* (pp. 43-60). Collected in J. Areen (Ed.), *Family law: Cases and materials* (3rd ed., 1992, pp. 85-92).

DeShaney v. Winnebago County Department of Social Services, 489 U.S. 189 (1989).

Dickens, C. (1857). *Little Dorrit.* London: Bradbury & Evans.

DiFonzo, J. H. (1995, Summer). Deprived of "fatal liberty": The rhetoric of child saving and the reality of juvenile incarceration. *University of Toledo Law Review, 26,* 855-900.

Doe v. Doe, 222 Va. 736, 284 S.E.2d 799 (1981).

Drinan, R. F. (1973). The rights of children in modern American family law. In A. E. Wilkerson (Ed.), *The rights of children: Emergent concepts in law and society* (pp. 37-46). Philadelphia: Temple University Press.

Drinan, R. F. (1992). The United Nations' new institute for children's rights. *America, 166,* 424-425.

Dugger, C. W. (1992, September 8). Troubled children overwhelm care system. *New York Times,* pp. A1, A15.

Dunlap v. Dunlap, 84 N.H. 352, 150A. 905 (1930).

Education for All Handicapped Children Act of 1975, 20 U.S.C. 1401-1454 (1975).

Edwards, J. N. (1987). Changing family structure and youthful well-being: Assessing the future. *Journal of Family Issues, 8,* 355-371.

Elias, M. (1993, February 25). How adoption echoes through family life. *USA Today,* p. 6D.

Ellis, J. W. (1996). Voluntary admission and involuntary hospitalization of minors. In B. D. Sales & D. W. Shuman (Eds.), *Law, mental health, and mental disorder* (pp. 487-502). Pacific Grove, CA: Brooks/Cole.

Elmer-Dewitt, P. (1994, April 18). The crucial family years. *Time,* p. 68.

Emery v. Emery, 45 Cal. 2d 421, 289 P.2d 218 (1955).

Erikson, E. (1963). *Childhood and society* (2nd rev. ed.). New York: Norton.

Erlen, J. (1987). The child's choice: An essential component in treatment decisions. *Children's Health Care, 15,* 156-160.

Evans, J. L. (1995). Are children competent to make decisions about their own deaths? *Behavioral Sciences and the Law, 13,* 27-41.

Evans v. Asphalt Roads & Materials Company, Inc., 194 Va. 165, 72 S.E.2d 321 (1952).

Ex parte Devine, 398 So. 2d 686 (Ala. 1991).

Fair Labor Standards Act of 1938, c. 676, § 1, 52 Stat. 1060 (1938).

Farber, S., & Green, M. (1988). *Outrageous conduct: Art, ego, and the Twilight Zone case.* New York: Ballantine.

Fare v. Michael C., 442 U.S. 707 (1979).

Farmer v. Farmer, 439 N.Y.S.2d 584 (1981).

Farson, R. (1974). *Birthrights.* New York: Macmillan.

Federal Child Abuse Prevention and Treatment Act of 1974, 42 U.S.C.A. 5101 *et seq.* (1974).

Feldman v. Feldman, 45 A.D. 320, 358 N.Y.S.2d 507 (1974).

Felner, R. D., & Terre, L. (1987). Child custody dispositions and children's adaptation following divorce. In L. A. Weithorn (Ed.), *Psychology and child custody determinations* (pp. 106-153). Lincoln: University of Nebraska Press.

Fine, M. (1992). Where have all the children gone? Due process and judicial criteria for removing children from their parents' homes in California. *Southwestern University Law Review, 21,* 125-153.

Finkel, N. J. (1995). Prestidigitation, statistical magic, and the Supreme Court numerology in juvenile death penalty cases. *Psychology, Public Policy, and Law, 1,* 612-642.

Flin, R. H., Davies, G. M., & Stevenson, Y. (1987). Children as witnesses: Psycholegal aspects of the English and Scottish system. *Medicine and Law, 6,* 275-291.

Foldi v. Jeffries, 93 N.J. 533, 461 A.2d 1145 (1983).

Fox, M. (1997). Federal education programs evaluation: Field study. *Congressional Testimony by Federal Document Clearing House* [page unavailable].

Fox, S. J. (1996, Winter). The early history of the court. In R. E. Behrman (Ed.), *The future of children: Vol. 6. The juvenile court* (pp. 29-39). Los Altos, CA: Center for the Future of Children.

Franklin, P. (1994). Children's rights: Straight talking. *Nursing Times, 90,* 33-35.

Friedrich, W. N., & Boriskin, J. A. (1976-1977). Child abuse and neglect in North Dakota. *North Dakota Law Review, 53,* 197-212.

G.A. v. D.A., 745 S.W.2d 726 (Missouri 1987).

Garcia v. Miera, 817 F.2d 650 (10th Cir. 1987).

Gardner, R. A. (1987a). *The parental alienation syndrome and the differentiation between fabricated and genuine sexual abuse.* Cresskill, NJ: Creative Therapeutics.

Gardner, R. A. (1987b). *Sex Abuse Legitimacy Scale.* Cresskill, NJ: Creative Therapeutics.

Gary W., et al. v. State of Louisiana, et al., 437 F.Supp. 1209 (E.D.La. 1976).

Gathing, J. T., Jr. (1989). When rights clash: The conflict between a parent's right of free exercise of religion versus his child's right to life. *Cumberland Law Review, 19,* 585-616.

Geneva Convention Relative to the Protection of Civilian Persons in Time of War. (1949, August 12). Art. 68, 6 U.S.T. 3516, 3560, T.I.A.S. No. 3365, 75 U.N.T.S. 287.

Gerber, M. S. (1993). Equal protection, public choice theory, and Learnfare: Wealth classifications revisited. *Georgetown Law Journal, 81,* 2141-2173.

Giampetro-Meyer, A., & Brown, T. S. (1992). Protecting society from teenage greed: A proposal for revising the ages, hours, and nature of child labor in America. *Akron Law Review, 25,* 547-569.

Gibson v. Gibson, 3 Cal.3d 914, 92 Cal.Rptr. 288, 479 P.2d 648 (1971).

Gideon v. Wainwright, 372 U.S. 335 (1963).

Goebel, B. L., & Lott, S. L. (1986, August). *Adoptees' resolution of the adolescent identity crisis: Where are the taproots?* Paper presented at the annual meeting of the American Psychological Association, Washington, DC.

Goetz, J. D. (1985). Children's rights under the Burger Court: Concern for the child but deference to authority. *Notre Dame Law Review, 60,* 1214-1232.

Goldstein, J. (1977). Medical care for the child at risk: On state supervention and parental autonomy. *Yale Law Journal, 86,* 645-670.

Goldstein, J., Freud, A., & Solnit, A. (1973). *Beyond the best interests of the child.* New York: Free Press.

Goldstein, J., Freud, A., & Solnit, A. (1979). *Before the best interests of the child.* New York: Free Press.

Goldstein, J., Freud, A., & Solnit, A. (1986). *In the best interests of the child.* New York: Free Press.

Gordon v. Gordon, 557 P.2d 1271 (Okla.), *cert. den.* 439 U.S. 863 (1978).

Gorney, C. (1989, June 26). The real-life dilemmas of frozen embryos: A Tennessee divorce case raises questions the law hasn't begun to confront. *Washington Post,* p. B01.

Goss v. Lopez, 419 U.S. 565 (1975).

Green, R. (1978). Sexual identity of 37 children raised by homosexual or transsexual parents. *American Journal of Psychiatry, 135,* 692-697.

Greenberger, E. (1983). A researcher in the policy area: The case of child labor. *American Psychologist, 38,* 104-111.

Greenberger, E., & Steinberg, L. D. (1982, July 28). Testimony before Congress on proposed changes to child labor provisions of the Fair Labor Standards Act.

Greenberger, E., & Steinberg, L. D. (1986). *When teenagers work: The psychological and social costs of adolescent employment.* New York: Basic Books.

Greenhouse, L. (1990, February 21). Justices limit parent's rights in child abuse case. *New York Times*, p. A11.

Grisso, T. (1981). *Juveniles' waiver of rights: Legal and psychological competence*. New York: Plenum.

Grisso, T., & Vierling, L. (1978). Minors' consent to treatment: A developmental perspective. *Professional Psychology, 9*, 412-427.

Grych, J. H., & Fincham, F. D. (1992). Interventions for children of divorce: Toward greater integration of research and action. *Psychological Bulletin, 111*, 434-454.

Guerrero, M. P. (1979). *American Indian Law Review, 7*, 51-77.

Hafemeister, T. L., & Melton, G. B. (1987). The impact of social science research on the judiciary. In G. B. Melton (Ed.), *Reforming the law* (pp. 27-62). New York: Guilford.

Haley v. Ohio, 332 U.S. 596 (1948).

Hall, A. S., & Lin, M. J. (1995). Theory and practice of children's rights: Implications for mental health counselors. *Journal of Mental Health Counseling, 17*, 63-80.

Hall v. Tawney, 621 F.2d 607 (4th Cir. 1980).

Hammarberg, T. (1990). The U.N. Convention on the Rights of the Child—and how to make it work. *Human Rights Quarterly, 12*, 97-105.

Hammer v. Dagenhart, 247 U.S. 251 (1918).

Hanover, D. (1996, September 1). The education of Kathy [sic] Lee. *Good Housekeeping, 223*, 68-71, 188, 189, 191.

Hart, S. N. (1982). The history of children's psychological rights. *Viewpoints in Teaching and Learning, 58*, 1-15.

Hart, S. N. (1991). From property to person status: Historical perspective on children's rights. *American Psychologist, 46*, 53-59.

Hart, S. N., & Pavlovic, Z. (1991). Children's rights in education: An historical perspective. *School Psychology Review, 20*, 345-358.

Hauser, B. B. (1985). Custody in dispute: Legal and psychological profiles of contesting families. *Journal of American Academy of Child Psychiatry, 24*, 531-537.

Hazelwood School District v. Kuhlmeier, 484 U.S. 260 (1988).

Helgeson, V. S., Goodman, G. S., Shaver, P., & Lipton, J. P. (n.d.). *Attitudes concerning the rights of children and adults*. Unpublished manuscript, University of Denver.

Helms v. Franciscus, 2 BlandCh. 544, 20 Am. Dec. 402 (1830).

Hentoff, N. (1988). *The first freedom: The tumultuous history of free speech in America* (Rev. ed.). New York: Delacorte.

Hetherington, E. M., Cox, M., & Cox, R. (1979). Play and social interaction in children following divorce. *Journal of Social Issues, 35*, 26-49.

Hewellette v. George, 68 Miss. 703, 9 So. 885 (1891).

Hibbett, A., & Fogelman, K. (1990). Future lives of truants: Family formation and health-related behavior. *British Journal of Educational Psychology, 60*, 171-179.

Hill by and through Hill v. Rankin County, Mississippi School District, 843 F.Supp. 1112 (1993).

Hoeffer, B. (1981). Children's acquisition of sex-role behavior in lesbian-mother families. *American Journal of Orthopsychiatry, 51*, 536-544.

Hoffman v. Tracy, 67 Wash. 2d 31, 406 P.2d 323 (1965).

Holt, J. (1974). *Escape from childhood*. New York: E. P. Dutton.

Hopkins, E. L. (1993, October 18). My turn: Abusing the rights of parents. *Newsweek*, p. 26.

Horowitz, R. M. (1984). Children's rights: A look backward and a glance ahead. In R. M. Horowitz & H. A. Davidson (Eds.), *Legal rights of children* (pp. 1-9). New York: McGraw-Hill.

Howell v. Howell, 304 N.Y.S.2d 156 (1969).

Howlett, D. (1993, September 9). Lesbian ruling stirs fury, praise. *USA Today*, p. 3A.

H.R. 867 (1997, November 18), amending 42 U.S.C.A. 671 (a) (15) *et seq.*

Hsu, S. S. (1997, February 12). Virginia aims to cut out-of-wedlock births: State officials push local effort with federal funds as reward. *Washington Post* (Metro Section), p. B06.

Huston, A. C. (1995). Policies for children: Social obligation, not handout. In H. E. Fitzgerald, B. M. Lester, & B. Zuckerman (Eds.), *Children of poverty: Research, health, and policy issues* (pp. 305-326). New York: Garland.

Huston, A. C. (1997). *Children in poverty.* Cambridge, UK: Cambridge University Press.

Ijams, M. N. (1976). Personality adjustment of adopted children in early adulthood. *Dissertation Abstracts International, 37,* 1488-B.

Ilfeld, F. W., Ilfeld, H. Z., & Alexander, J. R. (1982). Does joint custody work? A first look at outcome data of relitigation. *American Journal of Psychiatry, 139,* 62-66.

Individuals with Disabilities Education Act, 20 U.S.C. 1400 *et seq.* (1997).

Ingraham v. Wright, 430 U.S. 651 (1977).

Ingrassia, M., & Springen, K. (1994, March 21). She's not Baby Jessica anymore. *Newsweek,* pp. 60-66.

Ingulli, E. D. (1985). Grandparent visitation rights: Social policies and legal rights. *West Virginia Law Review, 87,* 295-334.

Inhelder, B., & Piaget, J. (1958). *The growth of logical thinking.* New York: Basic.

Inmates of Boys' Training School v. Affleck, 346 D.Supp. 1354 (D.R.I. 1972).

In re E.G., 133 Ill. 2nd 98 (1989).

In re Gault, 387 U.S. 1 (1967).

In re Green, 448 Pa. 338 (1972).

In re Guardianship of Myers, 610 N.E.2d 663 (Ohio Com. Pl. 1993).

In re Marriage of Carney, 24 Cal.3d 725, 598 P.2d 36, 157 Cal.Rptr. 383 (1979).

In re Marriage of Rosson, 224 Cal. Rptr. 250 (178 Cal. App. 3d 1094, 1986).

In re P.E.A., 754 P.2d 382 (Colo. 1988).

In re Petition of John Doe and Jane Doe, Husband and Wife, to Adopt Baby Boy Janikova (John Doe et al., Appellees; Otakar Kirchner, Appellant.), 159 Ill.2d 347 (1994).

In re Philip B. v. Warren B., 92 Cal. App. 3d 796 (1979).

In re Winship, 397 U.S. 358 (1970).

Institute of Judicial Administration–American Bar Association (IJA-ABA) Joint Commission on Juvenile Justice Standards. (1981). *Standard relating to abuse and neglect.* Cambridge, MA: Ballinger.

International Catholic Child Bureau (ICCB). (1995, February). *Facts about the United Nations Convention on the Rights of the Child.* Geneva, Switzerland: Author.

International conference on child labor ends. (1997, February 27). *Xinhua English Newswire* [page unavailable].

International Covenant on Civil and Political Rights. (1966). Art. 6(5), Annex to General Assembly Resolution 2200, 21 U.N. GAOR Res. Supp. (No. 16) 53, U.N. Doc. A/6316.

In the Matter of Kevin Sampson, 317 N.Y.S.2d 641 (1970), *affirmed* 323 N.Y.S. 2d 253 (1971), 328 N.Y.S. 2d 686 (1972).

In the Matter of Seiferth, 137 N.Y.S.2d 35 (1955), *reversed* 309 N.Y. 80 (1955).

In the Matter of Tara Cabrera, 381 Pa. Super. 100 (1989).

Itkin, W. (1952). Some relationships between intrafamily attitudes and pre-parental attitudes toward children. *Journal of Genetic Psychology, 80,* 221-252.

Jacobsen v. Jacobsen, 314 N.W.2d 78 (N.D. 1981).

Janis, I. L., & Mann, L. (1977). *Decision making: A psychological analysis of conflict, choice, and commitment.* New York: Free Press.

J.B. v. V.B., 161 W.Va. 332, 242 S.E.2d 248 (1978).

Jehovah's Witnesses in State of Washington v. King Co. Hospital Unit No. 1, 278 F.Supp. 488 (W.D.Wash. 1967), *affirmed* 390 U.S. 598 (U.S.Wash. 1968), *reh. den.* 391 U.S. 961 (U.S.Wash. 1968).

Jessica DeBoer (a/k/a Baby Girl Clausen), by her next friend, Peter Darrow v. Roberta and Jan DeBoer and Cara and Daniel Schmidt, 442 Mich. 903, 503 N.W.2d 444 (1993).

Joey T., et al. v. Azcoitia, et al., U.S.D.C. (N.D.Ill. 1994)[94C-4248].

Johnson, S. J. (1997, July 20). No jobs for kids? Try baby-sitting or mowing grass. *Omaha World Herald*, p. 17-G.

Josselson, R. E. (1980). Ego development in adolescence. In J. Adelson (Ed.), *Handbook of adolescent psychology*. New York: John Wiley.

Jupp, M. (1990). The U.N. Convention on the Rights of the Child: An opportunity for advocates. *Human Rights Quarterly, 12*, 130-136.

Kane, J. N. (1994). Dispositional authority and decision making in New York's juvenile justice system: Discretion at risk. *Syracuse Law Review, 45*, 925-961.

Kaser-Boyd, N., Adelman, H. S., Taylor, L., & Nelson, P. (1986). Children's understanding of risks and benefits of psychotherapy. *Journal of Clinical Child Psychology, 15*, 165-171.

Kaufman, A. (1990). *Assessment of adolescent and adult intelligence.* Boston: Allyn & Bacon.

Keating-Owen Act of 1916, ch. 432, 39 Stat. 675 (1916).

Keilin, W. G., & Bloom, L. J. (1986). Child custody evaluation practices: A survey of experienced professionals. *Professional Psychology: Research and Practice, 17*, 338-346.

Kempe, C., Silverman, F., Steele, B., Droegemueller, W., & Silver, H. (1962). The battered-child syndrome. *Journal of the American Medical Association, 181*, 17-24.

Kennedy, M. (1997). Reading trends like tea leaves for success. *Capital District Business Review—Albany, 24*, p. 6.

Kent v. United States, 383 U.S. 541 (1966).

Kerian, C. L. (1997). Surrogacy: A last resort alternative for infertile women or a commodification of women's bodies and children? *Wisconsin Women's Law Journal, 12*, 113-166.

Kirk, S., & Kutchins, H. (1988). Deliberate misdiagnosis in mental health practice. *Social Service Review, 62*, 225-237.

Kirkpatrick, M., Smith, C., & Roy, R. (1981). Lesbian mothers and their children: A comparative survey. *American Journal of Orthopsychiatry, 51*, 545-551.

Klaff, R. L. (1982). The tender years doctrine: A defense. *California Law Review, 70*, 335-372.

Kline, M., Tschann, J. M., Johnston, J. R., & Wallerstein, J. S. (1989). Children's adjustment in joint and sole custody families. *Developmental Psychology, 25*, 430-438.

Koch, H. L., Dentler, M., Dysart, B., & Streit, H. (1934). A scale for measuring attitudes toward the question of children's freedom. *Child Development, 5*, 253-266.

Koch, M. A., & Lowery, C. R. (1984). Visitation and the noncustodial father. *Journal of Divorce, 8*, 47-65.

Koocher, G. P., & DeMaso, D. R. (1990). Children's competence to consent to medical procedures. *Pediatrician, 17*, 68-73.

Kornhaber, A., & Woodward, K. L. (1985). *Grandparents/grandchildren: The vital connection.* New Brunswick, NJ: Transaction Books.

Ku, M.-C. (Ed.). (1979). *A comprehensive handbook of the United Nations: A documentary presentation in two volumes* (Vol. 2). New York: Monarch.

Lantos, T. (1992, February). The silence of the kids: Children at risk in the workplace. *Labor Law Journal*, 67-70.

Larner, M. B., Terman, D. L., & Behrman, R. E. (1997, Spring). Welfare to work: Analysis and recommendations. In R. E. Behrman (Ed.), *The future of children, Vol. 7. Welfare to work* (pp. 4-19). Los Altos, CA: Center for the Future of Children.

Lasch, C. (1992, October). Hillary Clinton, child saver. *Harper's Magazine,* pp. 74-81.

Last, U., & Benyamini, K. (1991). Children's rights in Israel: Current status and evolving issues. *School Psychology International, 12,* 259-273.

Lazere, E. G., & Ostrom, K. A. (1994). *Nebraska's families: Poverty despite work.* Omaha: Voices for Children in Nebraska.

Leach, P. (1994). *Children first: What our society must do—and is not doing—for our children today.* New York: Knopf.

League of Nations. (1924). *Declaration of Geneva.* O.J. Spec. Supp. 21.

LeBlanc, L. J. (1995). *The convention on the rights of the child.* Lincoln: University of Nebraska Press.

Legislature 1997: Locke signs ban on taxing business intangibles. (1997, April 25). [Tacoma, WA] *News Tribune,* p. A13.

Leiken, S. L. (1983). Minor's assent or dissent to medical treatment. *Journal of Pediatrics, 102,* 169-176.

Leo, J. (1981, September 7). Cradle-to-grave intimacy. *Time,* p. 69.

Levine, M., Anderson, E., Terretti, L., Sharma, A., Steinberg, K., & Wallach, L. (1991). Effects of reporting maltreatment on the psychotherapeutic relationship. In S. Kalichman (Chair), *Mandatory child abuse reporting: A research policy update.* Symposium conducted at the 99th annual meeting of the American Psychological Association, San Francisco. Available from Baldy Center for Law and Social Policy, State University of New York, 511 O'Brian Hall, Buffalo, NY 14260

Lewin, T. (1992, August 24). Legal scholars see distortion in attacks on Hillary Clinton. *New York Times,* pp. A1, A10.

Lewis, M. A., & Lewis, C. E. (1990). Consequences of empowering children to care for themselves, *Pediatrician, 17,* 63-67.

Limber, S. P. (1994, April). Universal rights for children. *Society for the Psychological Study of Social Issues Newsletter* (No. 193), 10-11.

Locke, J. (1980). *Second treatise of government.* Indianapolis, IN: Hackett. (Original work published 1690)

Loper, N. F. (1977). A comparative study of the personality factors and social histories of three groups of adopted adults. *Dissertation Abstracts International, 37,* 4691-B–4692-B.

Lowery, C. R. (1986). Maternal and joint custody: Differences in the decision process. *Law and Human Behavior, 10,* 303-315.

Lowry, M. (1979). When the family breaks down: Massive and misapplied intervention by the state. In P. A. Vardin & I. N. Brody (Eds.), *Children's rights: Contemporary perspectives* (pp. 53-66). New York: Teachers College Press.

Luepnitz, D. A. (1982). *Child custody: A study of families after divorce.* Lexington, MA: Heath.

Luepnitz, D. A. (1986). A comparison of maternal, paternal, and joint custody: Understanding the varieties of postdivorce family life. *Journal of Divorce, 9,* 1-12.

Lumpkin, K., & Douglas, D. (1937). *Child workers in America.* New York: International Publishers.

Macaulay, S. (1987). Images of law in everyday life: The lessons of school, entertainment, and spectator sports. *Law and Society Review, 21,* 185-218.

Mack, J. W. (1909). The juvenile court. *Harvard Law Review, 23,* 104-122.

Mandell, B. R. (1995). Shredding the safety net. *New Politics.* Reprinted as "Poor women and children need welfare." (1997). In C. P. Cozic (Ed.), *Welfare reform* (pp. 10-26). San Diego, CA: Greenhaven Press.

Mann, L., Harmoni, R., & Power, C. (1989). Adolescent decision making: The development of competence. *Journal of Adolescence, 12,* 265-278.

Marks, S. P. (1990). Children and human rights in the 1990s. In D. Nurkse & K. Castelle (Eds.), *Children's rights: Crisis and challenge* (pp. A12-A17). New York: Defense for Children International–USA.

Martarella v. Kelley, 359F. Supp. 478 (S.D.N.Y. 1973).

Martinez v. School Dist. Board Hillsborough County, Fla., 675 F.Supp. 1574 (M.D. Fla. 1987).

Maryland v. Craig, 110 S.Ct. 5157 (1990).

Mason, M., & Gibbs, J. (1992). Patterns of adolescent psychiatric hospitalization: Implications for social policy. *American Journal of Orthopsychiatry, 62,* 447-457.

Mathews v. Eldridge, 424 U.S. 319 (1976).

Matter of Baby M, 537 A2d 1227 (1988).

Matter of Hofbauer, 47 N.Y.2d 648 (1979).

Maurer, A. (Chair). (1974, March). *A bill of rights for children.* Ann Arbor, MI: SPSSI Committee on Children's Rights.

Maurer, A. (1981). *Paddles away: A psychological study of physical punishment in schools.* Palo Alto, CA: R & E Research Associates.

Maurer, A. (1990). Corporal punishment in the public schools. *Humanistic Psychologist, 19,* 30-47.

Mauro, T. (1986, March 3). Campaigning or off-color orating? *USA Today,* p. 2A.

McGovern, P. J. (1983). Children's rights and child labor: Advocacy on behalf of the child worker. *South Dakota Law Review, 8,* 293-305.

McKeiver v. Pennsylvania, 403 U.S. 528 (1971).

McKelvey v. McKelvey, 111 Tenn. 338, 77 S.W. 664 (1903).

McLaughlin, B. J. (1985). Public school searches and the Fourth Amendment. *University of Dayton Law Review, 9,* 521-533.

Melton, G. B. (1980). Children's concepts of their rights. *Journal of Clinical Child Psychology, 9,* 186-190.

Melton, G. B. (1981). Children's participation in treatment planning: Psychological and legal issues. *Professional Psychology, 12,* 246-252.

Melton, G. B. (1989). Are adolescents people? Problems of liberty, entitlement, and responsibility. In J. Worell & F. Danner (Eds.), *The adolescent as decision maker: Applications to development and education* (pp. 281-306). San Diego, CA: Academic Press.

Melton, G. B. (1991). Preserving the dignity of children around the world: The U.N. Convention on the Rights of the Child. *Child Abuse & Neglect, 15,* 343-350.

Melton, G. B., & Ehrenreich, N. S. (1992). Ethical and legal issues in mental health services for children. In C. E. Walker & M. C. Roberts (Eds.), *Handbook of clinical child psychology* (2nd ed., pp. 1035-1053).

Melton, G. B., Lyons, P. M., Jr., & Spaulding, W. J. (in press). *No place to go: Civil commitment of minors.* Lincoln: University of Nebraska Press.

Merriam-Webster, Inc. (1993). *Merriam Webster's collegiate dictionary* (10th ed.). Springfield, MA: Author.

Meyer v. Nebraska, 262 U.S. 390 (1923).

Miranda v. Arizona, 384 U.S. 436 (1966).

Mnookin, R. (1975). Child-custody adjudication: Judicial functions in the face of indeterminancy. *Law and Contemporary Problems, 39,* 226-292.

Mnookin, R. (1978). Children's rights: Beyond kiddie libbers and child savers. *Journal of Clinical Child Psychology, 7,* 163-167.

Mnookin, R. (1995). Medical treatment of the child. In R. Mnookin, (Ed.), *Child, family, and state: Problems and materials on children and the law* (3rd ed.). Boston: Little, Brown.

Monaghan, P. (1997, July 3). A crusader against corporal punishment. *Chronicle of Higher Education, XLIII,* A7.

Moore, K. (1976). The dilemma of corporal punishment at Harvard College. *History of Education Quarterly, Fall,* 335-345.

Muhlenberg Hospital v. Patterson, 128 N.J. Super. 498 (1974).

National Industrial Recovery Act of 1933, ch. 90, 48 Stat. 195 (amended and modified by Act June 14, 1935, ch. 246, 49 Stat. 375) (1933).

Neb. Rev. Stat. 43-247 *et seq.* (1993).

Neugarten, B. L., & Weinstein, K. K. (1964). The changing American grandparent. *Journal of Marriage and the Family, 26,* 194-204.

New Jersey v. T.L.O., 469 U.S. 325 (1985).

New Mexico v. Michael G., 748 P.2d 17 (N.M. Ct. App. 1987).

N.J.S.A. [New Jersey Statutes Annotated] 2A: 4A-26 (1987).

Office for Civil Rights. (1984). *Elementary and secondary civil rights survey, 1984: National summary.* Arlington, VA: DBS Corp. (Eric Document Reproduction Service No. ED 271 543)

Okpaku, S. R. (1976). Psychology: Impediment or aid in child custody cases? *Rutgers Law Review, 29,* 1117-1153.

Orenstein, J. R. (1989). Negligent failure to rescue: Liability under 42 U.S.C. Section 1983. *Hamline Law Review, 12,* 421-446.

Palmore v. Sidoti I, 466 U.S. 429 (1984).

Palmore v. Sidoti II, 472 So.2d 845 (1985).

Pamela Kay Bottoms v. Sharon Lynne Bottoms, 249 Va. 410, 457 S.E.2d 102 (1995).

Pappas, A. M. (1983). Introduction. In A. M. Pappas (Ed.), *Law and the status of the child* (pp. xxvii-lv). New York: United Nations Institute for Training and Research.

Parham v. J. R., 442 U.S. 584 (1979).

Peach, L. J. (1988, Winter). Why do I have to go to school? Legal literacy in the classroom. *Update on Law-Related Education,* 23-29, 65.

People in Interest of D.L.E., 645 P.2d 271 (Colo. 1982).

People v. Scott D., 34 N.Y.2d 483, 315 N.E.2d 466, 358 N.Y.S.2d 403 (1974).

Perry [now Walker], N. W., & Wrightsman, L. S. (1991). *The child witness: Legal issues and dilemmas.* Newbury Park, CA: Sage.

Personal Responsibility and Work Opportunity Reconciliation Act of 1996, P.L. 104-193 (1996, August 22) 110 Stat. 2105.

Petersen v. Hastings Public Schools, 831 F.Supp. 742 (D.Neb. 1993).

Peterson, P. E. (1993, February). Give kids the vote. *Harpers Magazine,* pp. 23-26. (Excerpted from "An Immodest Proposal," *Daedalus,* Fall 1992 issue)

Pierce v. Society of Sisters, 268 U.S. 510 (1925).

Pignatella, M. A. (1995). The recurring nightmare of child labor abuse: Causes and solutions for the '90s. *Boston College Third World Law Journal, 15,* 171-210.

Pikunas, K. (1994, March). *The child's right to object to psychiatric hospitalization: A survey of Michigan judges and hospital administrators.* Paper presented at the biennial meeting of the American Psychology-Law Society, Santa Fe, NM.

Planned Parenthood of Central Missouri v. Danforth, 428 U.S. 52 (1976).

Platt, H., Chrost, S. G., & Jurgenson, G. (1960). *The Inventory of Family Life and Attitudes: An adaptation of the PARI.* Devon, PA: Devereux Foundation.

Poverty rate gets higher in U.S. (1996, September 16). *Xinhua English Newswire* [page unavailable].

Prather v. Prather, 4 Desau. 33 (S.C. 1809).

Press, A. (1983, January 10). Divorce American style. *Newsweek,* pp. 42-48.

Prince v. Massachusetts, 321 U.S. 158 (1944).

Public Papers of the Presidents. (1996, August 22). Weekly Compilation of Presidential Documents, Public Papers of the Presidents, 32 (Document No. 1484).

Purdy, L. M. (1992). *In their best interest? The case against equal rights for children.* Ithaca, NY: Cornell University Press.

Rachel K. v. Gregory K., 18 Fla.L.Weekly D1852 (5th Dist. Ct. App. 1992).

Rae, S. B. (1994). *The ethics of commercial surrogate motherhood: Brave new families?* Westport, CT: Praeger.

Ramon, et al. v. Illinois State Board of Education, et al., U.S.D.C. (N.D.Ill. 1992).

Ray v. School Dist. of DeSoto County, 666 F.Supp. 1524 (C.D. Cal. 1987).

Rector, R. (1996). Welfare reform. *Issues '96: The candidate's briefing book.* Reprinted as "Welfare reform is necessary." (1997). In C. P. Cozic (Ed.). *Welfare reform* (pp. 45-80). San Diego, CA: Greenhaven Press.

Rehabilitation Act of 1973, 29 U.S.C. 794 (1987).

Reisman, J., & Ribordy, S. (1993). *Principles of psychotherapy with children* (2nd ed.). New York: Lexington Books.

Religious Freedom Restoration Act of 1993, 42 U.S.C.A. 2000bb *et seq.* (1993).

Rennie v. Klein, 462 F.Supp. 1131 (D.N.J. 1978).

Reppucci, N. D., & Crosby, C. A. (1993). Law, psychology, and children: Overarching issues. *Law and Human Behavior, 17,* 1-10.

Rex v. Delaval, 97 Eng.Rep. 913 (K.B. 1763) (Mansfield, C.J.).

Rex v. Greenhill, 111 Eng.Rep. 922 (K.B. 1836).

Reynolds, W. F., Levey, C., & Eisnitz, M. F. (1977, August). *Adoptees' personality characteristics and self-ratings of adoptive family life.* Paper presented at the annual meeting of the American Psychological Association, San Francisco.

Rizzi, D. (1994). *In re Petition of John Doe and Jane Doe, Husband and Wife, to Adopt Baby Boy Janikova* (John Doe et al., Appellees; Otakar Kirchner, Appellant.), 159 Ill.2d 347 (1994).

Robertson, J. F. (1975). Interaction in three-generation families, parents as mediators: Toward a theoretical perspective. *International Journal of Aging and Human Development, 6,* 103-110.

Rodham, H. (1973). Children under the law. *Harvard Educational Review, 43,* 487-514.

Rodham, H. (1979). Children's rights: A legal perspective. In P. A. Vardin & I. Brody (Eds.), *Children's rights: Contemporary perspectives* (pp. 21-36). New York: Teachers College Press.

Rogers v. Okin, 478 F.Supp. 1342 (Mass. 1979), *modified* 634 F.2d 650 (1980).

Rogers, C. M., & Wrightsman, L. S. (1978). Attitudes toward children's rights: Nurturance or self-determination? *Journal of Social Issues, 34,* 59-68.

Rohman, L. W., Sales, B. D., & Lou, M. (1990). The best interests standard in child custody decisions. In D. Weisstub (Ed.), *Law and mental health: International perspectives* (Vol. 5, pp. 40-90). Elmsford, NJ: Pergamon.

Rohter, L. (1992, July 8). 11-year-old seeks right to "divorce" parents. *New York Times,* p. A7.

Roller v. Roller, 37 Wash. 242, 79 P. 788 (1905).

Rosenberg, E. (1993). *The adoption life cycle: The children and their families through the years.* New York: Free Press.

Ross, J. A. (1981). Improving adolescent decision-making skills. *Curriculum Inquiry, 11,* 279-295.

Roth, A. (1977). The tender years presumption in child custody disputes. *Journal of Family Law, 15,* 423-462.

Russ, G. H. (1993). Through the eyes of a child, "Gregory K.": A child's right to be heard. *Family Law Quarterly, 27,* 1-29.

Sales, B., Manber, R., & Rohman, L. (1992). Social science research and child-custody decision making. *Applied and Preventive Psychology, 1,* 23-40.

Salter, S. (1996, January 14). The movement to make child abuse official. *The San Francisco Examiner* (News section), [page unavailable].

San Antonio Independent School District v. Rodriguez, 411 U.S. 1 (1973).

Santosky v. Kramer, 455 U.S. 745 (1982).

Saul, S. (1997, March 3). Adult punishment: Minors face death row for crimes young offenders on death row. *Newsday,* p. A05.

Saywitz, K. J. (1989). Children's conceptions of the legal system: "Court is a place to play basketball." In S. J. Ceci, D. F. Ross, & M. P. Toglia (Eds.), *Perspectives on children's testimony* (pp. 131-157). New York: Springer Verlag.

Schaill v. Tippecanoe County School Corp., 679 F.Supp. 833 (N.D. Ind. 1988), *aff'd* 864 F.2d 1309.

Schall v. Martin, 467 U.S. 253 (1984).

Schechter Poultry Corporation v. United States, 295 U.S. 495 (1935).

Schwab-Stone, M. E. (1989). Diagnostic issues: *DSM-III* and *DSM-III-R.* In L. K. G. Hsu & M. Hersen (Eds.), *Recent developments in adolescent psychiatry* (pp. 31-49). New York: John Wiley.

S.E.G. v. R.A.G., 735 S.W.2d 164 (Mo. Ct. App. 1987).

Shane, P. M. (1987). Compulsory education and the tension between liberty and equality: A comment on Dworkin. *Iowa Law Review, 73,* 97-107.

Sharon Lynne Bottoms v. Pamela Kay Bottoms, 18 Va.App. 481, 444 S.E.2d 276 (1994).

Sharp v. Sharp, 491 S.W.2d 639 (Ky. 1973).

Shaw, S. R., & Braden, J. P. (1990). Race and gender bias in the administration of corporal punishment. *School Psychology Review, 19,* 378-383.

Shepard, S. (1997, July 27). Champion asks aid for no-dad families: Evander Holyfield urges Senate to act as House votes down assistance programs. *Austin American-Statesman* [page unavailable].

Shiller, V. M. (1986a). Joint versus maternal custody for families with latency age boys: Parent characteristics and child adjustment. *American Journal of Orthopsychiatry, 56,* 486-489.

Shiller, V. M. (1986b). Loyalty conflicts and family relationships in latency age boys: A comparison of joint and maternal custody. *Journal of Divorce, 9,* 17-38.

Shogren, E. (1993, December 13). "Gun culture" runs deep among youth violence. *Los Angeles Times,* p. 31.

Simmons, W. V. (1979). *A study of identity formation in adoptees.* Unpublished doctoral dissertation, University of Detroit.

Simon, R. J., & Altstein, H. (1977). *Transracial adoption.* New York: John Wiley.

Skafte, D. (1985). *Child custody evaluations: A practical guide.* Newbury Park, CA: Sage.

Skeels, J. F. (1990). The right of minors to refuse medical treatment. *Loyola University Law Journal, 23,* 1199-1230.

Social Security Act of 1935. 42 U.S.C.A. 601 *et seq.* (1935, August 14) 49 Stat. 620.

Stanford v. Kentucky, 492 U.S. 361 (1989).

Stanley v. Illinois, 405 U.S. 645 (1972).

State ex rel. Watts v. Watts, 350 N.Y.S. 285 (1973).

State of New Jersey in the Interest of S.M., 211 N.J.Super. 675, 512 A.2d 570 (1986).

State v. Baccino, 282 A.2d 869 (Del. Super. Ct. 1971).

State v. Perricone, 37 N.J. 463, 181 A.2d 751 (New Jersey 1962).

Steinberg, L., & Dornbusch, S. (1991). Negative correlates of part-time employment during adolescence: Replication and elaboration. *Developmental Psychology, 27,* 304-313.

Steinberg, L., Greenberger, E., Garduque, L., Ruggiero, M., & Vaux, A. (1982). Effects of early work experience on adolescent development. *Developmental Psychology, 18,* 385-395.

Steinman, S. (1981). The experience of children in a joint-custody arrangement: A report of a study. *American Journal of Orthopsychiatry, 51,* 403-414.

Steinman, S. B., Zemmelman, S. E., & Knoblauch, T. M. (1985). A study of parents who sought joint custody following divorce: Who reaches agreement and sustains joint custody and who returns to court. *Journal of the American Academy of Child Psychiatry, 24,* 554-562.

Stewart, C. (1997, March 15). Child workers seek regulated conditions, education. *Ottawa Citizen,* p. B6.

Stewart v. Stewart, 521 N.E.2d 956 (Ind. Ct. App., 4th Dist., 1988).

Stier, S. (1978). Children's rights and society's duties. *Journal of Social Issues, 34,* 46-58.

Stogdill, R. M., & Goddard, H. H. (1936). The measurement of attitudes toward parental control and the social adjustment of children. *Journal of Applied Psychology, 20,* 359-367.

Stott, L. H. (1940). Parental attitudes of farm, town, and city parents in relation to certain personality adjustments in their children. *Journal of Social Psychology, 11,* 325-339.

Sullivan, M. D. (1991). From Warren to Rehnquist: The growing conservative trend in the Supreme Court's treatment of children. *St. John's Law Review, 65,* 1139-1161.

Sussman, A. (1977). *The rights of young people.* New York: Avon.

Swisher v. Brady, 438 U.S. 204 (1978).

Tancredi, L. (1982). Competency for informed consent. *International Journal of Law and Psychiatry, 5,* 51-63.

Taylor, L., Adelman, H. S., & Kaser-Boyd, N. (1984). Attitudes toward involving minors in decisions. *Professional Psychology: Research and Practice, 15,* 436-449.

Thomas, M. P. (1972). Child abuse and neglect: Part I. Historical overview, legal matrix, and social perspectives. *North Carolina Law Review, 50,* 293-349.

Thomas v. Atascadero Unified School District, 662 F.Supp. 376 (C.D. Cal. 1986).

Thompson, R. A., Scalora, M. J., Castrianno, L., & Limber, S. P. (1992). Grandparent visitation rights: Emergent psychological and psycholegal issues. In D. K. Kagehiro & W. S. Laufer (Eds.), *Handbook of psychology and law* (pp. 292-317). New York: Springer Verlag.

Thompson v. Oklahoma, 487 U.S. 815 (1988).

Tinker v. Des Moines Independent Community School District, 393 U.S. 503 (1969).

Tinkler, J. D. (1992, Summer). The juvenile justice system in the United States and the United Nations Convention on the Rights of the Child. *Boston College Third World Law Journal, 12,* 469-505.

Tinsley, B. R., & Parke, R. D. (1984). Grandparents as support and socialization agents. In M. Lewis (Eds.), *Beyond the dyad* (pp. 161-194). New York: Plenum.

Trattner, W. I. (1970). *Crusade for the children: A history of the National Child Labor Committee and child labor reform in America.* Chicago: Quadrangle.

Traver, N. (1987, March 23). They cannot fend for themselves. *Time,* p. 27.

Tremper, C., & Feshbach, N. (1981). *Attitudes of parents and adolescents toward decision making by minors.* Unpublished manuscript, University of California, Los Angeles.

Tremper, C. R., & Kelly, M. P. (1987). The mental health rationale for policies fostering minors' autonomy. *International Journal of Law and Psychiatry, 10,* 111-127.

Trop v. Dulles, 356 U.S. 86 (1958).

Tyler, R. S. (1990, July 16). Can law save the children? *National Law Journal,* 13-14.

Uniform Marriage and Divorce Act, *Uniform Laws Ann. #402* (1979).

Union Pac. Ry. Co. v. Botsford, 141 U.S. 250 (1891).

United Nations Children's Fund (UNICEF). (1993). *The state of the world's children 1993.* Oxford, UK: Oxford University Press for UNICEF.

United Nations Children's Fund (UNICEF) Child Rights. (1997a). *About the Convention.* Available: http://www.unicef.org/crc.

United Nations Children's Fund (UNICEF) Child Rights. (1997b). *How to help the U.S. ratify.* Available: http://www.unicef.org/crc/updates/us-how.htm.

United Nations General Assembly. (1948, December 10). Universal declaration of human rights. In M-C. Ku (Ed.), (1979). *A comprehensive handbook of the United Nations: A documentary presentation in two volumes* (Vol. 2, pp. 691-697). New York: Monarch.

United Nations General Assembly. (1959, November 20). Declaration of the Rights of the Child. In M-C. Ku (Ed.), (1979). *A comprehensive handbook of the United Nations: A documentary presentation in two volumes* (Vol. 2, pp. 744-746). New York: Monarch.

United Nations General Assembly. (1989, November 17). *Adoption of a convention on the rights of the child.* U.N. Doc. A/Res/44/25.

United States Committee for UNICEF. (1997). *United Nations Convention on the Rights of the Child: FAQ.* Washington, DC: Author.

United States v. Calloway, 505 F.2d 311 (D.C. Cir. Ct. App., 1974).

United States v. F.W. Darby Lumber Co., 312 U.S. 100 (1941).

Van Bueren, G. (1995). *The international law on the rights of the child.* Norwell, MA: Kluwer Academic.

Vardin, P. A., & Brody, I. N. (1979). Introduction. In P. A. Vardin & I. N. Brody (Eds.), *Children's rights: Contemporary perspectives* (pp. xv-xvii). New York: Teachers College Press.

Veerman, P. (1986, February 16-21). *Is compulsory education a right?* Paper presented to the Second International Congress on Psychiatry, Israel.

Vernonia School Dist. 47J v. Acton, 515 U.S. 646, 115 S.Ct. 2386 (1995).

Vessels, A. (1997, March 14). Fasting to help out the hungry world event attracts more teens this year. *Richmond Times-Dispatch,* p. E10.

Volgy, S. S., & Everett, C. A. (1985). Joint custody reconsidered: Systemic criteria for mediation. *Journal of Divorce, 8,* 131-150.

Voting Rights Act of 1965, 42 U.S.C.A. 1973 (1965).

Waddell, F. E. (1985). Borrowing child support payments. *Mediation Quarterly, 9,* 63-83.

Wadlington, W. (1973). Minors and health care: The age of consent. *Osgood Hall Law Journal, 11,* 115-125.

Waechter v. School Dist. No. 14-030 of Cassopolis, Mich., 773 F.Supp. 1005 (1991).

Walding, J. K. (1990). What ever happened to *Parham* and *Institutionalized Juveniles*: Do minors have procedural rights in the civil commitment area? *Law and Psychology Review, 14,* 281-302.

Walker v. Superior Court, 47 Cal.3d 112 (1988).

Wallace, A. (1994, March 7). Foes exploit Brown's omission on school crime issue campaign. *Los Angeles Times,* p. 3A.

Wallerstein, J., & Kelly, J. (1980). *Surviving the breakup: How children and parents cope with divorce.* New York: Basic Books.

Wallerstein, J. S., & Blakeslee, S. (1989). *Second chances: Men, women, and children a decade after divorce: Who wins, who loses—and why.* New York: Ticknor & Fields.

Warboys, L., & Wilber, S. (1996). Mental health issues in juvenile justice. In B. D. Sales & D. W. Shuman (Eds.), *Law, mental health, and mental disorder* (pp. 503-521). Pacific Grove, CA: Brooks/Cole.

Warren-Leubecker, A., Bradley, C. S., Hinton, I. D., & Ozbek, I. N. (1989). What do children know about the legal system and when do they know it? First steps down a less traveled path in child witness research. In S. J. Ceci, D. F. Ross, & M. P. Toglia (Eds.), *Perspectives on children's testimony* (pp. 158-183). New York: Springer Verlag.

Webb v. McCullough, 828 F.2d 1151 (6th Cir. 1987).

Weiss, C. P. (1996). Curbing violence or teaching it: Criminal immunity for teachers who inflict corporal punishment. *Washington University Law Quarterly, 74,* 1251-1289.

Weithorn, L. (1988). Mental hospitalization of troublesome youth: An analysis of skyrocketing admission rates. *Stanford Law Review, 40,* 773-838.

Weithorn, L. A., & Campbell, S. B. (1982). The competency of children and adolescents to make informed treatment decisions. *Child Development, 53,* 1589-1598.

Weithorn, L. A., & Grisso, T. (1987). Psychological evaluations in divorce custody: Problems, principles, and procedures. In L. A. Weithorn (Ed.), *Psychology and child custody determinations* (pp. 157-181). Lincoln: University of Nebraska Press.

Weitzman, L. J. (1985). *The divorce revolution: The unexpected social and economic consequences for women and children in America.* New York: Free Press.

West v. United States, 399 F2d 467 (1968).

West Virginia State Board of Education v. Barnette, 319 U.S. 624 (1943).

What the laws say. (1996, April 25). *Detroit News* [page unavailable].

White v. Rochford, 592 F.2d 381 (7th Cir. 1979).

Widener v. Frye, 809 F.Supp. 35, *affirmed* 12 F.3d 215 (1992).

Wilkins v. Missouri, 492 U.S. 361 (1989).

Wilson by Wilson v. Wilson, 742 F.2d 1004 (6th Cir. 1984).

Winick, B. J. (1991). Competency to consent to treatment: The distinction between assent and objection. *Houston Law Review, 28,* 15-61.

Wisconsin v. Yoder, 406 U.S. 205 (1972).

Women's Alliance. (1994, May/June). End poverty as we know it (not welfare!). *Resist.* Reprinted as "Welfare reform is a mistake." (1997). In C. P. Cozic (Ed.). *Welfare reform* (pp. 27-34). San Diego, CA: Greenhaven Press.

Wood, C. L. (1994). The parental alienation syndrome: A dangerous aura of reliability. *Loyola of Los Angeles Law Review, 27,* 1367-1415.

Woodard v. Los Fresnos Indep. School Dist., 732 F.2d 1243 (5th Cir. 1984).

Worsfold, V. L. (1974). A philosophical justification for children's rights. *Harvard Educational Review, 44,* 142-157.

Wrightsman, L. S., Nietzel, M. T., & Fortune, W. H. (1994). *Psychology and the legal system* (3rd ed.). Pacific Grove, CA: Brooks/Cole.

Wringe, C. (1981). *Children's rights: A philosophical study.* London: Routledge & Kegan Paul.

Wyer, M. M., Gaylord, S. J., & Grove, E. T. (1987). The legal context of child custody evaluations. In L. A. Weithorn (Ed.), *Psychology and child custody evaluations* (pp. 3-22). Lincoln: University of Nebraska Press.

Yerger, E. E. (1981). *The factors that influence an adoptee's desire to search.* Unpublished master's thesis, National Catholic School of Social Service of the Catholic University of America, Washington, DC.

Young and poor: A report shows that U.S. children lag far behind others. (1996, June 6). *Pittsburgh Post-Gazette,* p. A16.

Youngberg v. Romeo, 457 U.S. 307 (1982).

Zainaldin, J. (1979). The emergence of a modern American family law: Child custody, adoption, and the courts, 1796-1851. *Northwestern University Law Review, 73,* 1038-1089.

Legal Cases Cited

Bailey v. Drexel Furniture Co., 259 U.S. 20 (1922).

Baker v. Owen, 96 S.Ct. 210, 395 F.Supp. 294 (1975).

Baltimore City Department of Social Services v. Bouknight, 110 S.Ct. 900 (1990).

Battles v. Board, 95 F.3d 41 (4th Cir. 1996).

Bellotti v. Baird, 443 U.S. 622 (1979).

Bethel School District No. 403 v. Fraser, 478 U.S. 675 (1986).

Blissets Case, 98 Eng.Rep. 899 (K.B. 1774) (Mansfield, C.J.).

Breed v. Jones, 421 U.S. 519 (1975).

Breitwieser v. KMS Industries, Inc., 467 F.2d 1391 (5th Cir. 1972), *cert. denied,* 410 U.S. 969 (1973).

Brown v. the Board of Education, 347 U.S. 483 (1954) [*Brown I*].

Brown v. the Board of Education, 349 U.S. 294 (1955) [*Brown II*].

Burnham v. West, 681 F.Supp. 1160 (E.D. Va. 1987).

Carey on Behalf of Carey v. Maine School Administrative Dist. No. 17, 754 F.Supp. 906 (1990).

Commonwealth of PA v. Addicks I, 5 Binn. 520 (Pa. 1813).

Commonwealth of PA v. Addicks & Lee (Addicks II), 2 Serg. & Rawle 174 (Pa. 1815).

Cornfield by Lewis v. Consolidated High School Dist. No. 230, 991 F.2d 1316 (1993).

Coy v. Iowa, 108 S.Ct. 1798, 487 U.S. 1012 (1988).

Craig v. Selma City School Board, 801 F.Supp. 585 (1992).

Custody of a Minor, 375 Mass. 733 (1978).

Davis v. Davis, 842 S.W.2d 588 (1990), affirming Tenn. Ct. App. (1990).

DeShaney v. Winnebago County Department of Social Services, 489 U.S. 189 (1989).

Doe v. Doe, 222 Va. 736, 284 S.E.2d 799 (1981).

Dunlap v. Dunlap, 84 N.H. 352, 150A. 905 (1930).

Emery v. Emery, 45 Cal. 2d 421, 289 P.2d 218 (1955).

Evans v. Asphalt Roads & Materials Company, Inc., 194 Va. 165, 72 S.E.2d 321 (1952).

Ex parte Devine, 398 So. 2d 686 (Ala. 1991).

Fare v. Michael C., 442 U.S. 707 (1979).

Farmer v. Farmer, 439 N.Y.S.2d 584 (1981).

Feldman v. Feldman, 45 A.D. 320, 358 N.Y.S.2d 507 (1974).

Foldi v. Jeffries, 93 N.J. 533, 461 A.2d 1145 (1983).

G.A. v. D.A., 745 S.W.2d 726 (Missouri 1987).

Garcia v. Miera, 817 F.2d 650 (10th Cir. 1987).

Gary W., et al. v. State of Louisiana, et al., 437 F.Supp. 1209 (E.D.La. 1976).

Gibson v. Gibson, 3 Cal.3d 914, 92 Cal.Rptr. 288, 479 P.2d 648 (1971).

Gideon v. Wainwright, 372 U.S. 335 (1963).

Gordon v. Gordon, 557 P.2d 1271 (Okla.), *cert. den.* 439 U.S. 863 (1978).

Goss v. Lopez, 419 U.S. 565 (1975).

Haley v. Ohio, 332 U.S. 596 (1948).

Hall v. Tawney, 621 F.2d 607 (4th Cir. 1980).

Hammer v. Dagenhart, 247 U.S. 251 (1918).

Hazelwood School District v. Kuhlmeier, 484 U.S. 260 (1988).

Helms v. Franciscus, 2 BlandCh. 544, 20 Am. Dec. 402 (1830).

Hewellette v. George, 68 Miss. 703, 9 So. 885 (1891).

Hill by and through Hill v. Rankin County, Mississippi School District, 843 F.Supp. 1112 (1993).

Hoffman v. Tracy, 67 Wash. 2d 31, 406 P.2d 323 (1965).

Howell v. Howell, 304 N.Y.S.2d 156 (1969).

Ingraham v. Wright, 430 U.S. 651 (1977).

Inmates of Boys' Training School v. Affleck, 346 D.Supp. 1354 (D.R.I. 1972).

In re E.G., 133 Ill. 2nd 98 (1989).

In re Gault, 387 U.S. 1 (1967).

In re Green, 448 Pa. 338 (1972).

In re Guardianship of Myers, 610 N.E.2d 663 (Ohio Com. Pl. 1993).

In re Marriage of Carney, 24 Cal.3d 725, 598 P.2d 36, 157 Cal.Rptr. 383 (1979).

In re Marriage of Rosson, 224 Cal. Rptr. 250 (178 Cal. App. 3d 1094, 1986).

In re P.E.A., 754 P.2d 382 (Colo. 1988).

In re Petition of John Doe and Jane Doe, Husband and Wife, to Adopt Baby Boy Janikova (John Doe et al., Appellees; Otakar Kirchner, Appellant.), 159 Ill.2d 347 (1994).

In re Philip B. v. Warren B., 92 Cal. App. 3d 796 (1979).

In re Winship, 397 U.S. 358 (1970).

In the Matter of Kevin Sampson, 317 N.Y.S.2d 641 (1970), *affirmed* 323 N.Y.S. 2d 253 (1971), 328 N.Y.S. 2d 686 (1972).

In the Matter of Seiferth, 137 N.Y.S.2d 35 (1955), *reversed* 309 N.Y. 80 (1955).

In the Matter of Tara Cabrera, 381 Pa. Super. 100 (1989).

Jacobsen v. Jacobsen, 314 N.W.2d 78 (N.D. 1981).

J.B. v. V.B., 161 W.Va. 332, 242 S.E.2d 248 (1978).

Jehovah's Witnesses in State of Washington v. King Co. Hospital Unit No. 1, 278 F.Supp. 488 (W.D.Wash. 1967), *affirmed* 390 U.S. 598 (U.S.Wash. 1968), *reh. den.* 391 U.S. 961 (U.S.Wash. 1968).

Jessica DeBoer (a/k/a Baby Girl Clausen), by her next friend, Peter Darrow v. Roberta and Jan DeBoer and Cara and Daniel Schmidt, 442 Mich. 903, 503 N.W.2d 444 (1993).

Joey T., et al. v. Azcoitia, et al., U.S.D.C. (N.D.Ill. 1994)[94C-4248].

Kent v. United States, 383 U.S. 541 (1966).

Martarella v. Kelley, 359 F.Supp. 478 (S.D.N.Y. 1973).

Martinez v. School Dist. Board Hillsborough County, Fla., 675 F.Supp. 1574 (M.D. Fla. 1987).

Maryland v. Craig, 110 S.Ct. 5157 (1990).

Mathews v. Eldridge, 424 U.S. 319 (1976).

Matter of Baby M, 537 A2d 1227 (1988).

Matter of Hofbauer, 47 N.Y.2d 648 (1979).

McKeiver v. Pennsylvania, 403 U.S. 528 (1971).

McKelvey v. McKelvey, 111 Tenn. 338, 77 S.W. 664 (1903).

Meyer v. Nebraska, 262 U.S. 390 (1923).

Miranda v. Arizona, 384 U.S. 436 (1966).

Muhlenberg Hospital v. Patterson, 128 N.J. Super. 498 (1974).

New Jersey v. T.L.O., 469 U.S. 325 (1985).

New Mexico v. Michael G., 748 P.2d 17 (N.M. Ct. App. 1987).

Palmore v. Sidoti I, 466 U.S. 429 (1984).

Palmore v. Sidoti II, 472 So.2d 845 (1985).

Pamela Kay Bottoms v. Sharon Lynne Bottoms, 249 Va. 410, 457 S.E.2d 102 (1995).

Parham v. J. R., 442 U.S. 584 (1979).

People in Interest of D.L.E., 645 P.2d 271 (Colo. 1982).

People v. Scott D., 34 N.Y.2d 483, 315 N.E.2d 466, 358 N.Y.S.2d 403 (1974).

Petersen v. Hastings Public Schools, 831 F.Supp. 742 (D.Neb. 1993).

Pierce v. Society of Sisters, 268 U.S. 510 (1925).

Planned Parenthood of Central Missouri v. Danforth, 428 U.S. 52 (1976).

Prather v. Prather, 4 Desau. 33 (S.C. 1809).

Prince v. Massachusetts, 321 U.S. 158 (1944).

Rachel K. v. Gregory K., 18 Fla.L.Weekly D1852 (5th Dist. Ct. App. 1992).

Ramon, et al. v. Illinois State Board of Education, et al., U.S.D.C. (N.D.Ill. 1992).

Ray v. School Dist. of DeSoto County, 666 F.Supp. 1524 (C.D. Cal. 1987).

Rennie v. Klein, 462 F.Supp. 1131 (D.N.J. 1978).

Rex v. Delaval, 97 Eng.Rep. 913 (K.B. 1763) (Mansfield, C.J.).

Rex v. Greenhill, 111 Eng.Rep. 922 (K.B. 1836).

Rogers v. Okin, 478 F.Supp. 1342 (Mass. 1979), *modified* 634 F.2d 650 (1980).

Roller v. Roller, 37 Wash. 242, 79 P. 788 (1905).

San Antonio Independent School District v. Rodriguez, 411 U.S. 1 (1973).

Santosky v. Kramer, 455 U.S. 745 (1982).

Schaill v. Tippecanoe County School Corp., 679 F.Supp. 833 (N.D. Ind. 1988), *aff'd* 864 F.2d 1309.

Schall v. Martin, 467 U.S. 253 (1984).

Schechter Poultry Corporation v. United States, 295 U.S. 495 (1935).

S.E.G. v. R.A.G., 735 S.W.2d 164 (Mo. Ct. App. 1987).

Sharon Lynne Bottoms v. Pamela Kay Bottoms, 18 Va.App. 481, 444 S.E.2d 276 (1994).

Sharp v. Sharp, 491 S.W.2d 639 (Ky. 1973).

Stanford v. Kentucky, 492 U.S. 361 (1989).

Stanley v. Illinois, 405 U.S. 645 (1972).

State v. Baccino, 282 A.2d 869 (Del. Super. Ct. 1971).

State v. Perricone, 37 N.J. 463, 181 A.2d 751 (New Jersey 1962).

State ex rel. Watts v. Watts, 350 N.Y.S. 285 (1973).

State of New Jersey in the Interest of S.M., 211 N.J.Super. 675, 512 A.2d 570 (1986).

Stewart v. Stewart, 521 N.E.2d 956 (Ind. Ct. App., 4th Dist., 1988).

Swisher v. Brady, 438 U.S. 204 (1978).

Thomas v. Atascadero Unified School District, 662 F.Supp. 376 (C.D. Cal. 1986).

Thompson v. Oklahoma, 487 U.S. 815 (1988).

Tinker v. Des Moines Independent Community School District, 393 U.S. 503 (1969).

Trop v. Dulles, 356 U.S. 86 (1958).

Union Pac. Ry. Co. v. Botsford, 141 U.S. 250 (1891).

United States v. Calloway, 505 F.2d 311 (D.C. Cir. Ct. App., 1974).

United States v. F.W. Darby Lumber Co., 312 U.S. 100 (1941).

Vernonia School Dist. 47J v. Acton, 515 U.S. 646, 115 S.Ct. 2386 (1995).

Waechter v. School Dist. No. 14-030 of Cassopolis, Mich., 773 F.Supp. 1005 (1991).

Walker v. Superior Court, 47 Cal.3d 112 (1988).

Webb v. McCullough, 828 F.2d 1151 (6th Cir. 1987).

West v. United States, 399 F2d 467 (1968).

West Virginia State Board of Education v. Barnette, 319 U.S. 624 (1943).

White v. Rochford, 592 F.2d 381 (7th Cir. 1979).

Widener v. Frye, 809 F.Supp. 35, *affirmed* 12 F.3d 215 (1992).

Wilkins v. Missouri, 492 U.S. 361 (1989).

Wilson by Wilson v. Wilson, 742 F.2d 1004 (6th Cir. 1984).

Wisconsin v. Yoder, 406 U.S. 205 (1972).

Woodard v. Los Fresnos Indep. School Dist., 732 F.2d 1243 (5th Cir. 1984).

Youngberg v. Romeo, 457 U.S. 307 (1982).

Author Index

Subject Index

About the Authors

Catherine M. Brooks (J.D., University of Virginia, 1980; M.A., Fordham University, 1977) is Professor of Law and Director of the Center for the Study of Children's Issues at Creighton University in Omaha, Nebraska. Before joining Creighton's faculty, she taught at Seton Hall University School of Law. She has also been in private practice and served as Assistant Deputy Public Defender (1983-1988) for the New Jersey Department of the Public Advocate in its law guardian program. She is an editor and coauthor of *The Nebraska Juvenile Court Procedures Manual* and has published numerous scholarly articles on children and the law. She consults locally with child advocacy groups, family law practitioners, and social service agencies; is a member of the Nebraska Permanency Planning Task Force and the Board of Directors of Big Brothers Big Sisters of Omaha; and serves on the Nebraska Governor's Commission on Juvenile Justice.

Nancy E. Walker (Ph.D., University of Nebraska, 1982) is Postdoctoral Fellow in the Law/Psychology Program at the University of Nebraska–Lincoln. Formerly, she was Professor of Psychology and Codirector (with Catherine M. Brooks) of the Center for the Study of Children's Issues at Creighton University in Omaha, Nebraska. Before joining Creighton's faculty, she conducted psychological assessment, diagnosis, and treatment of children and adolescents with emotional problems. For 14 years, she has been engaged in research on developmental psychology and the law. The author of numerous scholarly articles and book chapters in that topic area—published under both her current and former (Nancy W. Perry) names, she was also coauthor (with Lawrence S. Wrightsman) of *The Child Witness*. The recipient of several awards for teaching and community service, she also serves as consultant, lecturer, and expert witness on children and the law.

Lawrence S. Wrightsman (Ph.D., University of Minnesota, 1959) is Professor of Psychology at the University of Kansas—Lawrence. He has been conducting research on legal processes for 20 years and is Director of the Kansas Jury Project. The author or editor of eight other books relevant to the legal system, including *The American Jury on Trial* (coauthored with Saul M. Kassin), *The Child Witness* (coauthored with Nancy W. Perry [now Walker]), and *Rape: The Misunderstood Crime* (coauthored with Julie A. Allison), he was invited to contribute the entry on psychology and the law for the multivolume *Encyclopedia of Psychology,* sponsored by the American Psychological Association. He has testified as an expert witness on several topics and has assisted defense attorneys in jury selection for trials as diverse as criminal murder cases and civil malpractice suits. He is a former President of both the Society for the Psychological Study of Social Issues and the Society of Personality and Social Psychology.

CPSIA information can be obtained at www.ICGtesting.com
Printed in the USA
241626LV00003B/55/A

9 780803 951044